Jéjee

Memoirs of Saint Giorgis

DECLARATION OF COPYRIGHT

ISBN–13: 978-0-578-26171-3

GK
Publishing

TABLE OF CONTENTS

INTRODUCTION

The story that you are about to read is true. Names have been changed for privacy reasons. Many people are still unaware Yahshua, as do His Angels and Saints, spiritually and physically exist. I am living proof of His Truth and I will proclaim Yahshua's Truth to whomever desires to listen. Our Holy Father, Yahshua or his angels may walk among humanity at any given moment; man will never limit His power.

I was born to serve Baba (My Father in Heaven) and his son Yahshua (Our Big Brother)

I am Jéjee: (Saint Giorgis)

I am The Dragon Slayer

My story inspires the faithful followers of our Father's and Yahshua's Truth and educate those who are still unaware of their eternal existence with humanity. Their supernatural experiences with man-kind were true in the past, present and forevermore. The moral of my story is about Faith, Courage, Love, Truth and Justice, even if it means that others will use my story to try to instigate hate or falsify my claim. The Truth sometimes instills fear and anger into others while providing His Love to many. There is no religion I am promoting.

The hidden chosen elites who instill fear and shed blood onto this world and bring hatred to others or their own are to blame. It may be the supposed powerful leaders, occult groups, Christians, Catholics, Muslims, Hindus, Buddhists, Scientologists or any other denominations or non-denominations or any other human; they all have their own beliefs or religions of how life should all come to be. In the end, the Word of Baba – will have the last Word and can instill Love or terror even toward the worst kind of human or Satan.

Love is the answer – the only answer – to all the problems in this world. The Love, compassion and devotion for Baba, Yahshua and to each other will bring everyone together no matter what creed, color or belief. In the end, ALL of us will be on our knees reaching for His bread. We are all the same flesh, as Baba had created us. Make peace with one another to understand His Word and you will understand each other. Set aside your cultural differences, color or status and live together with harmony as one voice praising His Love.

Help everyone who are in need and defeat the fear and hate we have against each other within our hearts. Embrace your family and friends to encourage Love to grow within their hearts so that they may spread the joy to their brothers and sisters in the world. Forgive the ones that have done you wrong, for they can be loved as well. Love will show them the true meaning of Baba's Word and He will open their hearts to let you in. Furthermore, Baba's words never will fail you or anyone else on the entire planet.

Humanity will have a choice to drink from the cup of His everlasting life *only* through Yahshua. No other will enter heaven if they will not accept His son who died for our sins. The ones who choose the lusts of this world and their evil deeds will perish into non-existence, erased from His book of life. Truth definitely will set you free; literally. His prolific Word will be for all to fear, love, praise and believe in our Holy Father's Love for us and embrace Yahshua's Love forevermore.

His Word is Love, His Word for all of eternity.

Abba - "Father" in Hebrew

Yahshua – Our Father's son

Baba Allaha – "Father God" in Aramaic

Eesho – "Yahshua" in Aramaic

PREFACE

Origin of The Name Jesus

The Name <u>Jesus</u> is a Modern Invention

Contributed by Dan Baxley

From the very beginning, I want to make it plain, the name JESUS, has only been around for the past 400 years. When the Apostles preached, proclaiming the Gospel message it was in a name given to our Savior at birth, by an Angel from God the Father (Luke 1:31).

A name given to Mary and Joseph to name Him, and that name was YaHshua (this being the transliterated form from the Hebrew into English) – the false name, Jesus, is not that name, it is not an "equivalent," it is a "replacement" for the *only Name found under heaven by which we must be saved* (Acts 4:12). This chapter will show, that the false name JESUS (IESUS) is a lie and a deception. "... *They perish because they refused to Love the Truth and so be saved.*

For this reason, God sends them a powerful delusion so that they will believe the lie..." (2Th 2:10-11). This writing, then, is not for those who refuse to see the Truth and want to argue about it; it is for those truly seeking the Truth and willing to follow the Spirit of Truth, as revealed to them, not by me but by Him. I could rattle on and on and unless He opens your mind to this Truth, removing the delusion, then none of this will mean anything to you. Please listen, I in no way question the sincere hearts of those seeking and called to YaHshua and to the Heavenly Father.

We are not born with complete knowledge. A baby does not know its parents' names or its family name until it learns to understand what the parents are saying. Like children, we go through a process, first we are calling on our "dada" and our "mama," but sooner or later, if we are moving through our growth toward maturity, we will understand which family we belong to. In this family is a big brother, the first of many, the "First Fruit," and it is His sacrifice that makes Him our Savior.

Sad, but too many have become stuck, some on purpose, some by plan and some by ignorance. There is a small calling to this Truth, I pray it is you – *John 6:44 and Mat 11:27.* His Name was never "Jesus," and I will spend the rest of this article presenting the Truth in this matter. But, as stated, the name most of Christianity accepts today is a fake, a false name, a deception and can be recognized as nothing else due to the fact this name never ever existed before 1611 AD.

Also, the birth name of our Savior has never been lost, it has always been around, just ignored and replaced. If His true name has always been available, then ask yourself, why use another name, a different name? I hope this article will help those looking or being led to this Truth.

His Name is Not JESUS, and it is not IESUS and it is not IESOUS

Jesus is not His name! I can prove it, and knowing this fact about his name does matter.

First, however, you have to approach this with an open mind. You and only you can control your final thoughts; sure, you can give your trust away and accept everything you are told or read, but in the end it is you, not me, not your pastor, and certainly not the TV evangelist, who you never should allow to do your thinking for you. Your personal responsibility in matters concerning your life, the way you see the world, the way you see the church or churches and to whom you pledge your spirit, your spiritual loyalty – it is all on you.

Please, allow me to present a verse that should be the final answer, it is not the only verse, but is a final answer, as you will see: *And the nations were angry, and thy wrath is come, and the time of the dead, that they should be judged, and that thou shouldest give reward unto thy servants the prophets, and to the saints, and them that fear thy name, small and great; and shouldest destroy them which destroy the earth.*

(Rev 11:18) If you look up the word "fear," as in "...fear thy name, "in Strong's or some other Greek dictionary, you will find a better choice for this word, such as, "to be in awe," that is to "revere"(Strong's G5399). There is coming a time when the "reward" of "eternal life" is going to be handed out to those called saints, servants, prophets and those that respect and revere His Name – those left out of this, much of the peoples of the nations, will be angry at this – the corrupt of the world, corrupting the earth by their unrepentant sin, hatred and Love of violence, destroyers of this earth.

The final Word of concern in this verse where YaHshua is proclaimed King of Kings is the word used for "destroy." This word would make more sense using other choices found in Strong's Dictionary for the word destroy –"corrupt, ruin, rot, perish"– we see the sense of those individuals not receiving the reward, those angry, as those "corrupting" the earth, bringing the earth to ruin by their rebellion and rejection of the one and only Savior, YaHshua.

These "corrupters" of the earth do not "fear the Name" of the Creator, the one having ultimate power over life and death. So, the Name is important, and it is a corrupt mind that allows corrupt thinking to distort this Truth. Again, it is your responsibility, not mine, for you to clear you mind of outside influences, of teachings that can be demonstrated as false, or in error, or misunderstood. Take your pick of any excuse you want, but, finally, in the end, decide to fight the concepts you have been indoctrinated into under false precepts and false Christ.

Examine your own heart and mind, please, and know if it is the Truth you seek or just a wonderful feeling of worldly bliss. Not my intention to offend anyone, but some will be, and I cannot help that. I pray, however, you wake up to the fact that a great deception has overcome this world – another messiah is preached all the while the preachers hold up the written Word of the Living God and proclaim another Christ, a Christ not named in the original writings but substituted by the blind or the deceiver that the God of Heaven is always aware.

Still, some will say their Bible has the name Jesus in it and that is the name all the verses of the New Testament use. They'll also look at all the miracles in that name Jesus, not to mention all the prayers answered. That is exactly my point; the deception runs deep and has been ongoing, in development for the past few hundred years. Make no mistake, the Bible and the message are true and faithful, and our Heavenly Father looks on the heart of the seeker and the convert, but a time is coming, and for some, is now, when He is going to uncover this deception.

Even now many in the Evangelical churches are using a name, Yeshua, that is almost right and true, but they use it interchangeably with the bogus name *Jesus*. If I have not scared you off at this point, please continue, with an open, Truth-seeking mind. I pray you will find this article informative and challenging and will give you concern for your spiritual well-being. Many of you already know and have accepted this Truth, and for you, this should stiffen your resolve not to waiver in the face of critics and those refusing this basic Truth.

I should not have to prove this in an age exploding with knowledge like never before, as everyone has access to the same knowledge at the same time. Most like to see themselves as people in the know, well-informed and intelligent and collectively, as a people, informed as no others since the time of our beginning. Still, the Christian community is not concerned about this truthful subject at all. There is a deafening silence when it comes to this deception. The ignorance from the pulpit is astounding, or it is a deliberate conspiracy by the preachers, teachers and scholars of the Bible to deceive those honestly coming to the God of the Bible, Baba, for answers and seeking salvation.

The deception concerning this all-important subject is demonstrated in the silence regarding to our Savior's proper *birth name* as delivered by an ANGEL from Heaven. The Angel messenger could not have given the name Jesus to Mary and Joseph for the simple reason the name, JESUS, did not exist then – no one, not the Romans, not the Greeks, and most of all not the Jews had ever heard the name Jesus before.

It was 400 years before anyone would hear the name Jesus proclaimed as the Savior of the world! The promotion of the "bogus" name *Jesus* continues without as much as a question of its origins. A name all must come to and through whom all **must be saved**, and no one is asking where the name *Jesus* came from? Yes, there are a few – very few – that are raising the question; it's amazing in this age of information that this Truth is still so covered and ignored. Yes, we are seeing more and more television preachers beginning to use the name Yeshua and Jesus interchangeably, but you can see they are not committed.

Listen to the Biblical scholars, do you hear it – total silence. One would think the schools of theology, the professors of Biblical education, would all be howling at the preachers and teachers to get it right. Know the bogus name Jesus is a great error and begin replacing it with the true name of our Savior and you will quickly see why it is so important. (Acts 4:12, Phi 2:11).

Considering the name Jesus is in error, replace the bogus name with His correct birth name, YaHshua. Little by little, some have heard a strange name mentioned, the Hebrew/Aramaic name of our Savior, the name given Him at birth, YaHshua (YH's Savior), but this has been ignored for the most part. After all, look at all the miracles preformed in the name Jesus. Dreams have been proclaimed and prayers answered, all in the name of Jesus. This is true, but every religion can make the same claim.

Miracles are preformed and prayer answered, but in the end even Satan and his agents are able to perform miracles and to even appear as angels of light (2 Cor 11:13-15, 2 Tim 3:13, Col 2:18). Be forewarned, not all in the Christian Church is from our Creator. If in the first century Church the Apostles saw the wolves and the greedy and the evil and advocates of angel worship and even the agents of Satan entering the flock, entering in among the called ones of YaHshua, then how much more does this occur today?

Satan has had 2000 years of infiltrating the Church, and look at it, full of every sin and evil imaginable and all done in the name of Jesus. I thank my God He saw fit to allow His Holy Name to be hidden, to only be revealed at His choosing and His time. We should not be too amazed at this, I suppose, the church becoming so polluted; we can see plenty examples of Christians following traditions easily proven to be pagan in origin, handed down by the Romans and the Roman Church, polluting the Christian faith by festivals inherited from the pagan religions of Rome.

Those claiming to be Christians do not seem too concerned as they go happily about observing these pagan practices and tradition. These traditions and festivals renamed to match places and names found in the Scriptures. This alone should send up red flags for the believers that something is wrong. When challenged by those outside their "church," they see the work of Satan tempting them – what they should do is see if it is true, if modern Christianity is a Pagan-practicing religion.

When someone is converted, cut to the heart, their mind opened to the Message of the Holy Bible, and they seek baptism and a desire to know more. They begin worship by putting all of their trust, as a child might, in the preacher or teachers of that group – forgetting the Message, no matter from whom it is heard, is from the Bible. The Bible is what the preachers and teachers should be promoting not their own work. This is natural, of course, but dangerous.

*Woe unto you, scribes and Pharisees, hypocrites! for you compass sea and land to make one proselyte (convert), and when he is made, **you make him twofold more the child of hell than yourselves.*** *(Mat 23:15)* Do you think this may apply to humanity? This is a charge our Savior laid at the feet of the Religious leaders of his days in the flesh. I think it applies today; the Message of Salvation is preached, and the new convert is then taught doctrine and customs and festivals that are not found in Scripture but can be found in the histories of Babylonian religions.

Very alarming to me, to see "called" people turn to the first group they encounter as their spiritual home. Understandable; but still alarming to witness the sincere heart of a new believer being turned so quickly to a false belief in a false hope, like the Rapture Doctrine. Certainly there are those hearing the "call" at a worship service and do feel some loyalty to that group but in Truth your loyalty should be to the Savior, to the calling itself, to the Word of Baba, the preachers are not the way but only an instrument and a fallible instrument at that.

I know of some that were called separate from any group or preacher, "called" by the reading of the Bible for themselves, their stony hearts crushed in repentance and immediately join with the first group of believers they encounter. The followers sometimes get entrapped by the doctrine and teachings of that group, being socialized into that group. People never questioning motives while giving up their freedom in the Messiah for the comfort of the group.

Once "called," your devotion needs to be to our Lord and Savior and your job is to be searching the Word, studying the words, not just reading *(2 Tim 2:15 – Strong's #G4704, to make effort, labor, be diligent, study).* You do not need a massive library, really; the Bible stands on its own. Men have spent lifetimes finding verses to cross reference with other verses with few or no Bible aides. Today, we are fortunate that we have the work of these men to help us, but they prove that all you really need is a Bible and to set your goal on knowing more about your Savior and Father.

Read, take notes, mark pages – the Holy Bible is a set of study books all bound together with everything you need to know about our Creator and Savior YaHshua. Not too many professing Christians seem to care; they are happy to just float along, take in the feel good messages, and go their way. They should care, they should be hungry to know more, hungry for Him, our Savior – once saved always saved, right?

When the initial excitement of conversion wears off, we are back to business as usual, for some, but for others it becomes a crazy ride of religious fanaticism *(from Latin, meaning "frenzy")* trying to get or hold that feeling of original conversion over and over again. Soon, you see this same kind of religious frenzy similar to pagan or primitive religions around the world – the jumping up and down, the swaying back and forth, the fits, the falling backward, and on and on it goes.

The emotional expression that some outsiders see as fits is all about confirming you or they have the spirit. Our Savior compared a person entering the Kingdom to a little child, and what is it a child does above all else? He or she believes their parents; without question they believe. What happens with a few, however, is they do not believe in their heart of hearts, so they need the physical confirmation. There are spirits out there only too willing to oblige by giving the seeker of such things as a very spiritual feeling, a child of the Living God is one of spiritual control as His Spirit is one of order and discipline.

Once the excitement of new knowledge, of being called, dissipates, our focus should be to know more, growing in knowledge about Him, and to do that, the Holy Bible is really the only book we need. In this age of increased knowledge, however, we have many other works to help us, but the primary book is and always should be the True Holy Bible.

Waging War in His Name

Praying to Baba (Baba Alaha) and his son Yahshua (Eesho) brings ease to your pain and suffering and feeds your soul with joy and much more. If you have no intention of at least eating His bread once, then you never will know the potential within yourself to shine for His Universe. Pray to our Holy Father who created the Universe, the father of Abraham, Moses, Ishmael, Isaac, Jacob, of Yahshua the Messiah, our Father. During the writing of my book, innocent Iraqi Orthodox Catholics, followers of Eesho, were being murdered, exiled or forced to convert to a religion other than their own.

The radical extremist groups that had taken over Iraq began the bloodshed in the name of Allah. Baba [Our Holy Father] has the *only* right to judge mankind as he desires. Man should never judge any other person on this Earth for their beliefs or creed. People have a right to choose their path; we cannot judge them for their path of choice. There will be judgment from the only Judge in the end for the path each human chose. Baba will have the last Word; He is all about Love.

Man never should use our Father's name in vain to conquer nations and instill fear on others with their own beliefs of right and wrong. If man chooses to shed blood of the innocent in His name, then they are disobeying Baba's commandments and face dire consequences. If radical religious groups decide to make their own religion righteous, then they arrogantly challenging Baba's Word. Religion was a mistake from the beginning, dividing nations, people and families.

Religion caused many wars among the nations, and extremists are presently decapitating innocent people and anyone else who is forced to convert in the name of Allah. Baba gave every human free will to choose their path wisely, choose the golden harmonious path of His Love. Baba hears the cries of the children and records the murder; uttering in the name of Allah by religious radicals. Alas; Baba is saddened and enraged. If He chooses to kill anyone or everyone on Earth in His own name, Baba can destroy any or many with a justifiable thought.

Within the Hebrew Torah, Yahshua the Messiah never shed anyone's blood other than His own for our sins. As a matter of fact, He performed many healing miracles in Baba's name. How many blind followers are unaware of the evil intentions of the radical extremists who terrorize this world? Humans are not born bad or evil; they are born with sin. Their parents or guardians teach them the ways of evil and hatred toward others who are unlike themselves.

When fear and hatred is taught to our young ones, Baba's original structure of peace and Love embedded in the child's DNA is ruined. The righteous who Love will realize the Love of Yahshua and Baba will bring peace to the world. They must stand up against the slaying of their innocent brothers and sisters who Love the Father and the Son. Baba is the creator, one Word, one Breath who brings prosperity and peace among all nations on this Earth. My relatives and other families alongside with Christian and Catholic-Orthodox ancestors in Iraq have suffered near genocide at the hands of the radical extremist.

People must realize that the devil's hatred of mankind controls those who draw the blood of the innocent. They are also the hidden in cloth of the clergy, the secret societies, Kan's decedents, the Barabbas voters and political agendas, bankers who are the warmongers. Controlling others as pets to create hate and fear against the nations to raise their sword and slay the innocent. Funding many nations to war made them guilty of breaking Father's Law.

They use corruption by way of force and threats to renounce one's true Faith of Truth, Love and Peace and to join the false doctrines of lies and murder. Religion is an excuse of war because it is easily used to control the masses that follow the supposed leaders of peace. What is said is heard while what is thought is silently hiding their sinister plan. Many of the clergy also have cloaked themselves with the devil's cloth to deceive the world of their true intentions of serving the evil one. Religion divides people and conquers them.

Religions that promote their own belief of Love and Truth are neither right or wrong; you must follow Yahshua's Truth because of His Word. Baba's Word is always true and never false. I am not promoting any religion in my book. Yahshua never had a religion; he had his Father's Love. We were instructed by Yahshua to follow him to his Father's Love. Where is the religion in that instruction? If the Love for Him and his Son is their religion, then I will march with my brothers and sisters when they arrive.

As we are all to march with Yahshua with Faith, Courage and Love. Your heart should be full of grace and devotion, humbly welcoming your brothers and sisters. From the beginning, He knew the ending of our journey on his bridge to join him in his kingdom. The story Baba had written in his book of life for humanity foretells his eternal Love for his children throughout the Universe. Yahshua always will guide you to His Father when you eat His bread and drink His Love. Your mission is to touch the hearts of many with the Love for and from Yahshua within your own heart.

No other individual on this planet can save you, only you can save yourself. When Baba opens the doors that you have knocked on to the path of His salvation, you have to take the initiative to better your life for the opportunities that are available for you. When will you repay your Father providing you the help that you need? When are you grateful? When you get what you ask for first or when you awake every morning?

Yahshua explained in His book of Truth not to have expectations for your desires and not to presume anything without the Truth. The advice given by your Teacher can be eaten as food for your mind and sustenance for your heart. When humanity finally realizes His authority upon the Earth, all will be on their knees and blessed for eternity. Yahshua will rule this planet with His father's authority, and all the angels and saints will be with him. We are all our Holy Father's saints, Yahshua's brothers and sisters walking on His path of Truth-Love-Faith-Courage-Justice.

The Ten Commandments

(Baba's Codes of Morals and Ethics)

1. I am your Father; you shall have no other Father before me.

2. You are forbidden to worship an idol in any form.

3. You are forbidden to use Father's name in vain.

4. Remember the Sabbath day, to keep it holy.

5. Honor your mother and father.

6. You are forbidden to commit murder.

7. You are forbidden to commit adultery.

8. You are forbidden to steal.

9. You are forbidden to lie.

10. You are forbidden to be envious of your neighbor's home, wife or property.

CHAPTER 1

Jéjee Is Awake

(Names have been changed for privacy.)

{The names' of my immediate family remained as is.)

Yawn....I awoke in Baghdad, Iraq, in the year 1973. The month and day of my birth were changed by my mother to hide my existence. However, I shared birthdays with my sister for many years. Truthfully; my birth by Baba's will was in April of '73. My earthly dad is not my father; Baba had written my name in his book from the beginning. I was placed into my mother's womb by the Holy Spirit through divine intervention.

Sandy, my older brother, was born one year prior to my arrival with the help of my earthly dad, Kalid. Unfortunately soldiers who are in active duty must return to base shortly after. My dad was part of the Paratrooper Special Forces in the Iraqi army while my mother was home caring for my brother. Ironically, my dad's skill trade is carpentry, similar to Joseph with Mariam.

My mother Mariam was instructed by my Holy Father, giving me the name Jéjee, the name for St. Giorgis. There is only one Jéjee, as there is only one John, Peter, Matthew, Michael, Gabriel, Raphael, Uriel, etc. I am who He made me to be for eternity. I am His living proof who allows me to witness the evil forces of this planet. The ones who wield their sorcery among the nations and especially against His followers. I am grateful my Father gave me patients and much more Love than the dumbass who is ruling this planet at the moment.

At the age of two, I was stricken with a high fever and taken to the hospital. To complicate matters further, a doctor mistakenly injected me with a supposed antibacterial shot. Paralyzing the left side of my body due to the side effects of the medication interacting with my high fever. The doctor who examined me explained to my dad that I would not have any use of the left side of my body for two years or never. My dad was determined to find a solution to my paralysis. However, in the early 1970s modern medicine and technology where unavailable in Baghdad.

My dad spoke with the director of the hospital who would be personally in charge of overseeing my electrotherapy recovery process. The nuns at the hospital had me wired to a muscle stimulating machine not intended for children with complicated conditions. During the nun's routine therapy rounds, they had forgotten to take me off the electro-therapy machine after the seven-minute time limit had passed. I was on the machine for at least fifteen minutes to which my heart could not tolerate the shock any longer and stopped.

After hearing the news of my death, my dad rushed to the hospital from the military base. My dad was furious, ready to bring the whole Iraqi army to destroy the hospital. It seemed my dad and Saddam were close, so he had some pull and push. As my dad arrived to the hospital, he rushed over to see my lifeless body for confirmation. He prayed to my Father, to Yahshua, to all of heaven to save me. My Father heard him and gave me a second chance.

My dad described a nun who appeared during my dad's prayer. The nun looked angelic and blessed with His love. After the heavenly nun held my lifeless body, I was once more awakened by His command. The entire hospital, not to mention the director, was ecstatic over my return. The director assigned me with the blessed nun who provided help for my recovery. The angelic nun was able to bring back movement and feeling to my left side within two months. After a swift and miraculous recovery, my dad wanted to show his appreciation to the nun; however, she was nowhere to be found.

The director stated to my dad that he had no recollection of the nun or assigning me with a nun. My dad frantically searched the hospital for the whereabouts of the angelic nun, questioning a majority of other nuns and staff working at the hospital, all to no avail. My dad never forgot that day, the day of the angelic nun who was sent to answer his prayers. Time progressed, and I began the struggles of physical therapy for a limping child. Being the one left behind or pitied takes a toll on the human spirit.

However, our Father's spirit gives us the strength to march on. Eventually my dad and mother finally received their visas to travel overseas. We said our farewells to our families and friends and we headed for Athens, Greece. The trip was swift arriving on a fast cruise boat. So there I was, a four-year-old living in Greece with all the colossal monuments towering over me. There was one named Acropolis the Parthenon on top of a mountain with stone steps that looked enormous, reaching to heaven. My family and I were touring Greece for memories, and what a memory it was.

I had difficulty trying to keep up with everyone due to the muscle atrophy on my right leg. The weakness was the result of being shorter in length than the left leg. Going up the steps of stone took a toll on anyone, let alone a handicapped child. I remember praying to Baba to help me walk up the steps of stone. As tired, battered, beaten and bruised as I was, I felt the presence of happiness and strength from Baba.

I felt the adventure of climbing that mountain of stone steps all on my own, with His help of course. As I looked up to climb the next stone I saw a black cat on the ledge of the mountain stone steps. The cat gestured at me to approach it. The elusive black cat started running up the mountain ledge when I approached to pet it. After repeated failed attempts, I was enraged. I gained the energy from my Father and warped drive up the stone steps after the strange black cat. I passed all of my family members and bystanders on my hands and feet as my mom was screaming in Aramaic, "Kalid, catch him!" yelled my mother.

Even the fastest person there was unable to catch me or keep up. "Jéjee stop!" screamed my dad. I looked up at the black cat that had stopped near the top of the stone steps and pointed at my dad. I glanced back at my dad and saw him approaching faster than anyone else who was trying to catch me; being in the military did my dad some good with strength and stamina. As my dad approached, he had terror, anger, relief and joy expressed.

I explained to my dad I was running after the black cat, while pointing at the ledge where the cat was sitting. My dad looked at the ledge next to me and all around with no cat in sight. I turned to look at the cat next to me while it was licking its paws and brushing its snout. "What black cat?" asked my dad. "The one right there!" as I was pointing at the black cat, it waved goodbye at me and jumped off the ledge. I was horrified, and my human instinct to save the cat made me leap over the edge after the cat. My dad reacted quicker and grabbed my ankle before I plummeted to my death.

I heard screaming from my family and people as my dad stopped me going over the ledge. I was in tears and pain from my ankle being slammed on the stone. When I looked over the edge, there was no black cat. I was confused as to why the cat jumped, why my dad was unable to see it and where did it go? Huh, no wonder black cats are revered as evil in most cases; the thing tried to kill me. Shortly after that incident we let the pain and memories subside.

But, do not let your guard down and think that it is over; always be alert and vigilant. However, this time I did not have to climb to meet my doom. Greece was such a calm and peaceful land back in those days, it makes you wonder who would ever harm a child in paradise. The harm toward me did not come from mankind; the harm came from an evil force that wanted me dead, from the dumbass who left. The tropical beaches in Greece are incomparable to the beaches of the world, bar none. The hot tropical sun beamed down on the sand and surf causing exhaustion to all its' visitors.

My family and their Greek neighbors decided to head home from the beach of fun and sun. When you are on a paradise island, you tend to keep your guard down because everyone is so laid back with no worries. However, our journey home was going to test our inner Faith and Courage. Automobiles in Greece were zippy, and everyone was in a hurry. Safety belts were unnecessary in the 1970s paradise island.

I thought I was safe sitting in the middle of the rear seats; at least everyone else and I thought that. I had the best seat in the back; –a crisp clear view of the road in front of us sitting next to my mother and her friend. There was no need to wear your seatbelts in paradise. The man who was driving was my dad's friend and he was fast. As we zipped along the road, I remembered the vinyl car seats were bouncy and slippery. Everyone was having a good time, life was good, the Love meter was full. Laughter and enjoyed filled our space while heading home.

That was soon to alter our brief existence on this planet. Life is short enough, buckle up. The driver of our fate was conversing with my dad in Greek while coming to an intersection on the road. I remembered our light was green and no idea how fast we were traveling. Inertia was going to introduce itself to me. While both men were facing each other talking, the woman next to me alerted the driver to stop just in time. The weird part was that the experience was all in slow motion for me.

I actually saw the evil look on the man's face in the other vehicle, as he deliberately slowed down and stopped in front of us. Our vehicle was coming to a screaming halt as I was flying toward the front windshield. Before my head touched the windshield, my hero saved me once more. My dad grabbed me with his super-fast soldier reflexes before I smashed through the glass and painted the road with my blood. What felt like eternity at a standstill can take micro-milliseconds for Baba to test your Faith and Courage. After a couple of years in Greece, my family and I finally arrived to Detroit in November 1979.

Experiencing snow for the first time for a boy from the tropics is a wow factor. My first visionary encounter with Yahshua the Messiah was during my first summer in America. I remember standing outside on the upper balcony of our two-family stacked home looking up at the bright blue sky with a hot, life sustaining sun. While enjoying the scenery, Yahshua's enormous head came down from the sky and floated a few feet away from me. He began to speak to me about what would happen in my life.

I could feel his breath hitting my chest, and His words entering my heart. Yahshua also mentioned I would be seeing him again in my mid-forties. I will not discuss that here; my message was only for me from Him. The message from my King was rather confusing back then at six and a half years old. Yahshua told me that I would have to go through life with pain until we meet again. Well, a bone deformity, leg length discrepancy, and a cut Achilles tendon should qualify for pain for quite a while. Anyone with those kinds of conditions could understand the painful days and nights of daily living.

After I was debriefed by my teacher, I immediately ran inside to yell the great news to my family. My earthly brother was first on the scene. After explaining the story about how Yahshua came to guide me through the journey that I had to endure through suffering. *Smack!* "Why did you hit me!" I screamed. "Because, so you would not forget!" my brother replied. We both yelled for our mother, who heard the commotion between us. She entered our living room only to hear the shocking news.

Slap! "Mom!" I screamed again as my mom was in smacking distance. "I am sorry habibi, come here and give me a hug. You have to follow Eesho, listen to what he has to tell you or show you and do not be afraid." "I will Mom, I will follow Eesho, I will not be afraid." I was in tears, in pain, confused and angry, yet I received hugs from my mother and brother to calm me down. One year later, someone very important arrived to our home. That day, I became His Truth to prove to me dad truth. I was an energetic young boy, a bit too energetic.

My brother and I were all playing as any children would play loud, company over or not. While my sister and mother were out shopping. However, that day was going to be a memorable day for my dad, brother and I. The man who came over had a very powerful energy surrounding him. I befriended him, yet deathly afraid of him. My siblings and I were usually playing that day, however; my dad began to reprimand me to behave. I did not understand why my dad was being so strict.

We had played loudly and vigorously with company over many times. However, I experienced my dad's anger and sadness toward me that day I would never forget. My dad yelled out in tears as he grabbed my arm and walked me to my room. "Oh dad, what did I do, I was just playing, I wasn't too loud?" I pleaded. "Stay in here until our guest leaves!" yelled my dad. "OK I will, I will" I was crying in tears and confused as to what I did wrong to trigger my dad's disciplinary actions. Moments later, my brother peeked around the corner into our room to see how I was doing.

"Are you OK?" asked my brother. "Yes, what did I do wrong, I was playing with you guys, you were just as loud as me, why aren't you guys in here too?" I pleaded. "I don't know Gandy." My brother sat next to me and hugged me to calm me down and keep me company until our guest leaves. While we were sitting there, I heard my dad arguing with our guest. "No, I can't; don't make me do this!" my dad begged our guest. "Do it now, or I will take him away from you!" demanded the guest.

"OK, OK, don't take him away!" I began to hear my dad crying while searching for something creating all that noise outside our room. When my dad came around the corner and into the room, I nearly pissed and crapped myself. "No dad, please don't, what did I do wrong? "Be quite, I have to do this!" cried my dad. "I'm sorry dad, I'm sorry!" -CLICK!- I was done for, I was doomed, I was incarcerated to my bunk bed with a steal chain around my left ankle with a lock. "Nooo! Dad! Nooo!" I screamed aloud.

"Dad, what are you doing, why are you doing this? cried my brother. "Sandy, you stay out of this and be quite!" "Oh dad, I love you so much, please takes this off me. I promise I will never be loud again. I promise; please!" I pleaded my dad. My dad was on his knees crying with his head hung low. While; my brother was resting his head on my shoulder crying as well. I looked up and noticed our guest watching us near my door while this was all happening. Then our guest revealed His Truth sealed within my heart for eternity.

"YH'!"

"Arrrgh!" "Nooo!" I shouted. Both my dad and brother turned to see why I   was   terrifyingly screaming and screamed also. "Nooooooooaaaah!" My beloved father Baba showed me his face that made me burst off my bunk bed and crashed out the window. As I leaped out our second-story window, I dragged the chain linked bunk bed with me while Sandy was still sitting on it. My dad and brother were screaming at me while I was in mid-flight tugging on my chain, trying to get away.

I was trying to pull the bunk bed out the window. "Jéjee! Jéjee!" screamed my dad. "Gandy, Oh my God, Gandy, dad help him!" "Jéjee look! Jéjee! Look where you are!" yelled my dad. I did not realize where I was until I noticed my wings and I looked down to see I was not falling. "Oh shit, Daaaaaad!" I felt like St. Peter walking on water with Yahshua until he looked down. I was imitating a cartoon character defying the laws of gravity until realizing there was no supporting ground.

Whoosh! Thud! "Ooooff!" Good thing my dad put that chain around my ankle, otherwise I would have fell straight down or flew away, huh. Instead, I abruptly slammed the side of our house and hung upside down until my dad pulled up into my room. When I was finally in the room, our Holy guest had vanished, however, our memories remained forevermore. That day my dad and brother witnessed His truth. We lived in Detroit until 1986 then moved to Warren, Michigan. I grew up a hectic and painful life yet an adventurous one nonetheless.

No obstacle or person stopped me from giving it my best with any sport or activity I participated in. Physical disabilities should never prevent you from giving your best to Baba. Your Faith and spirit will keep you going to seek His Truth. I performed average in certain studies and excelled in others. Life in school was difficult trying to look cool walking with a limp. Beer Junior High School was a memorable adventure I will never forget. Walking with a limp meant also running with a limp.

So there I was, thirteen-years-old on the school track and field, Mr. Speedy Gonzales, "Undele! Undele! Arriba! Arriba!" A never give up never surrender spirit flowed through my body. The Baton Relay Race event was about to begin. Schoolmates and teachers were either encouraging or deterring my participation. Humans are cruel or compassionate to physically challenged individuals. I was excited and honored to be part of this historical athletic school event, even though I was no athlete.

We were in groups of three on each of the four track paths. The runners who were to begin first had pipes in their hands. I thought they were about to battle, ha-ha. I was new to this sport, but comprehended the concept quickly. My team had a feeling we were about to come in last but cheered me on nonetheless. I felt sorrow for the ones who had to go through life being bullied and targeted for imperfections. Do not become a bully, jerks; He is watching you, and He will send for your surrender.

The competition was ready to begin, and my heart was pounding to escape of my chest, I felt like I was already running standing still. I did not realize how far a half mile was until it was my turn to give Him my very best. The crowd was going crazy cheering, I heard my family and friends cheering me on lifting my spirits. The second hand-off of this weird pipe to my teammate was on the way. I prepped my mind with prayer to my Father; my Brother, to all of heaven to give me strength. I glanced at my competitor's strong legs and imagined my legs were just as strong. "Roar!" shouts my spirit, "Roar!"

Here they come around the corner, we were in the lead because my teammates were faster than the others. "Come on! Run! Yeaaah!" I screamed cheering for my team. I began my pace and was ready to grab the metal baton and hobble into high gear. "Huff! Huff! Huff!" "Run Gandy! Run!" I heard the crowd yell. I was running for my life away from the other racers closing in on me fast. Hobbling along the half mile was brutal, exhausting and exhilarating at the same time.

I was gasping for air while feeling my heart beating to His spirit like the little drummer boy. I had never run so hard, fast or that far in such a short time in all my life; my guts were about to show me what I had for lunch. *Zoom! ran* the other sprinters past me as I was half-way to the finish line. However, on that day, my Father wanted to test my Courage and Faith. Losing my footing, I stumbled and took a dive on my knees, knuckles and chest, dropping the baton. "No!" "Get up!" "Get up!" I could not disappoint my cheering crowd, my audience of His Faith.

I was crying in pain and defeat, but heard Yahshua's voice, "Jéjee, get up and run, I am with you." I felt His immense power jolt me off the ground and boldly grabbed my scuffed baton; furiously hobbling the remaining distance with dignity and determination. All the while noticing everyone cheering and crying for my victory. "Gandy!" "Run!" "Go!" "Yeaah!" My eyes were filled with tears I could barely see the finish line. I exhaled my last breath across the ribbon that they held for me and nearly collapsed in my coach's arms.

"You did it Gandy, you did it! I am so proud of you!" "Thanks coach, but we came in last." "No Gandy, we all won because of you." I did not know how we won, but it looked like everyone was cheering for us as though we had finished first. I received my first athletic medallion and ribbon necklace to show my accomplishment in His book of life, I was honored to make my Father happy. Like I said before, never give up never surrender and give Him your all even if you fall; get up, brush your pain off and keep going.

That day was a memorable day, a glorious Yahshua day for the masses of empathy to witness His power in a young hobbling boy who never gave up. Always remember, He is always with you giving you strength and courage in your life whenever you need Him. Moving forward in my life after my heroic athletic popularity advancement, the next level was high school. My social life in high school was about being part of the crew; the people who were the "in-crowd" meant popularity with the friends and women at house parties. I decided one day that I wanted to have a house party of my own.

I finally got the opportunity while my mom, dad and siblings were away on vacation and I stayed home. People commented that it was one of the coolest house party ever. I was glad to have everyone enjoy themselves and remembered the good times we had. Especially when house parties get messy after the fun ends, host cleans. Mission successful, popularity level increased. Life on this planet lets you down or lifts you up; the decision to accept defeat will render you hopeless throughout your life. Never let any disability render you or rear you, have courage and faith and you will win in the end.

If you eat the food of man only and not of His bread, there is a higher chance that you will be left behind. Have no fear, eat His bread and drink His wine of salvation to find His Truth. I had my ups and downs in life, however I was constantly full with His mana. I also had my share of trouble with man's law. I have been incarcerated for possession of marijuana and discharging a firearm. "Forgive me for being half-human and reckless, Baba." I was charged for two separate crimes on two separate occasions.

The sentence for discharging a firearm was lowered to a misdemeanor. I had help from my lawyer, mother, uncle and brother. The 1990s were another memorable timeline for me. First and foremost, family who love you are more important than your street friends. Fake friends will leave you behind to rot while they enjoy their freedom and livelihood. Humans are unpredictable by nature separating each other with our inner thoughts. We cannot be read like a book by looking at its' cover. My dad was furious when he heard the news of my downfall.

I did not blame my dad for being angry at me, since I used his Walter PP7 handgun without his permission. The memorable anger from my dad yelling at me over the phone at the police station. "When I get my hands you, I'm going to kill you, I want you to return my gun you stole from me exactly where you found it, or don't come home at all, you understand me!" yelled my dad ripping me in half. "I'm sorry Dad, they will not give it back to me; they said they were going to keep it or destroy it." I was in tears and fear for my life, however my dad was not going to kill me.

He was justifiably expressing his anger and authority in our culture. We must all honor and love our parents, even if it means devastating their hearts by the actions do when we are young. All of us can make amends and leave our reckless past behind us to continue our path with Yahshua to His salvation. A long time was earned for my dad's trust; because his forgiveness was solider tough and gradual. The choices we make in our lives can turn out for the worst or have great rewards awaiting us. I made the wrong choice and experienced the taste of His bread that was bitter from my tears.

However, I was still on the path Baba prepared for me and that guided me back with Yahshua's light. For the record, no one was injured that night, besides my ego and my face from the deserved slaps of my dishonor. I learned a lesson of a lifetime about dealing with the wrong crowd. So I decided to hang out with people who were more laid back. I chose the mellow moments in my life and began smoking marijuana. However, even staying out of the lawman's reach whilst in the 1990s was bullshit.

The marijuana charge was not even my fault. I was just the passenger on my way home from work in my brother's five-speed manual Mustang GT. I was working the late night shift at a video store getting ready to close up for the night. Thirty minutes before closing, I received a phone call from my best friend wanting to hang out and smoke some hippy herb with me. My friend was getting dropped off at my work place, and I would drive him home after we closed the shop. Shonuf showed up and I was ready to get into chillaxed mode.

"Wasup Gan?" shouted Shonuf. "Wasup Shonuf?" I replied. "I got some bubonic chronic for the ride home bro." said Shonuf holding a bag of marijuana. "Bro, put that away before you stink up the whole store, hahaha." I said looking around for customers. "I see your brother let you drive his stang." asked Shonuf. "Yeah, my brother didn't feel like dropping me off at work while he was heading out with his friends" "Sweet, can I drive back?" asked Shonuf. "Bro, I am so tired from work, would you mind?" I said.

"Sure, I don't mind. I'm a bit rusty driving a stick though." replied Shonuf. "No worries, it's almost midnight, barely anyone is on the road." I explained. "OK, sounds good, you roll, I'll drive." replied Shonuf. After checking out the last customer; I finished my daily routine and locked up the store. Parking lot was empty so that gave Shonuf some room to practice. Driving a stick shift takes finesse and timing when shifting through the gears. My friend was still a bit off his timing and stalled the GT a couple times at the light. "Crap! Sorry bro, I'll get the hang of it."

"Shonuf, take your time, ease up off the clutch and give it gas at the same time, try not to pop the clutch." After a couple of miles driving and feeling the finesse, we were ready to spark it up. We puff-puff-passed the joint until we noticed some weird colored lights down the road. "Oh shit! are those cop lights up ahead?" "Shonuf don't freak out bro, chill out, just act natural." For the moment, we were in the clear from the two patrol vehicles that had pulled over another vehicle at the intersection.

Moronically I placed the marijuana joint we extinguished temporally in my cigarette box. Nervous and beyond paranoid, my friend was freaking out. "Relax bro, just remember to slowly ease up off the clutch; don't pop it." I said trying to instruct Shonuf. "I will-I will, I got this bro, Shit! Fuck!" yelled Shonuf. "Relax-relax, hurry, start it back up." My friend started the Mustang back up and but stalled it halfway through the intersection "We're fucked! We're fucked!" "Oh crap not again, shit-shit; one of them is pulling away, hurry bro hurry, start the car, start it up!" I yelled.

One of the patrol cars noticed our suspicious activities and decided to investigate. My friend finally got the car in gear and jerked our way to the speed limit. Shonuf looked in the rearview mirror and said; "Is he behind us, is he behind us?" "Yes, calm the fuck down and drive the speed limit!" I yelled. In about a half-mile, the police officer who was trailing us decided to investigate even further and turned on his strobe lights. "Fuck! Where should I pull over, we're on a main road?"

Shonuf was trying to find safe spot to pull over. "Just find a street and pull over before he thinks we are trying to get away from him." Out of all the places to pull over, my friend decided to pull over into church property. I am not a religious person, but I have morals and was not about liter the church grounds with drugs. On top of what we were about to go through, my friend decided to put the icing on the cake. "Throw out the joint before he gets out of the car." yelled Shonuf; "Are you serious bro, we are on church grounds!"

I had no idea how to react to following question. "Bro, you got to help me out, I don't want to go to jail!" Logically we were in a situation we had no control of future events, so I replied logically. "What do you mean go to jail, bro you just stalled the car, it's OK, just tell him your new at this, and it's my brother's Mustang." Shonuf replied with a WTF comment. "Bro, you don't understand, I don't have a license, it's suspended." Oh life, so full of surprises and so much drama. "Holy shit! Why the fuck are you telling me this now!"

I could not understand why Shonuf did not reply logically when he said: "Help me bro, let me borrow your license, it's dark, he won't see you, just look the other way." "Say what bro, I am sitting right the fuck next to you, it doesn't matter if it's dark; he has a flashlight. What if the gets us out of the car?" My heart was bigger than my brain at the time and could not bear to see my best friend terrified of going to jail. We used to enter night clubs while my friend Shonuf used my state ID and I used my driver's license; we had similar facial features.

Those door attendants had rocks for brains, my friend is six foot-two inches tall and I am five foot-two inches tall, huh. "Bro please, I don't want to go to jail trust me he won't look at you; I'll block his view." asked Shonuf. "OK, the shit I do for you bro. Out of all the places you pulled up in a church, and I still half a joint in my cigarette box." agreeing to Shonuf's idea. "Just throw it out before he gets out of the car." "I can't bro, you don't understand." I dislike loitering anywhere, especially on church grounds.

I handed my best friend my driver's license and prepared for my punishment. The police took his time getting out of his patrol vehicle. The reason —calling in for backup. The first officer did not get out of his car until his backup arrived. The 1st Officer approached the driver. "Hi, license and registration please." "Hi Officer, sorry about stalling the car, it's my friend's car, I'm just learning how to drive a stick shift." replied Shonuf. "Yeah, he's a little rusty." I told the officer. The 2nd Officer approached my door.

Tap -Tap - Tap "Lower your window." I lowered my window, and Mr. Officer shines his bright flashlight on my idiot face. "My I see your ID?" requested the 2nd Officer. I hand the officer my state ID that I had with me at the time. The 2nd officer looks at my ID and asks me to step out of the car. I look at my friend who is still in the car and is about realize these cops are not stupid. The 2nd Officer instructs me to stand at the rear of my brother's Mustang to empty my pockets.

"Anything in your pockets that may stick me like guns, knives, needles?" asked the 2nd officer. "No sir." I confidently replied. The 2nd Officer pulls out my cigarette box and sniffs the interior contents. "Smells kinda funky in here." "That's cause there's a roach in there." replying with a politically correct statement. "A what? A roach?" yelled the officer. "It's a small joint that has already been smoked." informing the officer of street slang terminology. "Why didn't you say that in the first place?"

"Force of habit, I guess, you said smells kinda funky in here, figured I'd reply in slang." The 2nd officer placed my possessions on the trunk of the Mustang and asks me to wait there while he speaks to his partner. I notice my friend is being questioned by both officers now. I had painful visions of what my family was going to do to me. Especially what my brother was going to do to me. Drugs in my brother's Mustang, I am dead meat. The 1st officer approaches me and asks me what was I thinking giving my ID to my friend?

"I'm sorry officer, I didn't want him to go to jail, so I tried to help him." I pathetically answered. "Well, now you're both going to jail." replied the 1st officer. "What! What for?" I shockingly asked. "For obstruction of justice." interrupted the 2nd Officer. I have never heard that term before so I had to ask. "What does that mean?" "It means lying to the police, like giving your ID to someone else to obstruct our investigation." replied the 2nd Officer. "Crap, I didn't know that!"

I was thinking I would get off with just a warning, like one of those non-stupid bouncers at the clubs used to give us and not let us in the bar. "Well now you know, so don't do it again, lesson learned. Now turn around and place your hands behind your back, please." instructed the 2nd Officer. I had no other words but..."Huff!" We were both arrested, and my brother's Mustang GT was towed. I was ripped in half by my family, and my clear record was tagged by the law. While on probation for my crime possessing marijuana, I had to check in with my probation officer on a weekly basis.

There were times that I had arrived late or was unable to arrive due to lack of transportation. My probation officer was quite lenient with me on many occasions, but on the last request to change the appointment to another day, he refused. I had no choice and no way of getting there and violated my probation that had ended my freedom. During arraignment, the judge convicted me and placed me in Macomb County Jail for almost a year. Marijuana had a grip on my life.

No matter if any of my friends or family advised me to stay away from my bad news friends, we still remained in contact with each other. Drugs have a very deep impact on a person. It may be over the counter or from the streets. The drug overcomes your emotional senses and rational judgment while inhibiting true Love towards people. Of course, marijuana has many medicinal advantages for those with severe medical issues. When used recreationally, though, it is no different that drinking or abusing any other drug readily available.

I have experienced irritating behavior from and toward individuals who were smoking Marijuana or not. This drug has a chemical imbalance mood altering effect. Clouding the mind with an addictive state of falsehood euphoria. I continued to smoke because of its natural properties to ease my ongoing physical pain; however, I gradually eased back on smoking. I despise man-made drugs of any kind. If my Father in Heaven was not involved with the natural creation of the remedy, then it is man's poison.

If you do anything in moderation you will be fine, any indulgence beyond what your body and mind can handle, you are asking for a shattered life. Picking up the shattered pieces takes minutes or years if you do not have His help. Prayers, belief and faith in Yahshua and Baba can help you with your pieces. Look up with your heart, He will heal you to spread your wings and reach out the others who need your help. Show them how much power He gave you when you are healed by his Love.

Samson prayed to our Father to help break his chains bonded by non-believers and the hypocrites. Men or women can receive the same power as Baba's son did when you strengthen your Faith with His Word. All people on Earth have their own free will; unfortunately, humanity's free will is no longer free. Their minds have been programmed by the media, their neighbors, propaganda, fear and force. Stand up and give your testimony when you are called upon, when the trumpets are blown start marching.

Your brothers and sisters will be there marching with you, Yahshua will be with us. Baba will cover us with His hands to defend us from the evil forces that control this world with the tyranny instilled into the hearts of many. Pray to Him who has the Word of salvation to feed us for eternity. Remember that in the end, you will be graded on your faith, your morals, your actions, your forgiveness toward others. The big reward in heaven will constitute on your merit here on Earth.

Everyone will get their chance in the Affairs and Accusations building in heaven. He will give you eternal life or death and justifiably judge you. Most people have the impression that they are not being watched when they commit their actions toward others or themselves. Every individual should be treated with the respect they are requesting to receive the respect in return. Do onto others as you would have them do unto you. For the record, marijuana was the depression, anxiety, pain and stress relief drug for me, and nothing else.

I kept using marijuana because it was less harmful than any doctor prescribed medicine. I started smoking when I was seventeen years old. I never smoked during or before school or while at work. It was only during late hours when I had the chance to relax and ease the pain with joint. When under the influence of drugs, you are unable to function properly and lose focus especially while communicating with others.

CHAPTER 2

Thou Forbidden Touch

My dreams of becoming a police officer were destroyed from having a criminal record from marijuana. I still had an interest for the Information Technology field, though. After a few general jobs later, I enjoyed working for a company called Computer Warehouse. The store was located two miles from home and dealt with sales of computers and electronic components to the consumers and clients of the businesses.

After one year working in the Computer Warehouse retail store, I was promoted to the corporate store. Working in the corporate store location was rewarding and frustrating because of the commission-based income. If you win bids with companies writing proposals or waited for customers to walk in to purchase, it meant that you had to wait to get paid. The year was 1997; I was working one Sunday afternoon at the corporate store.

The co-workers and owner were out to lunch while the cashier, accountant, computer technicians, and I remained. The environment was peaceful and quiet with no customers in the store. The measurements of the business were 152 feet in length and approximately 85 feet in width. The whole store consisted of aisles with five-foot high shelves and four-foot-high counters for desktop and laptop computers. There was an aisle in front of my desk leading from the front of the store to the very back alley door with no obstructions.

The long straight aisle had a counter off the one side displaying different models of laptops, and the other side was a wall with shelves storing boxed items. The other side of the computer store housed offices for technicians, the president of the company, the accountant and office managers. I was seated at my desk gazing at the "The Last Supper," painted by Leonardo Di' Vinci, as my background image on my desktop. I stared at the eyes of the painted image of Yahshua, thinking.

What is life supposed to be all about, why am I here, what I am supposed to do in my life? If every prayer of Love to Baba by humans is answered, then the whole world would revolve many issues on His Word, the Word of Truth. Faith, Love, Courage and harmony are the recipe of coexistence of many on this planet. The ones with metaphorical daggers from their mouths, stabbing the ones they communicate with daily; would eventually cease to return. My mind seemed connected to His presence at my desk.

At the right side of my peripheral vision, I noticed a figure standing by the laptops near me. I thought I had a blur in my eye, as I turned my head. I did a double take and noticed there was a man dressed in a suit standing there. I was curious where this person came from and how he entered to store unnoticed. I dismissed it rationally and gave the customer a few minutes before I approached him. He glanced at me a few times, giving an indication that he needed assistance with the laptop he was interested in.

I remembered our sales training of providing the customer with some personal space and not to approach too quickly. After a couple minutes had passed, I approached the professionally dressed man. His medium trimmed beard, shoulder length wavy brown hair and hazel eyes made him look as handsome as ever. He was a six-foot-tall CEO of a very important company. He wore a black suit, black tie, white shirt with alight khaki linen trench coat, and royal red velvet scarf.

He smelled like flowers and fresh water, with a hint of heavenly breeze. I remember him like we had met just yesterday; how anyone could forget a man with such a magnificent profile is beyond me. I introduced myself as Gandy the IT Consultant and attempted to shake his hand but noticed he was a bit hesitant and avoided doing so. I thought he had a touch phobia or did not understand the culture of shaking hands. He noticed I was confused toward not allowing me to shake his hand. "Can you explain to me what are these devices, and what do they do?" asked the CEO in the suit.

"Devices; oh you mean these laptops." I wondered how could someone with his stature of success ask me what are these devices and what do they do? Again, I dismissed his strange question and began to answer his question about the functionality of the laptop. After a couple of minutes explaining features, the tall gentleman glanced at me and asked me a question other than pertaining to the laptop. "Is there something that you want to tell me?" he asked me.

"Tell you? You mean something about the laptops? Hmm, I've explained most of the features, unless I forgot something?" He insisted that I tell him what was on my mind. I thought it was a rather personal and odd question to ask someone, however, for some reason I had the urge to tell him the Truth of what was on my mind. "It's OK you can ask me." "Forgive me, I am not trying to embarrass you or put you on the spot, but you look like Jesus." I shyly asked him. "I do?" the man in the suit replied. "Yes, you resemble the face of Jesus on my desktop image of the Last Supper."

The CEO and I approached my desk to confirm the comparison; not quite however. I had seen his face in the sky when I was a child in Detroit. "Yes, I do look like him; I get those comments of similarity a lot." said the CEO "Oh good, there were others who noticed, that's great, it wasn't just me." I was so relieved that he was not embarrassed or angry. We bonded a bit more and continued to discuss the features of the laptop. In the middle of the conversion, the tall Jesus look-alike gentleman showed interest of purchasing the laptops.

"How much would it cost if I bought fifty of these laptops?" asked the gentleman in the suit. "Fifty, wow, top of my head I would say $150,000 before tax." I replied to Him. I was shocked on his request; laptops were around $3000 - $5000 per unit in 1997, with a commission-based job, I felt like winning the lotto jackpot. After I heard the surprising request, I remembered my training and wanted to initiate physical contact to show the customer that I am their friend giving him an honest deal and would never cheat them.

We had no section in the textbook manual available from my employer that educated their employees about situations titled:

"Do Not Touch Yahshua the Messiah Without Asking For His Permission."

With my right index finger, I touched his red velvet scarf and immediately saw the wall behind Yahshua vibrate furiously. There I was, standing on top of a hill, slight gust of wind, the smell of dust, elements and the noise of the surrounding people. I was absorbing as much data as possible.

I observed two women on their knees to my left crying for Yahshua, as he laid on his crucifix on the ground. I realized instantly the two women were Miriam of Nazareth, the mother of Yahshua, and Miriam of Magdala. I turned my head toward Yahshua to see two roman soldiers knelt down tying his biceps to the cross-beam. I faintly heard the two soldiers discuss their next step; when the solider to the right of Yahshua reached for a hammer and thick nail.

I tried to move with the fullest extent of my wrath and every ounce of power I had within me. I managed to reach my right arm out from my frozen state toward the solider with the hammer and nail who was ready to strike. "Noooooo!" I yelled as loud as I could. Gesturing with my hand, as though I wanted to strangle the soldier's throat who was about to make his bloodline history. The Roman solider noticed my presence when I roared and reached for him. He turned to look at the other solider across from him, pointed at me with his hammer, spoke a few words, then they both looked at me.

Noticing the commotion between the two soldiers and me, Yahshua tilted his head back to look at me and sadly nodded to let me know it is OK, this must be done. I was unable to control my torment, my wrath, my helplessness hearing and seeing my Teacher, my Love, my Brother, my Beginning and End in agonizing pain as the nails pierced his palms and feet. After they had completed their treacherous duty, the Roman soldiers lifted the log upright and place the base into a hole then hammered in wooden shims.

The unforgettably terrifyingly realistic senses of my surroundings were so intense and vivid, they sealed my memorable experience for eternity. My heart was ready to explode as tears flooding my eyes. My gut wrenching stomach was in knots seeing Yahshua being crucified onto his immortalized symbol. The soldiers hoisted the tree log up and added shims to the base. I had never experienced anything so frightening. I looked up at Yahshua with such sorrow for what they have done to him. When he lifted his head, opened his eyes and noticed me looking at him.

I felt my body being drawn into Yahshua's eyes and I was back in the computer store. My tunnel vision focused on my surroundings with the vibration of the walls slowing down and eventually stopping. I flicked my head back as though dozing off for a split second to avoid falling over. "Whoa, I got dizzy for a sec, I apologize." "What happened?" asked Yahshua. "Oh I just dozed off for a sec, I'm probably a little tired, were you asking me a question?" "No, something happened to you, would you like to tell me?

I was very reluctant to tell him of what just happened. Was I going to lose the sale, lose my job, get labeled as a quack? "I'd rather not." Yet, somehow, I felt compelled to tell him the Truth again. "It's OK, you can tell me." asked Yahshua "Are you sure? It sounds crazy." I nervously replied. "Yes I'm sure. It's OK tell me." insisted Yahshua. I described in as much detail as I could remember of my experience to him and waited to view his reaction. "Are you OK now?" said Yahshua. "Yes, I am OK." I replied. "Are you sure?" asked Yahshua. "Yes I'm sure, does that sound crazy?" I asked.

"No; sounds about right. Can you tell me a little more about these laptops?" My mind raced with an explanation on what just happened. How could I be there when I was here? How could I hear, smell and sense the environment where I had gone? Why was this happening to me? I was trying to solve every question without displaying emotional distress. However, I was one hundred percent positive I was there. I am not epileptic nor had any dizziness, fatigue or hallucinations.

I absolutely had no drugs, alcohol or any mental instability in my system at all. I was a professional when I went to work, concentrating on sales and success. My experience on Mt. Olives with His people crying and moving about the hill top, the dust blowing around in the wind and the thunderous clouds approaching was epic. I wanted so much to help Yahshua, yet sadly I was there only to observe. I dismissed the occurrence, apologized and began describing the laptop features and functionality. After a few more minutes of talking about the laptop my King requested a total of a larger quantity purchase.

"How much would it cost if I bought one hundred of these?" asked Yahshua. My eyes opened wide after I heard him say that. "You want to know how much one hundred of these laptops cost? Are you serious?" "Yes, how much would they cost?" replied Yahshua. "Oh ahhh, I'd have to calculate that if you can give me a few moments." I was terrible in math. "Maybe later. Can you tell me a little more about them?" asked Yahshua gesturing to the laptops.

I wanted to hug him if he would have bought all those laptops; I felt like I had won an even bigger lotto jackpot. No new employee had ever sold that many laptops with one transaction at Computer Warehouse that I was aware of. I was stunned by his remarks on the amount requested, yet I felt the need to initiate physical contact once more. I was awakened for eternity on what happened next. I wanted to further our friendship and do business with him endlessly. I remembered my sales training of physical contact with the man who looked like the King of Kings.

Palms of Psalms

"It is Baba who arms me with strength and makes my way perfect." – Psalm 18:32

I waited for the right moment to place my right hand palm on his left chest where his holy red velvet scarf rested. I was immediately shocked into a drunken state and fell to my knees. The blur surrounding me was moving while the words from Yahshua were muffled.

When I fell to my knees, my Teacher had my left hand in his right hand. I was so weak, so happy, so drunk with joy. His image was coming into focus from the immense waves vibrating uncontrollably. Yahshua spoke to me through my drunken slumber I was experiencing. I felt underwater listening to a human figure above. After a few attempts of Yahshua contacting me, I began to tune in to his Love and comprehend His words. I was coming up out of the calming waves to show me an image of a man standing above me while on my knees. "Gandy, Gandy can you hear me?" asked Yahshua.

I was surprised to hear Yahshua speaking Aramaic to me as I was being baptized. How could He call me by my given name; I was trying to be logical, how blind I was. "Jéjee, Jéjee can you hear me?" "Yes, I can hear you." I groggily replied with a euphorically joyous feeling. "Do you know who I am?" I glanced up at Yahshua's face with a glorious aura around his magnificent figure dominating my minuscule existence. "Yes I do; you're Jesus."

With the gesture of his left hand, as though to stop me from speaking and his right hand on the center of his chest, he shook his head and said "No; not Jesus; my name is Yahshua; call me Eesho. I am here for you, everything is going to be OK." "Eesho! Oh Eesho, how wonderful; thank you so much." I said cheerfully. I was still on my knees feeling drained of energy after contact yet very happy, calm and safe with him. He moved my left hand to his left hand and placed his right hand on my left shoulder. "Jéjee, I would like for you to stand up for me." commanded Yahshua.

However, before I was able to stand up, Yahshua had stopped me with his right hand. "No, I want you to get up on your right leg." My heart pounded vigorously "My right leg?" "Yes." said Yahshua testing my faith. "I can't; I haven't been able to stand up with my right leg ever since I was little." I sadly replied. My right leg was still very weak due to the muscle atrophy throughout my toddler years. I managed in my condition as though I was as normal as anyone else on this planet.

"You know who I am, and you believe in me, correct?" proclaimed Yahshua. "Yes!" I replied with faith. "Then if you believe in me, you can do anything you want; now I want you to stand up on your right leg." instructed Yahshua. "WOW, I did it!" I yelled. Yahshua smiled and made me feel loved. "Do you see, whenever you believe in me, you can do anything?" said Yahshua truthfully.

His Words of Truth, Words of Love, Words of Faith, Words of Courage from Yahshua to my soul; forevermore.

For many years I had no strength to lift myself with my right leg. I consistently used 90% power from my left leg and 10% power from my right leg. I felt like His champion once more when His power flowed through my body using infinite-% power. I was ecstatic with my accomplishment of strength and my loving belief for Yahshua. I had no idea what was next or what he had planned for me for the rest of my life. My weakness became strength; my doubt became Truth and my sadness became joy.

The immense feeling of eating His Holy Bread of Life is beyond explanation on any earthly level. I had the feeling of being initiated into the most elite organization that I had ever dreamt of joining, an organization more important than Earth itself. With YH' being the creator of the Universe, the Father of my older Brother, there are no others I would ever join. Yahshua is my Brother, my best friend, my greatest Heavenly Love who has my heart and soul in his hand. There is nothing more blessed than to have the gloriously greatest teacher in the Universe preparing you for graduation.

The most magnificent Messiah ever to live on this planet, he can provide you the light that will never blind you for eternity. He can lead you on his path of Truth to Baba's kingdom. His embrace gives you the Courage and Faith that you need to succeed in your life. Let him be the one who can provide for you whatever you ask for. Be faithful to Yahshua and live a truthful life; when he comes for you be ready for your re-birth. Yahshua will provide you the Courage to face any opponent when battle ensues.

Your Faith and Love will conquer nations or planets with His Word. Continue your faithful adventure to the very end to claim your reward; your Father awaits you. People today who live their lives as though they have no purpose, getting by day to day with desirable content, lack Faith. What will you do when Yahshua arrives to talk to you? Will you have the Faith and Courage to follow him to his Father's kingdom? Will you have what it takes to win battles with His armor and strength? Whenever you feel like you have no one else who will hear your suffering. Contending with the pages of your life, chapter after chapter; speak to Yahshua; he will listen. We all have Baba's number; Yahshua is His connection who puts us on hold until he is ready to answer our call. Informing his Father of our Faith and Love.

Hugged Baba's Love

Yahshua can show you what the meaning of life is all about. I had no idea what life was about until he showed me His Truth. I was in a calm state in front of Yahshua after I had stood up.

His glory and immense energy was transforming my blood. I knew that I had made the right decision. With his left hand still holding my left hand, Yahshua let go and with both arms stretched outward toward me. "Can I get a hug?" requested Yahshua. "A hug?...Yes!" I gladly said. Without question or hesitation, I surrendered to His will and obeyed every Word He spoke. I embraced my Big Brother and my Father who is within him. Time and the space was irrelevant hugging Yahshua, who I had missed dearly. I felt the loving childhood memories when my mom and dad had calmed me down.

The feeling of a hug after crying uncontrollably from the sadness, pain and suffering. I did not want to let go; I was one with the Universe. Shortly after; Yahshua and I stopped hugging, he held my left hand again and placed his right hand on my left shoulder and turned my whole body ninety degrees. I did not feel my legs move like I while gliding across the floor, ending up facing the rear of the store. "What would you like to do right now Jéjee?" asked Yahshua.

Thinking of my childhood of being left behind, unable to keep up with my family and friends. "I want to run as fast as the wind." I replied. "That is good; you will be fast, strong and much more." said Yahshua. "Fast, strong and much more, wow." I replied in awe. "Now, I want to you to run as fast as you can down this aisle and when you get to the end come back." said Yahshua instructing me. Before Yahshua could finish his instructions, I was moving my legs as fast as I could; unable to move, my legs looked like a blurry propeller. "Slow down, slow down, stop!" shouted Yahshua.

I could barely hear Him from all the propeller noises my legs were making moving back and forth swiftly. I immediately stopped and felt as though I landed on the floor. "Begin slowly and then gradually pick up speed." said Yahshua gesturing with his hand. "OK, sorry about that." I embarrassingly said. "It's OK, are you ready?" asked Yahshua. "Yes, I'm ready." I quickly replied. I was not dressed for this athletic tryout; I was in a suit with wingtip dress shoes; nonetheless, I was ready.

I began slow and kicked it into high gear and was at the end of the store within seconds. Before I reached the back of the store, I realized that I could not stop, I was running on carpet. "Whoa!" *BOOM!* I hit the wall at the rear of the store with full force, stopping myself with my hands and body. I turned around to see Yahshua still standing there by the laptops counter near my desk. He was gesturing for me to come back to him. I peeked my head out of the backroom and made sure the coast was clear before I ran back to Yahshua.

I began slowly; however, no time was wasted to turn on some supercharged turbo, I Love supercharged turbo. I was running faster than the Warner Bros. Roadrunner, *Hmeep! Hmeep! Whoosh!* Approaching Yahshua rapidly. I noticed him gesturing with his hands and could not realize what he was trying to tell me until it was too late. I was getting ready to pass Yahshua in supersonic speed, but he slowed down time and space with His authority. During the slow-motion effect, I turned my head towards him and understood his slow down gesture.

Immediately after; I sprung back into full speed, turned my head in the direction of a huge pane glass window at the front of the store. I prepared for impact with no way of stopping except to slide to a halt like I did at the back of the store. *SMACK! BOOOOOMM! POP!* I slammed both my knees against a shelf that housed some CD's, books and manuals just below the pane glass window. Placing both hands in front of me to brace for impact, I smacked the giant eight-foot by twelve-foot glass window with my right cheek.

Miraculously, the glass window warped outward like a balloon upon impact. I witnessed a lady at the business next door purchasing something at the cashier's counter. She had seen me warping the window like a balloon and pointed at me screaming, causing the cashier to look at me and scream as well. Seconds after hitting the glass window, it snapped me back into the store, tossing me through the air and landing me on my butt. The receptionist turned around just as she had seen me flying through the air.

CD's, manuals and books were scattered in the air falling to the floor. "Oh My God! Gandy are you OK, are you hurt, oh my God do you want me to call an ambulance, I thought a car crashed through the store!" shouted Danielle. "No-no I am OK, it was just me, no car, no need for an ambulance." I quickly replied. While gathering the scattered items on the floor, I noticed the lady outside from the business next door walk past the front of my store with her hands to her mouth and pointing behind me in shock.

She probably saw Yahshua behind me. I gestured for her to enter the store, but she shook her head in fear, waved no thank you and slowly continued to walk away. She will not forget that day I am definitely sure. The accountant heard the loud noise and commotion and came out of his office yelling. "What's going on, what was that loud noise!" yelled Victor. "It was just me Vic, sorry about that, everything is OK!" I shouted. "Keep the noise level down out here, OK?" demanded Victor. "OK!" I shouted giving Victor a thumbs up.

I turned to speak to Danielle with glee and laughter throughout my body. "I was just running over to the bookshelf to retrieve a CD for a customer who is standing near the laptops over there." gesturing towards Yahshua direction. Danielle turns her head and says "What customer?" I immediately turned my head to see if Yahshua was still standing there for verification. "The customer who is standing by the laptops near my desk." I pointed at Yahshua. Danielle turned her head to take a second look. "There is no one standing there."

I thought, how could this be, how is she unable to see Yahshua yet I can? "Wait a minute; you can't see anyone standing there, you can't even see a guy with a suit on near the laptops?" "No, am I supposed to see someone there?" replied Danielle. Chills flooded my body, as I glanced over to Yahshua almost in tears, as he gestured with his palms up and shrugged. I turned to Danielle and stepped back a bit trying to hold my composure and contemplate what just happened. I was frightened to the core but did not dare show my emotions.

I was a logical professional, I was Spock. "He must be walking around the store. If you see a man dressed in a suit, black tie, red scarf, and a Khaki trench coat leaving the store, please stop him. I would like to talk to him before he leaves, OK?" I just wanted to move away from Danielle and head back to Yahshua to figure out what was going on. "OK; Gandy are you sure you are OK?" asked Danielle. "Yes, I'm fine, no worries, just let me know if you see him. You can get back to what you were doing, I'm fine I'm fine." I replied.

Walking back to Yahshua, I had flashbacks of the incident, fear was trying to consume me, confusion set in, excitement filled my heart and Baba's son was still standing there waiting for me. So as to avoid acting like a crazy individual speaking to thin air. I approached Yahshua and stood next to him using one of laptops opening programs and checking laptop settings, etc. Danielle kept looking at me with concern and fear, probably thought, "This guy has just lost his marbles." Danielle finally turned and faced her computer screen.

I spoke softly to Yahshua while preventing myself from turning to face him and get caught by Danielle talking to a ghost. I was speechless; I wanted to understand what just happened but did not know where to begin. "What's happening, why can't she see you?" I asked Yahshua. "Because I am here for you, others may not be able to see me, Are you OK, you hit the shelf rather hard?" said Yahshua. "Yes I'm OK, my knees hurt just a little bit though." I explained. "Just a little bit, OK good, maybe you should have a seat while I look around the store and if I need you I will call for you." instructed Yahshua.

I obeyed his command and sat to ease my pain. Immense excruciating pain in my knees let me know His Truth. The memorable feeling of a hammer striking both knees would never be forgotten as long as the Universe existed. Was this really happening to me? Did I just run as fast as the wind? Did Yahshua take me to Mt. Olives? Did I slam my body into that glass window? Why are my knees throbbing with pain. How could she not see Yahshua? Is he really Yahshua the Messiah?

Thinking Oh Yah Baba help me, what is going on, what am I going to do now? My thoughts were racing a million miles a millisecond in slow motion to the speed of light squared. Remembering his instructions for me to be seated until called upon, I patiently waited His command. Glancing momentarily at Yahshua to affirm my sanity, to my relief he was still standing near me. I was in a Twilight Zone moment after having physical contact with Yahshua. I stared at my monitor then at Yahshua, then the monitor, then back to Yahshua, until I finally back to my computer screen.

I noticed movement to the right of my peripheral vision of a man moving away. As I turned to look at Yahshua, who I thought was walking away, I was shocked beyond imagination. Yahshua had lifted himself off the floor a few inches, and his shiny black dress shoes had transformed into sandals, and he began to hover away. He was maneuvering through the store faster than I had, instantaneously performing ninety degree turns.

My jaws dropped to my desk, and my eyes were ready to pop out of my sockets like a cartoon character. Yahshua finally came to a sudden stop between the accountant and the president of the company's office. My Teacher's eyes had locked onto mine, and he had a surprised look on his face, perhaps because I witnessed him hovering through the store. I gestured to wait for me. Yahshua raised his index finger to his lips to hush me. I felt my head being turned with authority toward my computer screen back to the image of The Last Supper.

I could not even control turning my eyes toward Yahshua's direction. After my eyes fixated on the image of The Last Supper, I immediately snapped my head back to where Yahshua was last standing to see if he was there. He had vanished; I stared in his direction for a moment thinking perhaps he had ducked down to pick something up from bottom shelf. I focused my attention back to the monitor looking at man's interpretation of Yahshua's image hoping he would return, yep, I was dumb.

I did a few double takes and after turning the last time toward Yahshua's direction, my heart burst into joy once more upon seeing him standing there. "Wait, wait please, I beg you, please stay." I muttered. As I beckoned Yahshua to wait, he turned my head toward the monitor once more. His force was very strong, I was a youngling, a Padawan. After Yahshua adjusted my head, I quickly turned back toward his direction, and he was gone again. "That's it" I said as I rose from my chair and headed toward Yahshua's location all the while checking each aisle on the way there.

All aisles were empty including where he was standing last. I thought someone had played a joke on me. Where could he be hiding, perhaps in the account's room or the computer technician's lab? The president's office door was open and I verified no one was there. I walked next door to the technician's lab and rang the service bell located on the counter. One of the computer technicians appeared from the back room where diagnostics and repairs were conducted.

"Hi Gandy, how can I help you?" said the technician. "Hi, where is he, where is the gentleman wearing a suit?" I asked. "Where is who? Gentleman with a suit? What are you talking about Gandy?" questioned the technician. Having seniority over the technicians, I unlatched the counter's top lid and swung it over allowing me to walk to the back of the tech lab. I metaphorically examined every nook and cranny of the room without success of finding my Brother. There were two other technicians in the room fixing computers at the time. They looked extremely puzzled as to who I was looking for.

I pardoned myself for my rude behavior and left the technical lab. I had passed the accountant's office remembering that he had strict rules for anyone entering his office uninvited. I was hesitant to risk my job for barging into Victor's office, so I headed back to my desk. Before reaching my desk, I realized what a coward I was and built up my Faith and Courage and decided to risk my job. I marched right back to the accountant's office and opened the door startling Victor sitting at his desk.

"Gandy, what are you doing, I thought I told you never to come in here when I have the door shut!" yelled victor. "Where is he, where is the man with the suit? Did you see him, did he come in here, are you hiding him, are you two in on this!" Victor looked at me just as confused as the technician I had questioned. "Is there something I can help you with?" asked Victor. Ignoring his remarks, I looked around the office and noticed the television that monitored the store security cameras. "Aha, that's it!" I shouted. "What's it?" asked Victor.

I thought of reviewing the recorded footage of what just happened. I was determined to find Baba's Truth whom I seek. I placed a chair under the television and stood on it to reach the buttons on the VCR fastened underneath the television. "What are you doing?" shouted Victor. "I am looking for a man that came into the store, and I believe he had taken something and now he is gone, and I wanted to check the security cameras to verify where he went or what he took."

I felt so guilty, so ashamed saying those words about Yahshua in regards to having him steal. The only thing Yahshua stole was my heart and soul. I was stupid, it was the only quick remark I could think of to have Victor comply. Victor was puzzled watching me as I was pressing buttons on the VCR with no success. "What is going on, why can't this VCR stop playing or rewind?" I asked. "That's strange, it was working yesterday, Check to see if there is a cassette tape in the VCR." asked Victor. I pushed the latched door of the VCR where cassettes are inserted and gasped when I noticed it was empty.

"No, no, no, where's the tape? There's no VCR tape in here; you've always put a tape in here!" I yelled. "Oops, I must have forgotten to put a cassette tape in the VCR to today." said Victor. I snapped, I literally lost it and began pounding the television and VCR like a madman raging against the machine. "What are you doing, are you crazy!" yelled Victor. I jumped off the chair and threw it across the room, smashing other items in his office. Victor rose up off his chair out and stepped away from his desk in fright.

Victor was shocked on how hysterical I was and attempted to calm me down. I grasped his dress shirt with both hands and yelled in tears. "You don't understand, you don't understand, he was here, he was here and now he's gone, he's gone, come back, come back." I cried. "Who was here?" asked Victor. "Eesho! Eesho was here!" I yelled. "Eesho? Eesho was here?" asked Victor. During all the commotion, Danielle and the technicians showed up at Victor's door. They were wondering why I was banging the floor with my fists and crying like a child.

I was begging Eesho Msheekha to come back so I could apologize for whatever I have done to make him leave. Victor dismissed the staff and shut the door. After draining all of my tears and energy, I gathered my composure and picked myself up off the floor and apologized to Victor for putting him through this traumatic ordeal. "Gandy, are you sure you are OK?" asked Victor. "Yes, I am OK, I'm so sorry Vic, I didn't mean to destroy your office, I'm just going sit back down at my desk, is that OK? I'm sorry, can I go now?" I replied with exhaustion.

"Yes you can go." said Victor opening the door for me. "Thank you." said sad me. I headed back to my desk and heard Danielle at the counter asking if I was OK; I just nodded. The consequences of my actions walked into the store thirty minutes later. The president of the company arrived with an urgency to get to Victor's office. "Gandy, in my office, now!" yelled Winston. I gathered the scattered pieces of what was left of my puzzled life and began my frivolous journey of explanations to the lost people.

I came in and sat down with the saddest blank look on my face. "Gandy, what happened today? I heard you went into Victor's office and began destroying it? Do you mind telling me what's going on?" asked Winston. I lifted up the weight of a mountain head of mine toward Winston and replied to his question. "Do you want to know the truth?" looking at Winston with a raised eyebrow. "Yes, I want to know the truth." replied Winston. "Eesho was here, and I talked to him, touched him, hugged him, and now he is gone."

I explained in detail of what happened as much as I could before I was interrupted by Winston's doubt, ignorance and arrogance. "Eesho, are you serious? I think you are just exhausted from all that work and need some time off. Why would Eesho come to see you here?" asked Winston. "Yes, I'm serious. Why wouldn't Eesho come see me? He can see whoever he wants." Tilting my head at the president of the company with a raised eyebrow and utter disbelief of his reply. "You think I'm lying?" I asked.

"Yes, I think you're lying." replied Winston. "I just told you the Truth about Eesho being here. I spoke with him and hugged him and now you are calling me a liar?" "I think you are just losing it, Gandy. You're just stressed out from all the work and imagined Eesho was here when no one else could see him." I was horrified by his remark about Yahshua and wanted to excuse myself from his office. I did not understand how someone could not be ecstatic to hear the great news about Eesho, especially from someone who is of my culture.

"You could stay for the remainder of the day if you like; however, I insist you take some time off." instructed Winston. "Are you firing me? No, that's fine, it's OK, I quit." I quickly replied. "No-no, you don't have to leave right now, just finish the rest of the day then you can go, I'm giving you the time to stay as long as you can." insisted Winston. "Sure that's fine, OK, are we done here?" I asked. "Yes we're done here." replied Winston. When we ended our pointless conversation, I went back to my desk, rested my weary head on my forearms, and sobbed.

Danielle heard me crying and asked if I was OK. I remained silent and wanted only to speak to Yahshua. The day was over, my life was over and my mind, body and spirit were given Truth that no one on this planet could ever imagine. After leaving that day, I made my decision and quit. That quite sunny day at work is forevermore unforgettable. Yahshua showed me who I am and what happened on Mt. Olives; blessing me with His Love for eternity. He is with me, and I follow Him everywhere. I am Yahshua's brother, and Baba is my Father. I am eternally grateful.

I am Jéjee, born in Baghdad on April of '73, with a destiny that will be the greatest epic quest to change the world. My miraculous "Awakening" and adventures in the years on this planet and throughout the Universe were set in motion. My King Yahshua is thy strength, thy sword, thy armor, and I await thy words with open arms and a faithful soul. Everyone should embrace His words to be accepted into His family. Everyone should take the challenge to change their lives for the better. Have no fear from any person or obstacle in your life.

When suffering, think of when Yahshua bled and died for you, and He still loves you. His words will comfort and heal you, bringing out the best within you. He will transform you into the person he expects you to be. All you have to do is accept His help then Love your brothers and sisters and follow Yahshua to the ends of the Earth and beyond. In the end, who awaits to guide you to your destination is entirely up to you. Everyone on this Earth has a destiny, strange as it may sound.

My request in my younger years was to become like Michael the Archangel. I wanted to be part of the battle that would ensue against the evil in this world and any evil throughout the Universe. I wanted to join T.H.E.M. (Trinity of Holy Elite Membranes) to serve our Father of Heaven. When Yahshua arrived to see me, there was reason for my life. I must have been a part of His epic picture in some way, and He wanted to remind me. I am forever grateful. If you were a part of a moment in history, would you be honored to be included in the Universal plan?

You should have no doubt and no fear to be recognized by he who is the Lamb. So he may show you the way to out Father's kingdom. Never give up searching for the Truth, disallow anyone from steering you away from His Truth. If you stumble and fall, regain your spirit and raise your heart to heaven for strength and guidance and He will hear you and may reach out to bless you as well. You must deny the arrogance from anyone who denies Yahshua's Truth; they may be your family members, friends or strangers.

None of them will ever save you when your time for judgment is at hand. Just remember that there should never be trespassing on your part toward your neighbors. Pray for them for everyone is being judged daily in His Book of Life. Everyone must use their own free will wisely. People's fate will be between the Prosecutor of the Universe and the Judge. With their faith, He will shield them with his Love. With their rejection of His Son's Truth and Love, you will be erased. Do not be the one who is left standing outside His golden gates or walking into darkness.

The same principle applies on Earth with your man laws and your man morals, is the same in Heaven. When people break the law, where do they end up? What proceedings do they have to go through for their punishment here? Are they not fined, ruined, incarcerated or exterminated? You will face the Judge in the Affairs and Accusations building when your proceedings begin after your Earthly lesson. Your studies and attributes of morals and ethics on this bridge you walk upon will prepare you for your next level.

If you excel on this planet with Truth, Justice, Courage, Faith and Love, then you will be honored to be part of His existence. If Baba chooses to include you in his quest, set your affairs in order and suit up in His armor. Then upon completion of your quest's journey, you will wear the very last clothes you will ever need – His embrace. The materials and possessions on this planet all will wither away, but his Love for you will be everlasting. Do not accumulate worthless treasures in your hearts and household.

That behavior will instill animosity toward your family or friends and separate your connection with Baba. Most people on this planet are unaware of the connection they have with Him to always help them. The distractions are overwhelming to the mind of those with less compassion toward others or themselves. The simplest way to explain the base foundation of the connection we all have to our Father in Heaven is...your heart and mind's signal. The more Love you have for Him the stronger the connection and energy.

My life after meeting Yahshua the Messiah in 1997 was an experience I believe everyone should go through. Expressing a feeling of hugging Yahshua in words is unable to comprehend the magnitude of His Truth. However, make sure your heart speaks to Him if have that opportunity to hug Yahshua. Some people may give up or lose Faith because life gets too difficult when our prayers are not answered immediately. Just be patient, Baba is leading you to his direction.

CHAPTER 3

The Dragon

Years passed after meeting Yahshua, silent prayers and daily normal living went on. I gradually refrained from attending structural churches and concentrated on praying in the church that was within my heart, as our Teacher instructed. I continued the search for my brother Yahshua, being very patient and devoted to his plan for me. Each person on this Earth is part of His Big Picture, yet society chooses to lead its own show without Him directing them.

Why is it when people are ONLY in real desperate need of guidance, they call upon Baba or Yahshua? Yet, during society's everyday existence, they wait to get to church on Sunday (Sun worship) so that the pastor or preacher washes away their sins with a donation or prayer for the day (NOT). That is utter nonsense, yet it happens on a daily basis. Individuals that have that particular mentality tend to leave behind their prayers and morals in church on Sunday.

How can anyone think there is no time for the words of Yahshua the Messiah to them, their friends, their families, every moment of their lives? Be a good person, humbly grateful toward your Father in Heaven on a daily basis. Avoid breaking Baba's Ten Commandments and keep your sin in check. We falter with sin moments in our lives, ask for forgiveness. The act of forgiving and loving more has been a part of our lives for what seemed like an eternity, yet very few practice the feeling anymore. What does society comfort instead?

Spiteful revenge, hatred, lust, lies, ignorance, arrogance, infidelity, adultery, greed, violence, and the list goes on and on. I think those are but just a few of the most despicable behaviors toward even your worst enemies. Breaking a command against thy Father's forbidden laws toward your kind would get you incarcerated spiritually in purgatory. Man abides by man's law knowing that they may suffer the consequences with this planet's justice system at any given moment; there's no difference in His Kingdom.

Sometimes humans have the 'out of sight - out of mind' blockage when involved in immoral actions. Society is too blind to realize that He is everywhere and the people are just chess pieces on Baba's chessboard of life. It is pretty simple really – walk the path of Truth and Love, as you will be graded on your score of Faith and morals. In the end, our Teacher may graduate you from His school of life on this planet. Most who are unable to accept his Truth will be left behind while others will go on and meet everyone else at the graduation ceremony.

I believe suffering is a part of life, enduring the pain with every step of your journey causes you to build an everlasting bond with Baba and Yahshua. I suffered and still suffer for most of my life, there is only so much that loved ones and doctors can do for your pain. After a while, you must tolerate the pain and go forth –you must, as Yahshua did for you. My next encounter with the dragon was at the age of seventeen. Drugs speak the dragons' language with gibberish sounds. Conforming to fit in with the crowd was the objective no matter what it took.

The weekend arrived to gather with my friends and head out to the clubs and enjoy the night out. But that night was going to be different, another life altering different. After contacting my friends, they arrived at my home to pick me up and meet up with our others friends. I was smoking cigarettes at a young age of sixteen; however this smell was a bit different. I noticed my friends in the driver and passenger seats passing what looked like a cigarette. But smelled was like burning leaves. "What is that nasty crap smell?" I shouted.

"Maybe you shit your pants, hahaha." laughed Shawn. "I didn't shit my pants, dumbass. Seriously, what's that smell, can't you guys smell it?" I questioned my friends again. "Oh this?" said Phil. The odor was like someone had defecated in the vehicle. How anyone could enjoy the constant smell of excrement was beyond my comprehension. I wanted to fit in and not to be ridiculed for being a coward, and I wanted to try it once, even if the taste and smell was wretched.

Let me explain something to you first before you go ahead and put up your dukes to fight the dragon. If your Love for Baba and his son Yahshua is absent before you enter ring of drugs, then you are in a world of hurt. "What is that, is that what's making that shit smell?" I said. "I don't know about shit, but it sure tastes good." *Puff ~ Puff* replied Phil passing the joint to "Errr, errr, you wanna to try it?" said Shawn passing the joint to me. "No man, I don't know what that shit is, and I don't wanna smell like shit; I'm just gonna smoke my cig."

"No man, don't light a cigarette yet, wait till we're done with this joint!" shouted Phil. "Can you at least lower the window down all the way instead of just a crack?" I asked. "No man, why are you being a pussy?" replied Shawn. "I ain't no pussy!" I yelled back. "Well then try it." requested Phil. "I don't know bro, first tell me what It is." I ask. "It's a joint." replied Shawn. "I know that, you already said it was a joint, I mean what's in it –tobacco, shit, crack, what?" I ask. "It's marijuana bro." said Phil. "Mara-what?" "It's Hashisha, Ha-She-Sha."

"Say what, is it Mara-wanna or Ha-Shi-Sha, which is it bro?" I confusingly asked. "It's both, Marijuana is in English and Hashisha is in Arabic, but it both means the same." replied Phil. "Oh, I see." Unfortunately; I could not see my future of what was about to happen. "So do you wanna try it or not? Look bro, you're not gonna die, you'll get high." asked Phil. "Hahahaha! You ain't gonna die, you'll get high!" laughed Shawn. "Hahahaha! You ain't gonna die, you'll get high!" laughed Phil joining Shawn singing. "High, like up in the sky high, or like 'Hi what's up?" I ask.

"More like high in the sky, make yah wanna say hi to every gal and guy, hahahaha." laughed Shawn. "Hahaha, ah, makes you friendly, huh?" I laughed. "Yep, we smoking the peace pipe, brother, how you doin?" replied Phil. "I'm gooooood, how you doin?" I said. "You'll be much better than gooooood once you hit this jizzo in the hizzo." said Shawn. "Man, now it's jizzo in the hizzo, what the fuck bro?" I shouted. "Hahahaha, Gandy, you wanna hit it or not, it's almost out bro." laughed Phil.

"Is anything besides getting high gonna happen to me?" I ask. "Who knows, we won't know until you try it." replied Shawn. "Phil, Shawn, don't fuck with me, if I die, I'mma fuck you up, hahahaha!" I yelled before I puffed on the dragon. "Hahahaha!" laughed Phil. "Hahahaha!" laughed Shawn. "Ok, I'll try it. Do I smoke just like a cigarette?" I reply. "No, take a hit, a puff, and hold it in for as long as you can, then blow it out." instructed Phil. "Ok, that's it?" I ask. "Yep, that's it, then keep smoking till your high." said Shawn.

The route back to His path would be very difficult without Faith if you take a turn during that path. It was my turn to inhale this dragon breath; its grip was intoxicating and unavoidable. After inhaling three puffs and holding in the poison. "Arrrgh, Noooooo, Aiyeee, Noooooo, Gah-Gah-Gah, Oh No - Oh No - Oh No, Oh God, Oh God help me, God Help Meeeeeeeee!" I was screaming in the back seat for my life, as though I was falling from the sky without a parachute. I felt as though I was dying and that my heart was literally bursting out of my chest.

I looked up to see my friend's yelling at me and saw their faces had turned into monsters right before my eyes. "Noooooooooo!" I screamed. "Gandy!" yelled Phil. "Gandy!" yelled Shawn. "Oh shit Gandy, bro what the fuck is going on!" screamed Phil. "Gandy! Gandy! Phil pull over bro!" instructed Shawn. "Oh my God, oh my god, I'm gonna die, I'm gonna die, I can't breathe, I can't breathe, my heart, ooooh my heart!" I said. My friends panicked and pulled over to the side to see what was happening to me, as I was curled up on the rear floorboard.

All I could hear were my friends screaming my name. However, I thought they were monsters trying to kill me. Everything seemed unreal and terribly terrifying. If you have no friends or family that care about your well-being, then you are in deep doo-doo. You are left to alone to battle with your dragon, your demons, as the devil snares you into his domain of drugs. After what seemed like hours only took a few puffs to hook me into marijuana addiction for many years.

The pain went away, however I began to see a different side in people, and I had more Love and empathy for their lost souls. I battled this nasty dragon for a very long time, daily in fact, with the help of my Father Baba and my Brother Yahshua. Friendly and non-friendly bad influences were a major part of my life. I was drawn me back to the disgusting habit of smoking cigarettes, marijuana, drinking, sex, fights, and other disgusting habits that sadden my Father. I lost the battle against sinning for so many years, but Baba and Yahshua never gave up on me or let me lose the war.

You lose time, friends, opportunities and short term memory when you begin that long journey after inhaling that selfish, deceitful, disgusting, anti-social to other non-smokers drug. I was slowly losing the trust my family members had for me. Having constant arguments over the type of friends I should be socializing with, I disregarded my family's warnings and leaped into a hurt of trouble, again. I ended up in the arms of the law and was incarcerated for months for drugs and engaging in misconduct.

Bond, Jéjee Bond

I reached the age of eighteen and was considered an adult by law. My disobedience was now with my dad, yikes. My reckless actions took a turn for the worse this time. I ignorantly borrowed – err, stole –my dad's Walther PPK (that of a James Bond movie) handgun. My dad loved his special edition gun. One day I had come home and accidentally saw my dad putting his gun in his secret hiding place when he did not notice me. The time came when I decided that gun would help defend and destroy a life.

~Ring ~ Ring ~ Ring~

"Yo Gandy wasup, wacha doing?" asked Phil. "Chillin, wasup with you?" I replied. "We about to throw down with some punks." said Phil. "Say what! Now?" I yelled. "Yeah, but ain't no one packin, and I remembered you said your dad had a gun the other day." said Phil. "Yeah he does, bro, you want me to use my dad's gun, are you serious?" I was flabbergasted by his request.

"Just for tonight, we ain't gonna shot nobody, it's just in case they start shooting at us." begged Phil. "Shit bro, what if my dad gets home and notices his gun is missing?" I replied. "He won't. We'll be back before then, and you can put the gun back where you found it." said Phil. "Shit, we gotta do this quick, I don't wanna get fucked up by my dad." I agreed. "Bet, we'll be there in ten minutes." said "Bet." I replied. I wanted to use my dad's gun to protect my friends, who were about to fight at a house party.

We looked like hit men dressed all in black and black trench coats, intimidating our enemies. My puff the magic dragon friend had arrived to pick me up to take care of business. There were two others in the van with Phil, but I only recognized one of them. "Sup Gandy, where you able to get your dad's gun?" asked Phil. "Yo, wasup Gandy." shouted Simsim "Sup." yelled Tommy. "Sup Simsim; sup Phil; yo wasup. Yeah I go it, but we ain't shooting nobody, right?" I said. "Bro, it's just in case they're packin." said Phil. We drove until we reached our posse, who were already at the destination neighborhood.

We were looking for the punks who wanted to show how tough they were at various house parties. We finally found them at a house party approximately two miles away from my house. They were taking refuge after hearing we were looking for them. We were in Phil's van parked three houses away from the house. Simsim, Phil and I excited the van and stood in front of the van. Curse words and threats were exchanged between us and them; until...*BOOM!!*

Our other friends, who were closer to the punks, ducked, scattered and jumped into their vehicles and backed away from the house to the corner of the street. "Oh shit, did you hear that, that sounded like a shotgun blast!" I yelled. "Shotgun, no man you're crazy, it must've been someone hitting a bat against a trash can?" replied Simsim. "Bro, I fucking heard it too, do you think they were shooting?" said Phil. I looked around the neighborhood and noticed there were no garbage cans in sight that day. "What trash can, do you see any trash cans around you in the street? I am telling you, that sounded like a shotgun blast!"

BOOM!! Snap! Snap! Crack! Crack! Snap!

The shotgun pellets wheezed past the top of our heads just below the tree line snapping a few branches and leaves. "Holy shit, they're shooting at us, get done, take cover!" I screamed. I pulled out my dad's Bond gun and took aim it at the man shooting the shotgun. I estimated fifty yards away, but could have been further; it was dark. Good thing my friend was there just in the nick of time. "No!" yelled Simsim. "What the fuck are you doing?" I yelled "Don't shoot him, bro, you may kill him!" yelled Simsim.

"Bro, are you fucking serious, I'm not gonna fucking kill him, just scare the shit out of him." I replied. I yelled at my friend, as he slammed my wrists down after taking aim. So I reverted to a sound deterrent instead of aiming at the tree next to the shotgun desperado. I decided to discharge the firearm into the air with a few rounds. *Pop! Pop! Pop!* "Shit that was loud!" yelled Simsim. "Yeah, it's loud." I yelled. "Can I try it?" asked Simsim. "Promise not to aim at them!" I said.

"Bro, are you serious, I was trying to stop you." replied Simsim.

Bang! Bang! Bang! Bang! Click-Click-Click

My friend shot the remaining bullets in the air emptying the clip. I did not realize until we started driving away that I was in deep shit. I did not know where my dad kept his extra bullets. How was I supposed to explain an empty gun to my dad, tell him, *"Hey Dad, I kept your bullets as souvenirs?"* Everyone backed off that had caused a ruckus and either went back inside or entered their wheels and drove off.

What we were unaware of was that the neighborhood was watching us all along during this showdown shootout. We jumped into our van, during the scatter, and I ended up driving. We contacted the other crew and decided to gather at our local car wash to gloat about our so-called victory. I was again at the crossroads, the path to salvation or solitary in a cell. I was two blocks away from returning my dad's gun back where it was last.

Instead of turning left to drop off the gun, I turned right, and we kept up with the rest of the group. I blindly told my friends I would drop the gun later. With my dad's gun still in my possession, we pulled into a car wash and ended up in the last bay undercover from the searching police helicopter. We were all dumbfounded when the authorities pulled into the car wash and surrounded the exits. One of the passengers got out and surveyed what was going on. "Shit-Shit-Shit Five-O, Five-O!" I yelled.

"They are searching the cars; I think they are looking for the gun." said Tommy. I was about to turn myself in when one of my friends stopped me and suggested we get rid of the gun and deny we had one. "Where the fuck are we going to hide it?" I asked. "Tommy, take this and toss over the fence next door." instructed Phil. "Why would you do that, don't you think they'll find it, they have dogs you know!" I yelled. "Tell the cops there was no gun, unless you want to go to jail!" said Phil. "Fuck, I'm so fucked" I said. Lying is just another form of a shovel to dig you deeper in misery.

I regretted doing that, we were fooling the authorities and seemed like it was working. The police finally had additional backup arrive and approach our van. Everyone was ordered to exit the vehicle and were searched but no gun was found. Since the van was reported doing the shooting, everyone who was in the van were handcuffed. I was being interrogated in the back seat of the patrol car. The final question struck me where it really hurt the most. Police tactics that I would have never expected from an individual that stood for the Truth.

"Where's the gun?" questioned the police officer. "What gun, there was no gun, you must be mistaken." I said. "Neighbors reported someone from this van was shooting a gun in their neighborhood." said the police officer. "I have no idea what you're talking about." I replied. "Well that's too bad, because whoever fired that gun in the air, the bullets came back down through a roof and struck a little girl." said the police officer. "Little girl, what little girl, what are you talking about? Are you being serious right now?" I asked.

"She's in critical condition, and we don't know if she'll make it. If she dies, whoever fired that gun will be charged with murder." said the police officer. That did it for me, I was so heartbroken that I fainted in the patrol vehicle and woke up with a headache and neck ache. I envisioned myself burning in hell for eternity for killing a child. I was crying to the officer about the little girl, and he insisted that I tell him where the gun is. "Are you OK, tell me where the gun is?" asked the police officer. "Oh no, no, is she going to die? I don't want her to die!" I yelled.

"Then tell me where the gun is, so we can sort this whole thing out." asked the police officer. "OK-OK, there was a gun, but it was my gun, and I was the only one shooting the gun and no one else was." I said. "Where is the gun now?" asked the police officer. "I gave it to one of the guys in the car, and he threw it over the fence." I replied. The officer went to each patrol car to find out who threw the gun and where. When he found the guy I gave the gun to, he brought him over to car I was in.

"Tell this officer where the gun is; I told him I gave it to you to throw over the fence." I said. "Are you serious, why'd you tell them?" asked Tommy. "Just show them where the fucking gun is at!" I yelled. After a few moments of searching, the officer that was interrogating me came back to his car to inform me that they had found the weapon and showed it to me. "Is this the gun?" asked the police officer. "Yes, that's it." I replied. "OK good, sit tight, I'll be back." said the police officer.

"Officer, what about the little girl, have you heard anything back from the hospital?" I asked. "What little girl? Oh, I was just kidding, I just wanted to see if you'd give in with a sob story." said the police officer. I was both angry at the police officer for not telling me the truth and thankful to Baba that no one was hurt once more. I did not judge the officer since I was also lying about the gun. When you are in jail, none of your so-called friends know you anymore. You are on your own, and snitching on your friends was not going to happen.

My dad's gun was either locked away or destroyed because it was used in a crime. Once word got back to my dad, I was done for. I wanted to stay in jail; it was much safer than being in the hands of my dad. My mother, brother and uncle arrived at the police station to bail me out of jail. I was never so ashamed of myself for disappointing my loved ones for my actions. I deserved each slap from each of them that night when they arrived at the police station. However, that was not the end of it.

~ Ring ~ Ring ~ Ring ~

"It's for you!" said mom. "Hi, who's this?" I asked. "Who's this, huh? Where are you?" asked my dad. "Where am I?" I replied. "Yes, where are you right now?" asked dad. "I'm at the police station; Mom, Sandy, and Uncle are here to bail me out." I said. "No, you're not going anywhere, you stay right there." said dad. "Why?" I asked. "If you come home right now, I'll kill you myself, do you hear me?" yelled dad. "Dad, I'm sorry!" sobering back.

"Don't sorry me; eat crap dog! Ayreb-Ayreb!" yelled dad. "I'm sorry, I won't do it again, I swear." I begged. "Where's my gun?" yelled dad. "The police took it, they said they won't give it back." I said. "You bring my gun back with you or don't come home, you hear me?" yelled dad. "Dad I can't; they won't give back to me." I replied. "Did you understand what I just said to you or not!" yelled dad. "Yes!" I yelled. "Give me the phone. Kalid, calm down, enough, do you hear me, enough!" yelled mom.

After all that commotion, everyone was concerned for my well-being. However, the peacekeeper of the family had to step in and calm everyone down –my hero, my mom. Time passed, and I stayed away from the troublemakers, except a select few that I had closer ties with. It took a while for my dad to forgive me, my earned trust would be a long journey. My criminal record followed me on this prison planet like stinky body odor. Charges were dropped from a felony to a misdemeanor to a charge of Carrying-Concealed-Weapon without a permit.

There goes my law enforcement career path down the toilet. What criminal justice department hires someone with a criminal record? Criminals and criminal justice are not buddies, unless you are a mercenary. Saints and wannabe warriors are not buddies. Nonetheless, I continued my education in law enforcement and hoped for the best. College was great; I eagerly enjoyed gaining knowledge, social activities and expressing my talents.

Walking was still demanding for me, using 200 percent effort on my part due to my irregular bone, tendons and lack of muscle. Imagine how you would feel if you had only one strong leg while performing daily tasks. How difficult, how much pain, would you have to endure? The pain was part of my life on a regular basis, yet my tolerance was earned, so I kept going. The courage of others who are much more physically challenged than I gave me inspiration and motivation. They have the never give up never surrender attitude and I am no coward.

Before meeting Yahshua the Messiah in person, I was lost, and after hugging Him, I witnessed Baba's Truth – being His dragon slayer, His St. Giorgis, worth more than all the treasures combined together on this Earth or in the Universe; I am honored and grateful eternally. We are human, making mistakes and falling, it is up to us to get back up, brush ourselves off and keep going. When you overcome obstacles, you gain knowledge to succeed on your path to Yahshua's salvation. Sometimes this quest takes one lifetime, one year, one month, one day and one foot after another.

Pain is felt from within our hearts to upon our flesh from others in our life, turn your cheek to the other side, continue on His path and await your reward. Life is a schooling system developed by Baba; a required course in order to be chosen as a holy scholar to someday perhaps rule your own galaxy. If you prove yourself worthy of such an honorable stature of being a Saint for Yahshua. Spreading his Word and Love without fear of anyone or anything on this planet or in the Universe.

Then perhaps Baba may promote you to becoming a member or an Ambassador to the Trinity of Holy Elite Membranes throughout the Universe. Courageously upholding Justice-Truth-Faith-Peace and Love with your crew on your starship. Stronger, faster and much more superbly advanced than any other. Baba gives you access to the whole Universe to travel with His Holy Key in your heart. Abuse your children, abuse your family, abuse others and you will lose your keys to enter heaven or travel anywhere.

Remember, every human on Baba's chessboard is important to His next move that He has for you. The choice is yours to accept your position in His game. Give Him your all; aim to have your name in His book with a star next to it. The Quest given to you can be carried for generations to come. Every step of the way, Baba and Yahshua will be with you protecting you from the evil forces you battle. His Force grows within all of you with each faithful prayer to thou Brother and Father in heaven. Your metaphoric training as a Jedi Padawan starts with accepting the Truth, and only then will your Quest begin.

Carry His name within your heart, and Baba's Force will be strong from within for eternity. Remember to walk the path of Truth, Justice, Courage, Faith and Love. Our lifetime on this planet is a test of our worthiness to serve Him as Saints of his Faith. I am not an evangelist; I follow the Messiah whose true name is Yahshua. Pronounced and spelled in English with respect and honor to my brother Yahshua and my father, Baba. I still do not understand how people can be so disrespectful to pronounce or spell someone's name the way they see fit.

An Indian, Asian, African, Russian, Middle Eastern and individuals throughout parts of the foreign lands pronounce and spell their names in English. Yet, ignorance and arrogance rests in the hearts of all who think they are following the son of man named Jesus. People have the audacity to spell and pronounce foreign names of humans, yet ignore the name Yahshua sent to them from the Almighty, from our Creator, from our Father. You do not need know how to speak Yiddish or be a Hebrew to pronounce and spell Yahshua in the English language.

I am not degrading or disrespecting any Christian here. Humans should have common sense integrated into their DNA. People were led path to falsehood by the Roman Empire for 400+ years. Christians are aware that the Son of Man died on the cross for our sins. They know He is the Son of our Father of Heaven and Earth. They know He is the King of Kings, our Savior, our Beloved Brother, our Glorious Teacher. America decides to use silent letter this, different spelling pronunciation that, Latin bullshit.

Other non-English lands say what they mean in writing and vocal. The English language hath no sounds of meaning from the mouth, just silent letters. Speak His Truth and you will be born again; you have my word. Yahshua's book of everlasting Life, Love, Truth and Joy is His Word. People's true names should be pronounced respectfully during their existence from birth to death and beyond. Americans pronounce foreign names effortlessly; so there is no shame in pronouncing our Teacher's Hebrew name in English: Yah-Shu-Ah.

If people accepted Yahshua's true name then they would know His Truth. The memory of that day at Computer Warehouse when my Beloved Brother arrived echoes His words in my mind like an everlasting record. Yahshua was very adamant about his birth name when he corrected me upon my response to his question. Knowing a person is not just by any other name but their True name. Humans' true existence are commanded by our Father in birth.

Our names follow us in history to be recognized for generations about knowledge from the past. Change the name of the individual, and you will erase their true name over time. The distraction of truth has been accumulated throughout history and humanity has become blinded and led astray. Eventually, everyone will see His Truth and learn the Words of wisdom spoken by Baba's voice. We all deserve the know the truth about everlasting life. The answer Truth has been calcified by the poison of modern Earth.

CHAPTER 4

Disobedient Suffering

There is nothing beyond His power if you show how grateful you are to Yahshua. Spread Baba's Love to everyone around you to reap the rewards of what or who you are seeking. In 2004, my second major mistake was disobeying my mother's advice when it came down to marriage. My brother went through the exciting stages of marriage with his bride. I wondered, "When will be my turn?

Was I going to be left behind living at my mother's home for the remainder of my life?" How long would it take my search to find my true Love waiting for my prayers to be answered? I was still attending college studying law enforcement at the time and decided to settle down in marriage. I had prayed to Baba and Yahshua for guidance in my life altering path once more, praying for them to send me a woman to marry who would be compatible with my immediate family.

Unaware of what I was asking for, I was trying to please my family rather than having patience and seek with my heart for my twin soul. For many years, my sister's best friend would visit our home to socialize with my sisters and mother. At that time, I had never noticed this woman in any way other than a sisterly friend that I would tease during every visit. One day, a stranger approached my door, or so I thought. ~ Ding ~ Dong ~ "Hi, is Sandrella home?" asked the stranger. "No she's not home." I replied "Well, can I come in and wait for her?" said the stranger.

The woman grabbed the door to enter, and I immediately blocked her entrance. "Wait a minute, excuse me, who are you?" I yelled. "It's me, dork!" April replied. "Dork, who you calling a dork, holy shit, April?" I said. "Yeah, it's me Gandy, you like?" said April. "Like wow, what did you do, I didn't even recognize you!" I said. My sister's best friend had transformed herself into a fashion model. She had undergone plastic surgery, a visit to the salon, makeup and new outfit; all that was missing was the red carpet.

I remembered the prayer to Baba and Yahshua for marital guidance and immediately assumed that the woman that I was supposed to marry was my sister's best friend. Since my family knew her family from Iraq, I thought why bother waiting any longer when He answered my prayers, a woman who was loved by my family for many years. When you pray for help from Baba and Yahshua, whatever you do, avoid requesting to rush their answer to you because you will get to eat Luke warm supper.

My attempts to court this woman failed repeatedly; I misunderstood why I was being rejected, as I never was rejected from women I was flirting with. I ignored the warnings of incompatibility with her because my judgment was clouded by desire; rather than awaiting my prayers to be answered to be with thy princess Sabra. April's numerous remarks that she only loved me as a brother and nothing more was somehow going through my ear and out the other. I should have taken that comment and ended the pursuit right there and waited for my true soulmate.

"No Gandy, I don't see you like that, I don't wanna go out with you." demanded April. "Seriously, it's not a date, just a cup of coffee. I just want to get to you know you better." I asked "That's a date, Gandy." replied April. "Ok, if drinking a cup of coffee is a date, ok how about we just sit and talk?" I asked. "Wow, you really don't give up do you"? questioned April. "No I don't give up. Besides, I like you even if you changed the way you look." I said. "That's nice, I like you too, but like a brother and nothing more.

Besides, you can't afford me anyway." replied April. "Say what, what does that mean?" I asked. "It means you can't afford me, the things I want, the things you can't afford to get me, the lifestyle that I want." said April. "Are you serious, all you care about is money?" I asked. "Pretty much, and you don't have it." replied April. "I don't have it right now, but I can always get it. So what if we aren't rich, doesn't Love mean more than money? I asked. "What if you can't keep giving me what I want?" asked April. "What do you mean?" replying to April's question.

"If you can't afford me, then I will divorce you take whatever you have and make you pay for child support if we have kids." demanded April. "April are you fucking being serious right now?" I shockingly asked. "Very serious, are you willing to take that chance with me?" replied April. My desires blinded me even more. She looked beautiful each day. I was a smart man, I could get any job I wanted and support her. I was determined to marry her to be part of our family and let everyone be happy; I was willing to suffer.

April finally agreed to our courting; we were privately seeing each other for about a year without April's parents knowing, I thought was a big mistake. Lying to your parents is a big no-no, lying to Baba is a gravely no-no. Still, this first deception with my future wife went unheeded and disregarded. April's mother had a good idea of what was going on when her daughter kept visiting without my sister being around. Blinded to what was about to happen to my path of suffering, I asked my mother what she thought of April as my wife. However, her response was heartbreaking.

"She is not meant for you; she was meant for someone else, my Love." said mom. "Say-what?" I asked. "What? replied mom. "Hahaha; you're funny, Mom; I meant are you kidding me? laughing at my mother's zany response. "No I'm not kidding you." replied mom. I was confused why my mother did not want me marry April; after so many years of knowing her? My mother knew April's mother as though they were sisters, talking to each other almost every day. "Why Mom, what's wrong with marrying her? You already know her family." I asked.

"Her mind, heart and soul is not compatible with yours; she has a different intellect and personality." replied my mother. "Oh Mom, I don't understand, am I supposed to stay here forever? I'm thirty years old." I sadly said. How can anyone know who is compatible with whom? I ignored my mother's warning while she begged me to wait until she received Word of whom I was supposed to marry by divine intervention. "If you want, I can find out who you are supposed to marry." said mom.

"Who? How? When? Now?" I asked. "Don't rush into this, don't tell her you want to marry her; give me twenty-four hours, and I'll get you your answer." instructed my mother. I pleaded with my mother about not relying in any type of fortune telling, cup reading, card reading, or crystal ball reading misunderstood mumbo jumbo for my path of Truth. But I loved her and trusted her judgment to find out who my true beloved was to be. My mother obtained the answer I sought and demanded that I listen to her advice about the woman that was about to change my life for better or for worse.

I gave her my full attention and scrutinized the names she mentioned. The names were a blank in my mind, expect one. Each person has a compatible soulmate, however to obtain a genuine soulmate is only by divine intervention. I was stubborn, I was disobedient, I was an eager young man that leaped first and questioned later. The only name my mother instructed me to remember was a woman who had the letters CAR within her name, and she was to be around pizza.

"Car, Cara, Sarah, pizza, are you kidding me right now, Mom? I asked. "No I'm not kidding you. Do you want to know more?" replied my mother. "More?" I asked. "She will be able to feel you." replied my mom. "Feel me, what you mean feel me?" I asked. "Like if you touch a part of your body, she will feel it, too, sometimes differently." replied mom. "Mom! For real?" I yelled. "Yes for real!" yelled mom. "Show me, for example." I asked. "All I know is a few; I forgot the others my friend was telling me because I was too embarrassed to remember." said mom.

"Mom, you know how awesome that would be for a woman to feel what I am feeling?" I asked. "Yes I know; so do you want to know or not?" replied mom. "Yes, please tell me." I demanded. Well, my dear innocent sweet mother was explaining some jaw-dropping Soulmate info. I was so shocked when mom pointed at areas of my body my Soulmate would feel. Yet, I was so eager to meet her. My frustration was time, no one knows the time but Him and I had to wait for my no more sweet sorrow Love.

"How am I supposed to find a woman with the letters CAR in her name eating a pizza or working at a pizza store, then start touching myself to see if she feels me, hahaha that sounds so crazy mom." I said. "I'm not crazy, I'm telling you the Truth." replied my mother. My mother began to cry; her tears crushed my heart for hurting her feelings. So, I gave her a hug and kissed her for all she had done for me. "Mom, I'm so sorry, please forgive me, I didn't mean to hurt your feelings." begging my mother. "You will find her, but if you marry April first you will suffer before you do." replied my mom.

When she mentioned that I would find my twin either way, how bad would the suffering be? I embedded my Soulmate's characteristics into my mind for my sake. I ate my mother's words of Love for many years. The emotional strut for love that my mother and I had endured together that day, I never will forget. I fell to my knees and begged my mother to accept this woman as her daughter, I will accept my suffering. I was consumed by the thought that I would be the last one to leave my mother's home in marriage.

I was still confused as to why my mother was determined to have me avoid marrying April. After our emotional breakdown, my mother finally agreed to my plea and gave me her blessings. We courted for a year with no issues as life went on. The weekend arrived and my dad invited me to go with him to his cottage for some bonding. The drive north took almost three hours, so my dad and I had plenty of time to talk man to man. "Dad, I want to marry April. We've been dating a year, and we think it's time to get married."

I said "Don't. She will make your life miserable, she is not for you, her personality is not the same as yours, don't marry her." replied my dad. "Dad, are you serious? Mom said the same thing about April." I said. "There's one more thing –the woman you are supposed to marry may cause you to take your own life." replied my dad. "What? What the fuck are you talking about; what do you mean 'take my own life,' like kill myself? Dad, answer me, Dad!" I shouted. "Yes!" yelled my dad. "Holy shit!" I said in grief.

I was shocked; my own dad was saying the same thing my mother said, but he added death. He did not know my beloved's name, however said that she would find me before tragedy. My dad added that my soulmate would not know I was hers until later on. I would have to go through another ordeal that would have me suffer, if not die, for her Love. "Dad, will she find me before I kill myself?" I asked. "Yes; she will find you; in the end you will win." replied my dad. "Win, win what, Dad?" I asked.

"I don't know." said my dad. I did not understand what he meant; how could I win if I killed myself? My dad received Word from his clairvoyant sources that I would be suffering during my Quest to seek true Love. Why was I the only one left in the dark? All I thought of was Love; how can anything go wrong in a marriage when you have Love supporting your foundation? That would be true, if both partners had mutual unconditional Love for each other.

However, if either of the two had to learn to Love unconditionally and fail, then my dad was correct. My dad's advice also resonated within my soul for many years. I blame no one but myself for my actions of disobedient disregard of my mom's and dad's advice. I swallowed their advice with a pinch of salt rather than jumping into the ocean and drinking His Truth. I continued courting April, and we were engaged to marry the following year in June 2005. So far so good, I thought, nothing out of the ordinary. No conflictions between my fiancé and I except a jaw dropping ultimatum from my soon to be wife.

"Change your career or forget about the wedding. I don't want to worry every day about my husband being shot and killed as a police officer." demanded April. "April, are you serious, I've been going to school for this long, and now you want me to change careers?" I asked. "Yes, I'm serious. If you love me, then you'll do it." said April. "Get shot, why would I get shot, I am going to work inside the police department for a couple years and then join the F.B.I." I replied.

"I said no. If you really love me and want to marry me, you will change your career." requested April. I was tongue-tied, frustrated, heartbroken, and clueless about how to reply, except to please her once more by agreeing with the terms, despite almost two years of education and tuition. I diverted my law enforcement career and attended ITT Technical Institute and graduated an associate's degree in computer networks. She was happy, and I was happy, or so I thought. There were few things that you start to notice from a person when you get to know them better.

To save my fiancé the embarrassment, we did not go dancing while dating because she had two left feet. Occasional movies, dinner, mall shopping (gag), family gatherings, and hanging out were all normal. I had shelved my Quest for my Soulmate. I was too busy living my current life with the woman that I thought would make me and everyone happy. The advice of your parents and sometimes grandparents are to be cherished and acted upon.

When your time arrives to make that big decision, remember their voices. In summer 2005, my fiancé and I were married. It was an expensive $30,000 fairy tale wedding with almost four hundred guests with all the trimmings included. When your bride demands a lot, the man must provide plenty to keep her. I was still attending the technical school, and we were both working. Preparing for the wedding was difficult and frustrating at first. Almost everyone goes through the nervous jitters and second thoughts before they take the big leap of fate.

The moment arrived and lasted 24 hours, and longer for others. We all had fun with no worries and plenty of dancing. Finally, we were married newlyweds on our way to Cancun for our honeymoon. I had no "get a passport" on my to-do list. So, I decided to use my driver's license and American citizenship credentials to travel. "Passport please." asked the gate attendant. "I don't have a passport, American airport security said I could use my American Citizen papers and ID to enter Mexico." I replied.

"Ha-ha, señor, you need a passport to enter Mexico." laughed the gate security attendant. "Sir, we just arrived from the United States on our honeymoon, here is our marriage license." I pleaded. "That does not matter, you still need your passport." replied the gate security attendant. "Wow, this is bullshit, can I speak to your supervisor?" I asked. "OK señor, please have a seat and I will get a supervisor for you." said the gate security attendant I waited to see a security supervisor to what seemed like forever.

My wife was worried that we would have to be sent back to the United States. I was not going to waste hours of flight and money just to be turned away for lack of a passport. "Señor, do you wish to speak with me?" asked the security supervisor. "Yes I do, your gate security is not allowing us to enter Mexico, and we are on our honeymoon." I replied. "Where is your passport señor?"asked the security supervisor. "I don't have a passport; just my American citizen papers." I replied. "Señor, you need a passport to enter Mexico." "So what happens now?" I asked.

"You will have to get back on your plane and go back to the United States." replied the security supervisor. "Is there any way you can help us out?" I asked. "If you and your wife can follow me please, I'll see what I can do for you." instructed the security supervisor. We followed the supervisor to a small interrogation room. The supervisor was seated and two other security officers entered the room. "Señor, how do you want us to help you?" asked the security supervisor. "By letting my wife and I enter Mexico to go on our honeymoon." I replied.

"We can't allow you to enter unless you help us first." said the security supervisor. "How do you want me to help you first?" It seems that bribery is a normal thing visiting Mexico –pay up or have them send you back on the same plane back to the USA. That is their way of thanking you for entering Mexico. It was my fault for not applying for a passport before our honeymoon. I was the next victim in line to pay up or get out. "The only way to enter Mexico without proper papers is with dinero." said the security supervisor. "Dinero, what's that? I asked.

"Dinero is money." said the security supervisor. "You want me to pay you money to enter Mexico? I already paid for our plane ticket and hotel." I replied. "No señor, you have to pay us to enter Mexico. You wanted me to help you, so I'm helping you, but first you have to help us." said the security supervisor. "How much; like $50?" I asked. "$50, ha-ha no señor, more than $50." laughed the security supervisor. "Well then you tell me how much?" I asked. "How much do you have on you, señor?" asked the security supervisor.

"You want me to give you what I have in my pocket, I have $200 in my pocket, are you serious? I asked. "Unless you want to be deported back to the U.S., señor." replied the security supervisor. I had no choice in the matter, I reluctantly give the immigration supervisor $200 to stay in Mexico for our honeymoon. After the whole ordeal, we missed our shuttle and had to take the funkiest cab in Cancun to the hotel. I had a painfully memorable honeymoon. I spent four agonizing days in our hotel room with second-degree sunburns.

The Mexican sun was scorching near the poolside. I was in the pool while engaging in hotel coordinated activities without sun tan lotion. *Oy vey,* as the Hebrews would say. Was I to receive more suffering because of my disobedience to my mother and dad's warning? It was an accident, I thought; anyone can get second-degree burns playing in the sun for that long. Just make sure you do not have a Mexican pharmacist prescribe you itching cream instead of burn ointment. Obviously, there was a language barrier between us.

They were unable to understand the English vocabulary of second-degree sunburn even after showing the pharmacist my skin condition. Was the pharmacist that stupid or cruel enough to be part of my suffering or should I have popped the puss out of my blistered skin in front of them for proof, hmm? We made the best of the remaining sensitive skin days of our honeymoon in Cancun before heading back home. April and I decided to seek a shopping market to purchase honeymoon gifts. Of all the souvenirs I purchased in any vacation,

I came across the one to pass on to generations. Sitting on the top shelf of a gift shop was a three-dimensional detailed sculpture of the Last Supper with Yahshua and his twelve disciples, a wonderful and intricate work of art. The artist expressed his love for Truth through his masterpiece. The new heirloom will be a great addition among family. We did not break the bank on our honeymoon and we still had an exciting time there. Our marriage was financially stable even before I graduated ITT Technical Institute.

Early job placement at ITT was very helpful, as I was immediately hired by a company that took interest of my skill trade. I began my career before graduation with a family-oriented company called Empire Wire and Supply, Inc. as an IT Coordinator. They really made me feel like family, and I loved working there. Months later, we purchased our first newlywed home and began our life together. Our agreement between each other was to wait to have children and build our nest-egg before taking another huge life-leap.

However, the mission was comprised by double agents. I was not anticipating my title change so soon into our marriage. "Tell me when you're about to, OK." asked April. "OK I will, I love you." I said. "I love you too." replied April. "No-no stop, let go, wait, don't, wait, stop, let go, let go...oh no why'd you do that!" I felt as though my soul was being pulled out of my body and into my wife's womb. My wife locked her legs around my waist preventing me from moving before copulation. "I'm sorry Gandy, I'm sorry."

"Oh my God, you're pregnant!" "What are you talking about, how do you know that?" "I felt my energy leave my body and into you, I know, trust me I know." "Oh Gandy, I'm so sorry; they showed me how, I didn't want to be an old mother." "Who showed you? Are you serious April? Old mother? You couldn't have waited two or three more years until we had children?" "No, I wanted children before I was thirty." "Oh my God, we have to pray." "What, pray, now?" "Get down here on your knees and pray for our children to be healthy and give them to Baba Alaha, now!" I shouted. "OK-OK!" yelled April.

After our prayer; I asked my wife why would she do such a thing so soon? She replied that she wanted to be a mother before she was thirty years old. I could not believe what I was hearing, we were just married; both working in lots of debt and now with a child on the way. In just a few months of marriage I became a father, forcefully. The deed had been done, signed by my DNA. The suffering was to commence, just as my mother and dad had predicted. We had to pray for our children to our Father in Heaven to protect them in this world.

My ignorance and disobedience from parental warnings blinded my judgment; but Love was still there preventing disaster. I was devastated and ashamed of myself for not using a male contraceptive. I should have undergone a vasectomy sooner. We were both emotionally exhausted from the whole ordeal. April apologized for her actions, but what was done was done. However, because half my DNA is Baba's DNA, I forgave her for what she had done because I really loved her.

I had to swallow my pride, my anger, my ego, my betrayed heart and replace with a soon-to-be fatherly Love. My mind was set at ease knowing that I would give all my children who I would father to Baba. I begged Baba to take my children into His hands and mold them as He sees fit. I prayed and prayed hoping that my plea would be answered; only time would tell. In whatever condition our children were born; I was still grateful to Baba for his blessings. Months passed and we were doing well financially and emotionally.

On the first day of July 2006, Prince Xander David Kachucha was born Defender of Mankind. To this day, he still amazes me on how brilliant, brave and beyond strength he has become. All things on Earth come to an end; they were never meant to last forever —only His Word and His Kingdom lasts forever. The repeating arranged economic bullshit bubble burst was initiated. We had lost our jobs, lost our home, our finances, our vehicles, and our lifestyles.

Without Yahshua in your heart, life would be empty of emotion and would be very difficult to continue. Family members will also help you along the way when you fall. In my case, my family helped Xander, my wife and me multiple times. I was beginning to see a pattern of resentment in our relationship, even after our second born. We were not making as much income as we used to before we had children. During the economy crash in 2006; keeping a lifestyle we were accustomed too was illogical.

We were determined to push on and make the best out of what we had. Another soul offering to my Father, on January 2009 –Princess Lexi Hope Kachucha was born as the beat to my heart and Hope to Humanity. Sacrificing both our children to Baba, Yahshua and the Holy Trinity was a wise decision on our part. In the end, Baba owns our souls and judges us of our actions towards others. Most people who bear children are hesitant to let their Father of Heaven protect them at the beginning stages of their lives.

Instead, the parents suffocate them with erroneous morals and values by allowing the media to raise them. Parents these days do not have the time or energy for their children anymore. They would much rather feed them boxed dinners, sitcoms, locked doors, deception, betrayal, resentment, hatred, abuse, drugs or whatever floats their tiny boat. Children begin understanding words and sentences by listening to their parents and the characters on television they watch.

I wanted to do something a bit different with my children at a young age. Introduce your children to Yahshua. In our Middle Eastern culture, we call him Eesho, and see what happens to their personality toward everyone else. Their eyes will light up with excitement from the stories of Yahshua, Moses, David and Goliath, Noah, Samson and Delilah, stories of miracles and adventures of the renowned. My son would say "Daddy, daddy please read us another story from the Bible before bed."

"OK, I will continue where we left off yesterday, try to stay awake just a bit longer, OK." I would reply. "OK Daddy." choired in Xander and Lexi. I was unable to finish the stories most of the time because of the harmonious words of Truth I was reading to my children put them to sleep almost instantly. I felt really great giving the Love I received from my Earthly and Heavenly family to my children who were eager to eat my Love. I believe they will grow to become glorious human beings with His Love protecting them in this world and beyond.

Prevent yourself from waiting until your children are in private school or need to attend catechism to understand who Baba, Yahshua the Messiah and the Holy Trinity are all about. If you do not know, educate yourself and pass along Yahshua's Truth to your children. If you procrastinate, then your ignorance, arrogance and doubt are to blame for whatever happens to your children in the real world.

My wife and I endured continuous financial struggles in addition to arguments about our children's behavior while I was away from home. Children need to vent; they will scream joy during their play sessions. They will have what seems like endless amounts of energy. Like Yahshua said, "If you can't beat them, join them." Our marriage was falling apart because I wanted instructions on raising our children followed instead of being challenged.

Mine were absorbing too much television, too much junk food, too much arguments, and not enough Love. Mother's take on plenty of mental stress from children who are young. The frustration blocks the mind; unable to figure out a problem with a toddler logically. It was quite simple – when children have a confrontation with each other – defuse the childish situation within minutes with authority without expressing any emotions. Kind of like a referee in a sporting event, do not choose sides, justify penalties, consequences and timeouts.

The stern tactic works every time and takes little time to gain the results you seek from your child. Once their lesson has been learned, hugged and smothered with kisses; take them out for ice cream. When you are young parents, stress levels are at their highest because you are new to the parental responsibilities and constantly worrying about the dangers your children may run into. Our first parental trauma was when Xander was riding his bike in the parking lot of our apartment complex.

The neighborhood children were all playing around spraying each other with water guns. When one of the kids decided to blindside Xander with water in his face; causing him to slide on a patch of dirt. He ended kissing the asphalt forcefully. The impact caused Xander's teeth to pierce his upper lip. Who knows if that was a deliberate act; or just boys will be boys, only He knows. The icing on the cake was when I received a call of Xander's injuries from my wife.

I urgently instructed my wife to immediately contact the ambulance to take him to the hospital. We only had one car to share in our family that I was using at that moment. April's car was wrecked from previous an accident while her mom and Xander were passengers; they were all ok. She agreed to call per our conversation. Utter disappointment and betrayal occurred when I arrived home. My wife decided that she would ignore contacting the ambulance.

She took it upon herself to confirm that Xander's injury was a non-emergency situation. When I arrived to our apartment, I found my son laying on the couch bleeding from his mouth. An argument immediately ensued about my whereabouts and delay, even after I instructed my wife to contact the ambulance. They would have arrived quicker than I would have. Ugh! "You let Xander lay there on the couch bleeding until I got home, are you crazy!" I shouted.

"Yes, I let him lay there; he isn't that bad. I told you I was waiting for you so we can go to the hospital as a family." replied April. "As a family? Are you serious? You're such a bitch; why didn't you call the ambulance like I told you!" I yelled. "Because this is not an emergency!" yelled April. "How the fuck is this not an emergency? He is fucking bleeding on the couch; his lip is ripped open!" I immediately picked up my son, and we all sped to the hospital, as a family. We arrived at the nearby hospital within ten minutes.

Xander's mishap triggered suspicion at the hospital; perhaps child abuse was the cause. One of the hospital staff that greeted us at the emergency doors raised his eyebrows. He began asking delaying questions about what happened. He came really close to seeing who I really was; he was judging me. Fortunately for him, I had my son in my arms. "Tell him what happened, Xander, it's OK." He couldn't even talk he was in so much pain.

His lips were pierced by his teeth; how do you expect a child to speak without agonizing pain? Their questions were irrelevant and obstructive to the urgency at hand. They would rather play detective at the door. "He's hurt, he can't talk; he was riding his bike at our apartment's parking lot and kids playing with water guns sprayed him in the face. He road over a dirt patch, lost control, and went down face first." I informed the hospital aid. He continued asking more questions, however I was frustrated with his delays and suspicious remarks and turned to my wife with a blank stare.

Just a few sentences more, and I was about to hand my son over to my wife while taking out my frustration on the hospital detective. "I'm taking my son inside so they can take care of him, you can ask her questions!" I demanded. Terror in my son's eyes and the screams for help during the stitching process was too much for my wife to bear. She began to faint and left the child emergency room.

I felt helplessly frustrated, furious and frightened for my child. I understood the pressures of parenthood. "Just hold still, Xander; the doctor wants to look at your lip. He is going hold your head still, OK?" calmly instructing my son. "OK daddy." replied Xander. The doctor, his assistant, and I were unable to keep Xander from swinging his arm at the doctor for getting too close to his wounds. The doctor advised we tightly strap down Xander-King-David's arms to administer a local anesthetic.

Also to prevent injury to his lips or the doctor's face. "Xander, Xander, stop baba, the doctor is trying to help you!" I shouted. "Arrrgh, Noooooo, he has a needle daddy, tell him stay away!" screamed Xander. "Oh habibi, don't be afraid; we're just trying to help you." I replied. My heart was in flames burning so hot that hell was freezing. After strapping down Xander, he still managed to free one of his arms and take a few swings at the doctor and assistant. We were all stunned and wowed with his strength.

The assistant had to strap Xander down once more. I secured his body straps down with my own body. Baba's child, what more can I say, he gives them the power to defend themselves. Time passed, wounds healed, lessons learned and memories and scars remained. Children are tough if you let them be; they will fall, pick them up, brush them off, kiss their wounds, and release them again with Love and Courage. The first incident with my daughter, was at my in-laws' home, ohff.

If you knew that your infant began to roll while sleeping, why would place them in a bed that was more than two feet off the ground? I advised all of them that if Lexi sleeps, place her on the floor with pillows around her to prevent her from rolling over onto her face. The fact is, most women will not take the advice from a man unless he gave birth to the child. I was constantly being challenged for the logical advice provided to the same team –duh, same team.

I am Jéjee, who forgives others for their wrong doing to my family, friends and me – unless you shed our blood, then you are mine. The reason I forgave so much is because He created me. Have no worries –worrying tends to stress out the human body so we lose years of our lives. Instead of taking my logical advice, my wife and in-laws decided to rest my daughter on top of an elevated box-spring and queen-size mattress with pillows around her. Well, at least they used pillows, right? Lexi rolled off the bed and fell on the hard wood flooring.

Imagine, a six-month-old with a fragile skull impacting the floor from that height. Remember when I mentioned earlier about sacrificing your children to Baba and Yahshua for protection? Situations in life where you are not always there to protect your children is the reason why. Lexi ends up landing on her butt with just bumps and bruises and nothing more. Metaphorically, she is mentally sharper than any blade on or off this planet. Still, we as parents have to be on constant alert.

Soon after that ordeal it was round two for Xander, who had another miracle of protection by His hand. If you intend on leaving someone in charge with your child other than yourself, make sure you pray to Baba before leaving. What does my mother-in-law request from her schizophrenic son? To take my son to a nearby neighborhood park so that she may clean her house without interruptions. A person taking on seven individuals' full load of cooking and cleaning up after them makes you a rather bitter person from the inside out.

My brother-in-law took my son to the playground and sat on the bench conversing with the voices in his head. I do not blame him for his mishap, as his parents signed his pill popping fate at an early age. The dumbass doctors started filling him full of pills to stop him from hearing voices. Even though he was taking his medication, he still heard voices in his head. If you make children suffer, you will suffer for your negligence and cruelty. Someone with a fearful mental instability will not be a suitable guard to keep children safe when an enemy draws near.

They are unable to distinguish the differences in character of the individual, and his response to my questions were. "What do the voices in your head talk to you about?" I asked. "They tell me that someone will get hurt, that they want to hurt Xander and Lexi." said Bruce. "What do you mean they want to hurt Xander and Lexi or are they telling you to do that for them?" I asked. "No, I would never hurt my niece and nephew, I love them." replied Bruce. "Oh that's good. Just let me know if they ask you to do anything to harm my children or anyone else, and we'll go from there."

I said. "OK I will." said Bruce. "This will be my warning to you, you hurt my children, I will hurt your whole generation, I will wipe them clean off this Earth, do you understand what I'm telling you Bruce?" I informed Bruce. "Yeah I understand." replied Bruce. Keep in mind; when someone stops taking mind-altering drugs, what is their initial reaction? The withdrawal of a psychosis chemical is anger and poor judgment, no matter what is said.

Xander's uncle was sitting on the bench watching my son play at the toddler section of the playground. However, anti-social behavior and psycho-pills are buddy-buddies. Along came a neighborhood mother and children playing in the same area as my son. Everything was OK until the older children playing with Xander decided to move to the big kids' playground located behind the school. Xander, the adventurous being he is, followed the group disregarding his uncle instructing him to stay. Bruce continued to hear voices in his head and froze on the bench.

When you snooze you lose, as the saying goes; and in this case Bruce snoozed and Xander lost, or did he? My son decided to climb the more advanced metal jungle gym despite his small stature. When Xander reached the top, he could not reach the bottom triangle bars of the dome and was unable to hold on much longer with his weak grip. I was not there to catch Xander and neither was his uncle available; my Father caught him.

Xander falls to his fate and gashes his exterior eye socket a quarter inch wide just above his eye against a sharp object. To keep him from crying uncontrollably, the mother of the other children allows Xander to ride one her son's bike. Xander acted like nothing happened to him; he was so happy to ride a strange three-wheel bike, ha-ha, Yah Habibi. He went to the hospital once more for stitches to add to his book of life. "Don't worry Dad, I'm used to it now, I can take the pain from stitches." said Xander. "Wow really, are you sure, even the needle, you're not afraid anymore?" I asked.

"Nope, watch me Dad." replied Xander. "You're so brave Xander, I love you very much." caressing Xander's head. "Me too Dad." With the rage that I had, no man or machine could stop me. I was hungry to smash some bones in payment for my son's pain and anguish. My fists were going to meet someone else's body to add their gash to their book, err pamphlet. The cut was deep; however, he was much stronger this time and built up his pain tolerance.

Baba and Yahshua calmed me down again and showed how much he loved my son by not taking his eye and giving him a quarter-inch scar to remember that day. I forgave them all because Baba wants me to, Yahshua wants you to trust in his Father to protect your family and let time pass to heal wounds and mend hearts. I last counted twenty-seven stitches my son had endured during his life as a toddler. Xander has earned an unimaginably high tolerance for pain; I praise you, Baba. My suffering was to continue on another level, a deeply emotional suffering.

Sadly, in 2006 my mother found out she had colon cancer, and the doctors gave her three months to live. My heart was crushed for my beloved, who may never see my second born before Baba calls her to join Him. I pleaded to my Father Baba, "How could You this happen to my mother; Your vessel of my birth." Life was unfair. I became frustrated at the doctors, my family members, even my mother, for keeping her vital health issues from me. Maybe I should have spent more time with my mother; forgive me, Mom.

I finally calmed down and realized that everyone's time on this planet must come to end. We must take into consideration that we do not live forever on this plant for a reason. My monarch, Mariam Bazi, passed away in October 2009. By the grace of thy Father, He let her live for three more years to witness the birth of my children, my brother's children, and my sister's wedding. Baba's plan is very difficult for humans to understand; we only use approximately 10% of my mental capacity to comprehend His Divine Truth.

Eventually all of us will learn His language on Earth as it is in Heaven. Growing up as a family, times were getting tough financially. We ended up getting shuffled around from our homes in Chesterfield, Macomb, Troy and Rochester Hills. However, our constant moving was frowned upon by my wife, but we had no choice but to move from one location to another. In the end, Baba always had a home for us to live. Before my mother had passed away, my younger sister was getting married.

However, mom was nearing her last days of her life and was in no condition to attend the wedding ceremony. So, my sister decided to put on her gown and head to the hospital before the wedding. My mother wanted to see her daughter all grown up before she met Baba, Yahshua, the heavenly angels, and all her passed loved ones. So, my sister decided to have my mom watch the recorded church ceremony right after it was completed. She personally delivered the video in her wedding dress.

I thought that was a very unique and kind gesture to allow mom to have some fun, too; even though she was not physically there, she was happy. Well-done, sis. The journey was emotional for all of us to see our foundation wither away to this family-destroying disease. Cancer is a profitable disease that flipped the world upside down. Cancer feed the money hungry doctors, cancer institutions, and pharmaceutical companies. The drugs doctors prescribe humanity prolong life until the human body is unable to tolerate the foreign poison. They will be judged by the Creator for poisoning His children.

I will wipe the poison off this planet if or when He gives the command, get ready. There is a cure or preventive measure for any disease known to mankind, they just do not care or it is not profitable. Who decides who stays and who goes to balance out population? Yet, they have such little Faith to allow Father to tend to his children. If the elite disclosed any condemning evidence to the public, their control over the population would end. They need someone drug dependent to feed their dragon.

The drugs and chemotherapy that the doctors had provided to my mother just made her wither away much slower for the companies to gain more profits. Dependency on drugs, no matter what form, makes our minds cloudy to communicate with our hearts to each other. Holistic medicine and natural remedies that are present in the world today and for thousands of years; are never spoken of because the pharmaceutical industries do not have patent rights to a plant from Earth. Vitamin B3, B14, roots, herbs, healthy diet and daily exercise is naturally preventative to diseases.

Avoiding processed foods, fast foods, high fructose corn syrup, as overconsumption of any substance is never good for the human body. Even drinking too much water can be detrimental to our health. Where do we draw the line to live hundreds of years like Noah? You do not, human; He draws the line for you when we talk to Him more often. You have to be mentally resilient against the temptation of an early death by disgusting habits and lethargically glutinous diets.

Break the habit of gluttony, use the power of will He gave us all to keep our vessel clean. Shine like Baba's eternal star on Earth to be placed in His Universe. The pain of exercise is far better than the pain you will feel throughout your body of poor diet. People think they have to purchase expensive workout machines or gimmick pills burning fat. People will even go to the extreme of siphoning out the fat cells from the body via vacuum procedures. The gluttony started in your brain, not your tissue; unfortunately, there is no siphon for mental ignorance.

CHAPTER 5

The White Monarch Buck

In the years after my dad had divorced my mother, I kept in contact with him on and off. I never held any grudges toward anyone for very long because of their past vulgar behavior. So there I was, my time to bond with my dad again like we used to. My dad and I had many things in common when it came to the outdoors. I enjoyed fishing, camping, hiking, biking and sitting around the campfire exchanging stories.

During the cold hunting season, my dad and his nephew would invite me to go deer hunting with them. We gathered with our relatives exchanging hunting stories of the big buck. I have never gone hunting before nor owned a rifle for that matter. So, my dad decided that he would gift me my first rifle for my birthday. It was the best Remington 3006 semi-auto, with elk and deer engraved into oak wood stock. It cost $600, excluding the scope, sling and rifle case.

The thought of the bonding gift was priceless. Rifle season for hunting deer was approaching; but first, crossbow season. I purchased an identical crossbow as my dad's. I had never shot or killed a deer before but enjoyed the taste of deer meat. After a day of crossbow practice in the backyard of the cabin, I fine-tuned my aim and was eager to land my first buck or doe. My dad, cousin and I decided to build deer blinds made out of plywood and one-inch thick bullet-resistant glass. Both built 6' x 6' deer blinds while I was stuck with a 4' x 4' deer blind.

I could not understand why I ended up with the smaller deer blind; we had plenty of material. Was it because I was a rookie? I could barely maneuver my crossbow within my blind, which was so small. That afternoon before the hunt, we baited our hunting areas with apples near our blinds. Nightfall arrived, and the excitement and adrenaline flowed through my veins for the next morning. We bonded by the campfire and our discussion of tactical deer hunting techniques was memorable.

I awoke at four a.m., as instructed, to wake up my drunken cousin and dad. Have you ever tried to wake up someone who has only had four hours of sleep after drinking a bottle of cognac? My attempt was futile on both of them. I had to use the good old pan and spoon tactic. *BANG-BANG-BANG-BANG-BANG!* "Get up, get up, get up, let's go, let's go, let's go, the deer are waiting for us, let's move!" I got my point across when my cousin fell out of his bed. However, my dad was pissed; he reached for his pistol, oops, sorry Dad.

I felt like a black-op on a mission to bring home the meat. We headed out to our grounds, tuned on our two-way radio transceivers, and began walking to each of our deer blinds. They were located in a triangular formation between each other. I reached my deer blind almost losing my breath from all that smoking and binge drinking. Oh, it was so cold and silent; all of nature was in slumber. All around was pure darkness; I could barely see the path to my deer blind. I was forced to use a flashlight and expose my presence.

I settled in my somewhat cushy chair and positioned my crossbow for the kill shot. That hunk of metal filled the deer blind. I wondered how I was going to maneuver this thing around in here without the deer noticing me and bouncing away through the woods. The weather in November is unpleasant when you have to sit for hours waiting for deer to cross your path. If deer smell the scent of humans downwind, upwind, east-way wind, or west-way wind, you can count on the deer heading to your no-way wind.

The first couple of days of hunting were frustrating for us because there were no deer in sight, at least not on the fourteen acres we were hunting. In my opinion, the deer would arrive after we left the woods for the day, eat the apples, poop all over the place, and wait for more to arrive. We were being outwitted by deer; that was classic. Sunday was the last day hunting; someone had to land a deer or we were going to be laughed at by our other friends at their hunting grounds. Once more I needed Baba to aid me in this hunting adventure.

I had never seen a deer closer than on television or nearly missing smashing into them on the road driving. While sitting in my deer blind, I closed my eyes and began to pray to Baba and Yahshua quietly. When you send a prayer request, it is near impossible that you will be answered immediately; however, I think Baba made mine a special request. Baba has to move a few chess pieces until the right moment occurs for your prayers to be answered, be patient.

"Yah Baba Alaha, Yah Eesho I know you can hear me, I need your help, can you send a deer my way, you have my Word I will not kill the deer, I will not shed its blood, I just want to see one up close." I prayed. All was quiet on the snowy northern Michigan front; it was the sound of deafness. I heard whispers on my radio, but could not make out who was speaking, my dad or cousin. *Tish-Beep-Tish–Beep* "Deer-deer." sounded the voice on my walkie-talkie. "Come in – over ~ *Tish-Beep* ~ come in – over ~ *Tish-Beep* ~ can you hear me?" I replied to the voice.

There was no deer in sight, let alone understood who said it or the direction to look, this way or that way. I could only aim my crossbow in one direction and that was it...*jump in front of me deer, hey deer, right here, now stand still, huh.* "Where-where, who is this, which way- which way?" I asked. "Heading your way Gandy, heading your way." replied my Dad. Chills ran down my whole body, I almost froze stiff above the November chill adding to my suffering.

~ *THUD! ~THUD! ~ THUD! ~ THUD!* ~ I thought, "Earthquake!" "Oh Baba – Yah Eesho, was that you, did you do that, did you send me that deer?" I whispered. The Earth was shaking beneath me with every thud. I heard my dad frantic again over the radio trying to get a hold of my cousin. The deer was heading my way from my dad's direction. We were slightly fifty yards away from each other. I had no luck contacting my cousin to help site the deer. "I can't see a deer, Dad, are you sure it's heading my way? Dad, can you hear me, Dad?" There was no reply from my dad.

I looked down at my radio to see if maybe I had lowered the volume or changed the channel accidentally. I felt my hairs stiff all over my body. The frightening terrible chill made me lift my head and notice a figure in the woods. The most magnificently glowing, pure white, monarch deer flying through the air with every leap. So glorious and massive, the deer came to a halt landing ten yards in front of me with a thunderous ground-shaking thud. I counted twenty points on his antlers; I counted more than once.

"Oh my God, oh my God, Dad, Dad, Dad come in, ooh my God -*Tish-Beep*- Dad come in!" I whispered through my grinding jaws, clamping shut my mouth from all the excitement and fear. The beautifully memorable monarch that stood before me glowing freakish white in the wooded field was terrifyingly glorious. I had never seen a pure white deer before, especially in Michigan. I froze still in tears, as I watched Baba's buck rear its massive neck looking for something. "Grunt! Grunt! Grunt! Grunt!" ~ *THUD!* ~ *THUD!* ~ *THUD!* sounded the magnificent White Monarch Buck.

The behemoth buck shook the ground and grunted his dominance with every stomp; his sound was echoing throughout the woods bouncing off my face. After a few moments of dead silence, a young deer that was following the brilliant buck was possibly for my taking. The kill shot was there, however, betrayal never overcame my heart to draw blood from Baba's creatures unjustifiably. Besides, I gave Him my Word. The young deer may have been Yahshua following his Father.

I avoided releasing my arrow and instead observed Baba's buck with all of the beauty and power He had over me. What will stay forevermore in my memory was the way the deer stared at me, as though Baba was speaking to me telepathically, "Here I am Gandy, magnificent enough for you?"A few minutes later, the gigantic white buck shook the ground once more, leaping away in the woods for the last time. After a few minutes my Dad showed up to my deer blind to see what had happened.

We were both shocked during the appearance of a never before seen White Monarch Buck in Michigan. My Dad and I debated on how many points were on the buck's rack; I counted twenty and my Dad stated eighteen. The memorable excitement between us was priceless. We could not wait to share the news with my cousin. Hiking up the trail to reach my cousin's deer blind; we tried contacting him through our radios. We received no reply from him; I thought perhaps his radio battery was dead. We approached the deer blind to find; my cousin lazily snoring away during the miracle.

My dad and I will never forget that day of Baba's Magnificent White 20-point Monarch Buck that arrived that chilly morning. He gave us a glimpse of His power over humans and creatures alike on earth as His authority over the cosmos. Monday morning, we arrived home with awe flowing throughout our veins. The experience I never would trade anything for in this world except to sit with Yahshua and Baba. His loving presence in the woods makes you see life in a whole new perspective again.

Sometimes, that affection goes a long way and begins to touch other lives for the better. They notice you are more cheerful, energetic and humble. If everyone had the same feeling daily, imagine what this Earth would blossom into? I believe it would benefit everyone on this planet for generations to come. Working together to resolve worldly issues is a must for the survival of our species, otherwise "we the people" may become our own doomsday weapon and destroy each other. Unfortunately, most of the people in the world are hesitant to be included in His quest He has for them.

Fear, arrogance and ignorance is stopping humanity in its tracks and preventing humanity from spreading their wings and soaring to greater heights. Only a few individuals are meant to soar high, while others were meant to fall below. Humans have free will, yet lack to use their common sense. Many people suffer in this world and many have the opportunity to help one another; yet do they? I have seen Baba's creatures having more compassion toward humans than humans toward humans.

CHAPTER 6

Suffering and Praying

Why would a person act cruel toward others? Are they not aware that it is their own self they are harming in the end? Whose side will you choose – the ones who destroy with words and weapons or the ones who Love, heal and prosper with kind words and hugs toward greatness with His Word? You have free will; choose wisely, Padawan. Every human has Baba's Force within them to battle the evil empire.

Use your Light Saber of Faith to fight the good fight alongside your brothers and sisters. Strengthen your force as warriors through prayer for Yahshua's salvation. With every path I walked in my life; I have learned to become an optimist and have more trust in Baba. With Yahshua's light leading the way; how could anyone get lost? Baba can move the Earth for you when you are in contact with Yahshua. He can touch your heart and transform you into Love allowing you to see His Truth with every step of your life.

There is a reason for everything and everyone in Baba's plan, and man-kind's mental capacity cannot comprehend the cosmic translation. The translation of His loving embrace towards humanity. The individual needs to accept the fact that they are a part of Baba's plan and to follow the path He prepared for them. Maybe, just maybe, receive what He rewards them with for being obedient and faithful. Even as my marriage was slowly dissolving in salt water, I kept my hopes up and continued the path to my destiny.

Flashback memories of my mother and dad resided in my thoughts about how my life was going to unfold page by page. I witnessed my dramatic life play out before my eyes. People have to continue to try, try and try again to fix any marriage no matter what it takes. When children are involved, continuing to Love them is a necessity to the future of this planet. When my dad left our family, my older brother became the father figure of the household. He had the most responsibility out of all of us in our family of five. Having the responsibility of a role of son, brother and dad all in one was too much to handle.

My brother and I argued almost daily because of my Mother's and Dad's divorce, and I did not blame him. He was under a lot of stress with his new role in the family. Yahshua reminds us to "Turn the other cheek," so I did when my brother and I were in a physical confrontation. I returned the wrath on the streets at the punks that touched me without my permission. Heed my warning wisely when I say, "Don't touch me or else He will touch you." If you touch Yahshua without being true to yourself and the Love you have for Him, then you may go insane or perhaps die right on the spot.

He has an infinite amount of Love and Power; the Universe justifies His authority. I shared my story with people about having physical contact with the most Holy Brother man has ever known. Their comments: "You should be dead"; You're crazy"; "You're lying"; "Prove it"; "Show me magic"... WTF? Honestly, I think they are all crazy, and I am sane and brave enough to hug Baba's Truth when He arrived to help me. I am an IT professional by trade, a handyman by hobby and a born saint, so I am sane.

In fact, I consider myself very intelligent because of Him. After the initial physical contact with Yahshua, everything became clear to me on how the Universe all became. Anyone else with ridiculously doubtful excuses toward my encounter with Yahshua may contact me to reassure them of His Truth. If you are one grain of sand on your own, you stand alone, weak. If you are one grain of sand on a beach, you are strong with your brothers and sisters united. Accept Baba's and Yahshua's awesome power and Love he has for you to become the sand on his eternal beach.

Humans are unable to comprehend how their power works. You must understand how to Love, then you will begin to learn their powerful language that can heal the world. To make my point come across to the non-believers, doubters, and opinionated mockers, Yahshua the Messiah manifested himself by slowing down his vibration for me to see him truthfully. In my case, though, I did not accept him at first as Yahshua.

I thought He was an individual who resembled Jesus and was interested in laptops – until I touched his crimson red velvet scarf with my finger, then with my palm, and finally a hug sealing my fate. I have eternal Faith and Love for my brother Yahshua, forevermore. The feeling of receiving Love from our Holy Teacher is like having uncontrollable shivers flowing through you with every prayer. Sometimes you have to spread your wings and share His immense energy toward your loved ones.

I wrapped my wings of Love around my children and their reaction shows through their happiness to see me every time. I have also showed my Love to my wife, yet oftentimes Love had stopped being returned unconditionally. Stale bread makes any relationship dry and cumbersome. Especially if one gives so much love only to be given crumbs in return. Unfortunately, only a few couples are truly compatible. If both attempt to outdo one another with unconditional Love and sacrifice, then their foundation becomes as solid as a mountain. In my case, Sabra is my Earth, and I live within her Heart.

My past marital foundation was built on stone that cracked; that I attempted to repair with cement that in time crumbled; that I replaced with wood that in time rotted and finally stood on glass waiting to shatter into pieces cutting our souls. The weekend came, and my family and I decided to visit my sister and her husband at my mother's home. Reminiscing the past and kicking tires for the future was at the discussion table. "I don't like this house." said April. "Why? It's big enough to grow our family." I replied.

"Because it's not my house with my memories or a new house for new memories. It is your mother's house with her memories." answered April. "But you were part of her memories and this house. Remember, I lived here, too, before I married you." I said. "It doesn't matter; I still don't like it." demanded April. Our backyard was a good size with soft dirt; I thought I may as well grab my shovel and bury myself alive back there, as during our social visit, my brother-in-law blurted a topic that should have been kept a secret between him and my sister.

My brother-in-law stated with glee that they were planning on moving soon and have not kept up with the mortgage payments for the past six months. Oh, I was charging full speed with my sharp lance on that remark. My sister was sitting across the couch and had the surprised look of: *Did you just give away our plan of letting this house go to the bank?* It was kept a secret until my sister and her husband saved enough funds to purchase another home. After they had moved out, we were left to deal with six months of late mortgage payments with the bank that could care less about any family's situation. Screw you Chase Morgan; one day I will take your empire.

I was puzzled on how any of my siblings forgot to mention a will during her sickness to deal with her affairs and estates. Was I at fault for not getting involved with my mother's personal affairs? I had my own issues to deal with. I was always last to hear the family news, even when my mother had cancer. But there was no blame towards anyone on my part. We cannot live on the hate and bickering because of personal issues.

You have to deal with the present in a logical manner for a better future. In this case; approximately $6000 to $7000 in late payments the bank wanted up front instead of moving the late payments toward the end of the mortgage contract. That sounds logical to me; but the heartless bank have little to no empathy or morals for that matter, in my opinion. I was unable to refinance my mother's home with my credit or my wife's. Furthermore, I could not even take over my from my late mother's account. The bank was unaware my mother had passed away.

After Chase Bank heard the tragic news, its greed rang in. ~ *Cha-Ching* ~ free home! It was only a matter of time until they kicked us out of our home. We tried to save as much as possible with the allotted time we had left until the foreclosure occurred. In the meantime, everything kept getting difficult to make ends meet. I was so down and out that I even attempted to grow marijuana in my mother's basement to use the proceeds to buy the home. It was a race against the bank's decision to eat us alive or feed them money.

The marijuana growing lasted four months; sometimes the yield was minimal, and I ended up breaking even with expenses or losses. The smell was unbearable for my family, even after filtration. Take my advice, do not grow marijuana in your home if others who live with you cannot bare the stench. Stress over money can lash out to discipline children for their excited, energetic and sometimes normal childish behavior. The stress level of mothers and fathers raising toddlers attacking each other takes discipline and plenty of unconditional Love.

I even tried to explain the easy process of defusing the situation in any argument before battles began. Some individuals avoid being advised how to raise children and decide that they have it under control until tempers flare and they make the first strike. Causing fear, confusion, anger and betrayal toward your seed(s) only will result in heartaches in the future your own children will direct toward you. Your children will feed you what you feed them emotionally or physically.

The children just wait until they are older and stronger to return your recipe from before. How, you may ask? What happens when you cause fear, confusion, anger and betrayal toward another adult, colleague or family member? You get to eat a hurtful dish of resentment. Do you want to eat that bitter dish? Try more Love, logic, hugs and a heaping portion of kisses. Try a recipe of Spock-spread, a kind of stern personality yet very logical with a dash of Kirk. When defusing the firecracker waiting to go off between your children, pour some water over their heads; that will snap them out of it.

If they react with anger or fear, pour the water over your own head and get a joyous reaction. No choosing sides or showing emotion, just Spock logic. Be the referee of the childish circumstance. Sometimes parents try to play the role of bad cop-good cop. Avoid using the bad cop-good cop method; no child should choose between the two. If you teach your children to be humble Baba warriors, you will no longer have disobedient behavior for very long.

Children blossom into Love when you provide them unconditional Love daily. Mind you, show them Love even if they anger or let you down. Then, listen to how their little hearts thump the beat of forgiveness. The encoded human emotion of mercy will trigger Love instead of unwanted hate. They will bond with each other as Baba commanded. Telling bedtime stories from the Bible about men of renown and adventures to your children really does make everyone feel good. Baba loves you for continuing his legacy to your seeds.

Pray the correct pronunciation of our teacher's name –Yahshua –and continue your lessons in the school-of-life. The excuse of children needing to attend catechism or they will get confused about faith is absolutely absurd .If people decide the "Book of Truth" is a waste of time, then they seal their own fate when Judgment arrives for the Affairs and Accusations proceedings. Ignore blabber and continue with the stories to your children about the biblical glory showing them the way to Yahshua into their hearts to never let Him go.

Xander "King David" Kachucha and Lexi "Hope for Humanity" Kachucha were sent by Baba. I would advise to always sacrifice your own flock to Him, always. Baba will watch over them, have no fear. My younger years had plenty of worldly abuse which made me chose one of two directions, praying or retaliation. I chose praying, because it is the backbone of humanity for our survival on this planet, so why stop now? When people attack others, they may win the battle, but when they do not fight fair, they will lose the war by His last Word of judgment.

He will strengthen the ones who follow Yahshua faithfully. People suffer immense pain, ridicule, frustration, depression, doubt, loss, loneliness and much more. Just bow your head down then hold your head up high and finally open your heart and let Him in. Baba may send His guardian angels to aid you in your journey through your game of life. If you fall, get up; if you doubt, look up and pray to Yahshua and he will lead you to Baba's kingdom.

He will hear you and send the help you need; be grateful and praise Him eternally. Believe in faith as Yahshua believed in his father. Our Father will provide you the Love and strength to conquer your enemies and win the hearts of nations. Forevermore, your path to salvation will be brightened by His glory. The key for a stable and secure household foundation is an understanding, unselfish, unexpected and unconditional everlasting Love. Will you forgive their mistakes and offer them a hug in exchange for their forgiveness?

Will you embrace His Truth of divine bread and share with others? Consider yourself an author writing your own book to tell your story to Him. We are all his characters in His Book of Life. When will you awake to live out your adventure? It's never too late, even at the last breath. Supplement your food for your heart with His literature. You will be fulfilled spiritually and mentally with His every Word. For even words spoken from your heart can be heard throughout the Universe. Speak up; don't be afraid.

CHAPTER 7

The Battle

Battles nowadays are fought cowardly –with missiles, bombs, guns, daggers, sticks and stones that break bones. Humans lost the ability to fight with Courage, like real men of renown with Iron Fists. Any piss-ant pee-shooter can fight from afar and try to call themselves heroes justifiably. The battle to any war will always be won when Baba empowers you to battle your enemies with your heart and mind.

He can give you the strength you need to be victorious. You just have to accept the fact that Baba is doing what he is doing because he loves you. Just like a parent disciplining their children with guidance when they are unaware of the dangers. The Love for Baba and Yahshua will empower you with the strength and Faith to keep you going in any situation; good or bad. Never fear any man or demon, you will always defeat them in His name for eternity for His Word is eternal.

I truthfully can say Baba and Yahshua have helped me in numerous occasions from near death situations, path choices and battles. They will empower you with their Truth and strength at any given moment for flight or fight encounters. Some earthly professionals classify those encounters as just an adrenaline rush; they are as clueless as scientists. So there I was, at a nightclub in downtown Detroit called Clutch Cargo at Fox Theater.

My friends and I were in our early twenties out for a night of fun. We were the clique with chips on our shoulders – Chaldeans who were avoided by others in confrontational situations at bars most of the time. They made a reputation for themselves; however, I am no Chaldean, I am half Assyrian and half 'Yah.' I am Jéjee-The Dragon Slayer, forevermore. I have always tried talking at first; it is rude to touch anyone without asking questions to why they would like to battle. For example; one day one of my good friend's cousin, let us call him Jo-Jo, started the battle unknowingly. We were standing near a skin head dance mosh pit.

The DJ was playing a heavy metal song in which a bunch of skinheads bash into each other on the dance floor and call it dancing; it was rather funny. We both had pitchers of beer in our hand; mine was three quarters full, and Jo-Jo's had his half full. Oh if there was ever a Kodak moment that would have been the icing on this guy's cake. "Watch this!" yelled Jo-Jo over the loud noise blasting away from the speakers. "Watch what!" I yelled back. *"Gulp"* - *"Gulp"* - *"Gulp"* as Jo-Jo swallowed a few gulps from his drink.

Already drunk; he decided to throw his pitcher of beer in the middle of the mosh pit onto a bunch of already pissed off skinheads. "What the fuck did you do that for!" I yelled. "Ha-ha-ha-ha-ha!" laughed Jo-Jo. "Bro you just fucked us up!" I shouted. I looked at him and while he was laughing it off and enjoying himself thinking no one had seen him throw his beer. The small group of skinheads looked our way as I was drinking my pitcher of beer. They pointed in our direction, I pointed my thumb at the idiot next to me.

I turned to look and was alarmed to see Jo-Jo's five-foot-two stature was bear hugged by a steroid-injected six-foot monster club security. Yep; looked like someone did see him throw his beer picture into the pit. "Gandy, help, help me!" screamed Jo-Jo trying to escape from the club security. "You're a dumbass!" I shouted. "Hurry, get the others and meet me outside; let go of me you motherfucker.!" I continued to drink my beer and gave Jo-Jo a thumbs up while I watched him being carried away like a sack-o-kicking-potatoes.

He pleaded for my help to gather up the crew and defend his stupid honor. Well, there went my night of fun, why me? I attempted to gather up the rest of our friends and leave as a group. Just because of one moron, our night was ruined. I was able to find a couple of friends and instructed them to head to the front of the club to help Jo-Jo who was being beaten to a pulp by bouncers. I had to finish my beer that I had bought, to enjoy what was left of our night out before we were all kicked out.

Who would toss a good tasting beer at someone? An idiot would, what a waste. There was such a riot in the nightclub. The bouncers were outnumbered and about to experience the SHTF everywhere. The arrogant beer thrower set off a chain reaction between the two clans like they have been feuding for generations. I just wanted to leave; I had nothing to do with their stupidity. I tried to leave, or so I thought. I ended up by the bar near the entrance doors to get a refill, since it was not yet last call.

A few moments later, Jo-Jo's cousin Zee approached me. "Gandy, where's my cousin?" asked Zee. "His sorry ass was being dragged out to the front doors; he's probably still out there waiting for us." I replied. "Let anyone you know we're outside and hurry up, we gotta help my cousin!" yelled Zee. "Sure thing Zee!" ~Gulp~ When Zee exited to the lobby, I heard some commotion that peaked my interest. I entered the lobby with my beer pitcher and witnessed two bouncers tussling with skinheads and Chaldeans.

It was a hilarious sight as to how they were getting tossed out like cats and dogs, lol. One of the club security personal who stood at the corner of the lobby noticed I had a pitcher of beer and approached me. "Hey you, you can't have that out here!" yelled the club security. "Who me, oh this, it's OK, I'll finish it out here before I leave, it's too rowdy in there." I replied. "OK that's fine." replied Braveman. As we were conversing, we ended up befriending each other, when I was interrupted once again. *BOOM!* sounded the entry doors to the club.

We both glanced over to investigate the loud noise, only to see a six-foot skinhead pointing at me. It looked as though his head was on fire and I was his extinguisher. The raging tree wanted to stomp on any middle eastern looking individual. "Hey!" yelled the Koo-Koo skinhead. "Who me?" I replied. "Yeah you, you're the guy who was standing next guy who threw the beer pitcher!" yelled Koo-Koo. "OK?" I said. "I'm gonna fuck you up!" shouted Koo-Koo. What was I to do? I was not going to run anywhere from anyone. So, what would you do, cower or battle?

Just before you react, though, you better know what you are doing or call upon Yahshua's help. "Could you hold this for me, I'll be right back." I asked. "Sure." replied Braveman. Baba took over and allowed me to battle truthfully.

~Wrath!~ *Whoosh!* ~ *Thud!*

I close lined Koo-Koo with Baba's wings full force spinning him in the air like a propeller until he landed on his back. Leaping at Koo-Koo to finish him off, my fist met his jaw. I had to slap the unconscious Koo-Koo a few times to wake him up. There are more drastic ways to wake up a person in their deep sleep. I started applying professional pressure points around Koo-Koo's neck to snap him out of sleep. "Hey, stop, you're killing him!" yelled Braveman. "No, I'm not, ~*smack*~ ~*choke*~ I'm just trying to wake him up, wake up motherfucker"!

"Warning: Refrain from Touching Me While I Am in Wrath Mode; You Will Only Get Hurt."

I was unaware who grabbed me at first. The Braveman felt sorry for my punching bag and bear-hugged me off him. As the bouncer was restraining me from doing any more harm to Koo-Koo, I was getting pissed off. I began to twist his grip free from my chest until I unlocked his hand and flipped the Braveman over me and grabbed his wrist. "No stop, please don't, don't break my wrist, oh God, please don't!" shouted Braveman. His plea to my Father let me know that he was on my side, and I realized he was the good guy just trying to save the other guy.

So, I let go of his wrist before snapping it and lifted him up off his knees. "I'm sorry, I didn't know you knew God." I said. "It's OK, where are they?" asked Braveman. "Where are who?" I replied. "Where are you wings?" asked Braveman. "My wings, what wings, are you sure you are OK? I asked. "Yes I'm OK." said the Braveman. We gathered ourselves and stood by a corner counter trying to figure out what happened. My beer was still cold...Ahhh. Moments later, the Braveman gestured to look behind me to see a stumbling human. "Wow, it's about time."

~*Arrggahhh*!~ "What happened, hey you, get over here, I'm not done with you!" yelled Koo-Koo. "Are you serious?" I asked. "Wait, I have an idea." said the Braveman. "What's that?" I replied. "I'm going to grab you as though I'm on his side and hold you for him to kick your ass." instructed Braveman. "What kinda idea is that?" I asked. "Trust me, I'll hold you and when I say now, kick as hard as you can." said Braveman. "Huh, OK." I agreed. Just then, the bouncer grabbed me with a bear hug, lifted me up and instructed me to get ready.

"I got him, I got him, get over here and kick his ass!" yelled Braveman. "Are you sure this is a good idea?" I asked one last time. "Trust me, get ready." replied the Braveman. "Ha-ha OK." I laughed. "Hurry I got him!" yelled Braveman. "Get ready." whispered the Braveman to me. We waited until the groggy punk ran close enough for Brave-Knight to initiate his plan. He lifted me up as I was pretending to break free. "Let me go, let me go, ha-ha, arrgh!" I yelled. OUFF! - down went Koo-Koo. "Shit, I think we killed him."

"Nah, he's all right; look he's still breathing." replied Braveman. "Oh yeah, huh, that was a good plan; thanks." I said. "Thanks, that was a good hit, you knocked him out cold, hahahaha." laughed Braveman. "Thanks, hahahaha, what a dumbass." I laughed. After finally finishing my now warm beer, we gave each other a brother to brother handshake, and I headed for the outer doors. "Hey!" yelled Braveman. "Yo!" I yelled back. "Thanks, I'll see ya!" yelled the Braveman. "You're welcome, see ya bro!" I yelled. While gesturing a Kung-Fu shaolin monk peach hand sign to the club security Braveman.

BOOM! sounded main entrance doors. Just as I reached the doors; an even bigger bouncer slams open the entrance doors. I thought, *Are you kidding me, you too?* He tried to grab me, so I crouched; ready to lunge and show humanity once again; Father's Wrathful Truth. He leaped back against the door as though he had seen a ghost and froze on the spot. I prepped for the next attack until..."Arrrgh Noooooo!" yelled the Goliath club security.

"No, leave him alone, he's OK, he's with me!" yelled Braveman. "Oh OK." I replied. "OK! I'm...with him." yelled Goliath. I could not help myself to give Goliath one last move to put him in check. "Boo!" I yelled. "Arrrgh!" screamed Goliath. I laughed, and that made Goliath angry at me and wanting to test his strength with me until Braveman stepped in and instructed the frightened Goliath not to attack. I waved goodbye to them both and laughed on my way out. My friends were waiting outside for me yelling as I exited the entrance doors.

"Where were you? We thought you were getting a beat down." said Phil. "No, I'm fine, you should have seen the other guy, hahahaha!" I laughed. "What other guy?" asked Phil. "Never mind, the bouncer got him." I replied. I thought for a second, *Nah, do not tell them.* Those were good times, good battles, however; I would much rather stand next to His crew rather than beer pitcher tossing idiots. Avoid going around thinking you are tougher than everyone else.

First and foremost, avoid any physical confrontations that may come your way. In most cases, training is involved when you battle one on one. However, cowards that stab with sharp objects, pull triggers, sucker punch, or use other tricks of their trade, meet their fate also. They may sometimes meet me, their fate. Some cowardly ran while others laid silent, unable to move until I shook and slapped them to awaken and fight another day, or not. When you have His Word in your heart, the strength of His breath resides within your soul to win the war.

Sometimes; you may be tested of your human strength with another opponent that may fight dirty. Keep the Faith, and you will survive. Show no fear, and He will allow you to spread your wings to knock that bully into senseless slumber until the following year. If you are challenged to a duel, talk your way out of it. If they insist on having a battle with you, then you will have two choices. Choose wisely and pray for escape or victory.

Your decision would be beneficial to you if you kept your Faith within your heart on a daily basis to keep you on your toes. Fighting should be the absolute last resort in any situation, unless for self-defense. Even then you should reconsider before getting into a confrontation with them, last-last resort. Violence and hatred have no resolution other than more contempt toward or from that person or country. Religion or creed should never be an excuse for any acts of violence because of their beliefs. Religion and resources are the excuse that we currently wage war.

Religion is the water cannon disbursing a crowd protesting against tyranny. The religions separate people and nations, turning them against one another. Institutional Religion forces brother against brother to pick their secular churches of who is better and bigger in their congregation. Massive amounts of blood has been shed for their religiously fanatical prophets. Some extreme religious groups seem to think that their prophet worthy of bloodshed for their cause.

Innocence killed during war causes Baba to sadden and rage against humanity for such cruel acts toward His children. Humans need to be reprimanded for their actions, only because they sent forth their children to the world damaged mentally, physically, emotionally and spiritually. Bullying parents who reared their children as bullies for the future are losers themselves. The daggers that are released from their mouths are the same as poisoning the whole world with terrorism. However, the losers are in disguise as sane and polite enough on the outside.

Only to show their true nature on the inside behind closed doors. They raise their hands to the weak and helpless children to instill fear. The bullies of this world begin their lives at home. The children always will be saved by our Father's Love, forevermore. Every human on this planet have their own habits leading them to a path. The choices they make during their lives are recorded second by second. If, for example, people are disgusting with the way their live in their home, there is a place for you. If you are a bully, there is a place for you.

There is a place for everyone who deliberately makes the lives of others more difficult to cope with. The majority of the humans live their life as though no one is watching them, out of sight, out of mind. When in His reality, we all will face Truth of actions here on Earth. Remember to be humble toward others, to help the elderly. You will all come of age, and the next generation will treat you the way you treated others in your life. Dish out a good plate for others to eat; you will eat well in return.

Invite them into your heart to have a seat waiting to sit with Him. Remember, we only have a few years on this old planet. Why would you waste your time being aggressive toward others? Our energy can be directed toward the better of mankind. Advancements in growing organic foods and architectural engineering would excel our society into an era of kindness. Our stages of grow depend of the willingness of humanity to take that path.

CHAPTER 8

Failed Death

The greed for power and money makes no sense to us all. Envy resides within the hearts of the lost who think wealth will suffice their appetite. The cure to end all war is Love and peace toward your brothers and sisters of this world. This world; that humans do not own; but live to experience emotions and leave behind memories. However, never deny the son of our Father, or he will deny you entrance into His kingdom when your time arrives.

Whatever you do, avoid having a physical confrontation with your family, friends or strangers. That aggression is frowned upon anywhere on this planet. You may think you are behind closed doors unnoticed – until you realize the end drawing near for your reward of power over the defenseless. Try your very best effort avoiding touching anyone else inappropriately. Baba has plenty of time and power; bullies have very little.

The most disgusting act toward your seeds or keys to your salvation is an act of condemning your soul. Would you rip up your ticket to the gates of heaven; the one who gave you the gift of life to keep safe from destruction? When He comes to collect and reward you, will your children be available to vouch for you to enter? We entered my mother's home to make our own memories. As time passed; I realized I was about witness the suffering that my mother and dad had talked about.

I feel sorrowful when the people I Love and respect give me advice and I do not follow through; forgive me I am stubborn at times. I kept having flashbacks my dad's warning of my marital decision's outcome of suffering. I rushed love into my life to spend the remainder deprived of receiving the same love in return, making me work overtime to win theirs. Earning their Love and having true Love is as different as night and day. To push your human emotional limits to the brink of hopelessness during a marriage is never healthy for either partner.

Each will begin to avoid caring about what the other will say, request or do for that matter. You might as well seek help, come to a mutual compromise, or end it for health of each individual's sanity. Being defensive or offensive by either person makes no room for Love. I was at a breaking point when my wife left with my children to her mothers' home. My emotions were drained and I was at my breaking point to self-destruction. I was about to go through with it, I had the pills in my hand ready to swallow.

My family had left me, I was alone, broken and lost. There was no reason to go on living on this stupid Earth. I was unsure how to go about ending my existence and going home, escaping this prison planet. So, I searched online for ideas, I was analytical, I was logical, yet, I was empty from within. I wanted my sentence to be swift and clean. I had no weapons within my home, other than knives, too messy. I did not have any rope; nylon string is too weak. Water was cleaner, but I did not have a pool. The only other quick and clean solution?

I searched online for what was the necessary amount to kill a person with 500mg Motrin aspirin. I checked my fridge and found a container of pills that shook full. This will do it for me, nice and clean, deep sleep, no wakey-wakey. I prayed to Baba and prayed to Yahshua and pleaded for forgiveness on what I was about to do. I cried and cried until I had emptied my tears and my river flowed no more. I was ready, and my rest area was prepped; my time was up. I checked twice and trice the quality and quantity of the pills that would be my checkmate.

I prayed once more, just in case I had left out any prayers and pleas for any of my wrong doing and trespasses against my brothers and sisters. The fate of humans or Saints are not really controlled by their own hands but the hand of our Father. Baba moves universal forces on his board to intercept your move. He will show you have much he loves you even during hopeless times of your life He has in his hands. My hands had all the pills rested in my palm. I wanted to make sure I had enough to do the deed.

I was unsure if I was to end that day or I just miscounted more than once. I thought there was enough, however, I was shy five pills to make it final, otherwise I would have ended up in the hospital getting my stomach pumped and labeled unstable. No one other than my wife knew about my suicide attempt; why worry the rest of my other family members? My suicide attempt failed; I prayed and prayed and prayed and cried and cried until I fell asleep in bed. Then I was taken – taken to thy Father and Brother and every Saint sitting at my Father's table.

The blonde-haired angel had taken me to His debate amongst the good and bad, Satan sat across from us next to Father. They were conversing of what was soon to become of me and all of humanity. The female angel who was floating in the air to the left of me; was informing me of my Quest for thy true Love. I was excited to hear the description of her glorious green eyes and interrupted the counsel. The big man sitting to the right of me nudged me with his elbow and hushed me.

So, I nudged him back and hushed him. Our Father heard us arguing and interrupted us all. I leaned forward to see Yahshua also leaning forward with His index finger to His lips to hush me. I apologized with my heart for my rude interruption and noticed my Father in anger flicking His right index finger at Satan and pointing His left finger at me. Satan was bowing his head, as our Father's facial expressions toward the fallen one was terrible. I thought my Father was angry at me; but He pointed at me with a gesture as "He will do it."

Perhaps Satan asked Father who will challenge him? I will dumbass, I will. Oh believe me, if my Father wants me to spear that dragon and toss him into his eternal pit, I shall. There are plenty of other individuals who have had dreams of premonitions sent to them by our Father, and they can comprehend the visions blessed to them. Yet, my encounter with the counsel was no vision, as His Truth was to be witnessed the following day. I woke up and took a cold shower since I had no hot water in the home and soon to be no electricity.

I did not realize what had happened to my body until I met up with my separated wife. She was shocked to see my stature had transformed into His Truth. "Gandy, is that you?" asked April. "Ah, yes, what do you mean?" I replied. "You are tall; you don't see yourself in the mirror?" asked April. "Yeah I know; I've always been tall." "Are you serious Gandy? What the fuck is going on?" demanded April. "I have no idea what you are talking about." I said. After a few moments, my wife and I decided to visit my brother's home to see if we could resolve our marital issues.

When we entered, my brother had a very surprised look on his face. My previous five-foot-five short was now six-foot-tall hugging my brother. "Hi Gandy –Gandy, is that you? asked Sandy. "Hi Sandy, yes it's me, you don't recognize me? I asked. "Yeah, but, but you're tall." said my brother. "I've always been tall, what are you two talking about, are you guys OK?" I asked. In my mind; my tall stature was normal; I was awake. When Baba awakens you, stand with your truthful existence.

That day was memorable to me, my brother and April, however, others may suppress their memories in denial; what can I say; they have free will. My wife and I left for the night and went our separate ways. I went back to my mother's home and she went back to hers. The suffering was normal for me; however, I would rip my heart out of my chest if my children had to suffer at home. My wife no longer loved me, leaving me to bleed. I accepted Yahshua the Messiah as the answer to all my problems and lived for our Father on a daily basis.

Seeking help from them was never wrong. I tried to keep the family together but knew the banks would salvage my mother's home because everything was past saving. I decided to destroy the second harvest of marijuana growing in the basement and figured perhaps marijuana was the reason my wife hated me so much. I had smoked pot since I was seventeen years old; it eased my depression and pain caused by physical deformity. When you are in pain, depressed, have anxiety or the jitters, it does help.

But there is a better drug, much safer, much healthier. Guess what that could be? Prayer. Prayer is your cure. You make think prayer has no power. Oh but you are wrong there my friend. The connection you have with prayer takes on a form of answers to your questions. Be patient, you may have to pay the ultimate price of sacrifice and suffering to get the best reward you will ever receive from anyone in your life. I made to call to my wife, asking if they had room for one more at her parent's home.

I had to swallow my pride for my children's sake because they needed daddy to protect them from the bad people in this world. My in-laws liked the idea that I wanted to save my marriage from ending. My stay lasted two years, three jobs later and not enough savings to purchase a home. I felt like I was trapped in my own nightmare and was unable to wake up. The money was never enough from the beginning of the marriage, as soon as the money came in, it was gone before I could empty my pant pockets.

Finally, I received Word from my wife's cousin that a computer repair shop needed a technician. Since I was an IT Professional, I began GK Services, LLC an IT and Security Consulting company. I began working at a local computer company called IT Network Solution and started learning the trade of CCTV security systems. Working for myself was my goal; I have entrepreneurship running through my blood. I trained there for about year learning all about the new technology I was eager to learn.

Then IT Network Solution was later sold to a previous employee there later named ITNS Computers. I relocated GK Services, LLC office into a local radio station office located just behind ITNS Computers. Voice of Future Radio has a nice sound to it. It had a variety of programs from political, medical, musical and poetic discussions. Everything was going smooth, and I was beginning my clientele list to build a successful company to make everyone proud of me. Patience is a required virtue to any business while the drive and determination is the key to success starting a business.

Statistically speaking, 8 out of 10 business fail because people just give up when the going gets rough. I had never quit, but my wife and in-laws needed results fast, the pressure was piling up. Living conditions for eight people in a four-bedroom household was crowded. My father-in-law, brother-in-law, and sister-in-law had their own room. I kept insisting that my mother-in-law to sleep in her own bed while I lay mattresses on the floor. However, grandma refused the idea of beds sprawled along her floor where her grandchildren rested.

It was just carpet, not filthy dirt; her house was spotless. I believe she wanted what was comfortable for her grandchildren, and I am grateful for her kindness. Upset that she had to suffer while we were sleeping in her room on her own bed. Couches were not made to be slept on every day. Time passes, children grow up and become much more difficult to manage without the proper guidance. The elders remain in their past and do not conform to social change to keep up with the modern day child's requirements to maintain sanity.

Many humans are willing to change with the world or surrounding environment and refuse to be left behind to comfort or conformity. Being too comfortable or conforming to tyrannous ways equals lack of Courage and Faith. When I was at my in-laws, I felt like Yahshua was reminding me that if I chose relaxation or reliance, then I may end up turning my face away from His Truth. Whenever someone gives you advice about what you should have, would have or could have done this way or that way. Ask them where their knowledge resides; in their pockets or in their hearts?

If they are successful spiritually, then take their advice with a grain of salt. If He sent them to you then prepare to jump in the ocean. I tell you this – if they are arrogant and ignorant with their advice. Then, forget about having them board your galactic starship heading to your own galaxy to rule as a King with your Queen. Like Yahshua said, Earth is but a bridge, pass over it, for Earth is just temporary, and Baba's Truth is eternal forevermore.

Our Father has your everlasting home waiting for you; hold Yahshua's hand and let Him guide you through the cosmos to his father. I had many brief visions and encounters of my future shown to me by Yahshua and His angels. I was online searching for zodiac symbols I ended up at a psychic website and began chatting via text to a woman named Melody. Oftentimes when psychics give advice, people will incorrectly interpret the advice. Like gambling with 50/50 odds, you will get the good and bad.

If you wait for your Soulmate patiently, your prayers will be answered on His own time knowing you will be ready for your beloved. After conversing online with Melody, she requested that I speak to her on the phone. She was hysterical because she had seen my past life and was ecstatic and terrified. "Oh my God, oh my God, it's you, it's you, oh my God, oh Sire." shouted Melody. "Huh, what are you talking about Melody, what do you mean it's me, why are you calling me *sire*?" I asked.

"Oh Sire, oh Sire, it's me, your servant." replied Melody. "Say what? *My servant,* are you ok Melody?" "Yes Sire, I am, I'm so happy to speak to you again." cried Melody. "It's OK Melody, can you please call me Gandy, I'm not sure why you keep calling me sire." I asked. "I'm sorry; please forgive me sire, I mean Gandy." replied Melody. I did not know of physic abilities –I followed His Word– she was genuine and honest with her speech. She knew me, knew my past, knew my future.

I wanted to test her psychic powers; I was a skeptic from the get-go with psychics. The guides in my life are Baba and Yahshua. She even predicted my company logo, my divorce, my beloved, my kingdom, my title. She mentioned I was going to divorce my wife, that friends and families were going to stab me in my back and deny His Truth, and last but never least my past royal bloodline. I was eye rolling, huffing my waste of time with her remarks. "Either you are crazy or you are trying to feed me some bullshit for me to hear and keep calling you back." I said.

"I'm so sorry Gandy, it's true, it's all true, you are St. George." replied Melody. "Say what, St. George, seriously?" I asked. "Yes, you had a kingdom and a queen. You loved riding your horse through the desert, and I was your servant." said Melody. "I was riding my horse through the desert? I love horses." I replied. "Yes, you loved riding your horse through the desert, magnificent horse you had, Sire." explained Melody. "Why would I divorce my wife? Don't say that, we just recently got married and have a two-year-old son." I said.

"Because you will in the end, but she will find you, your soulmate." instructed Melody. "Wow, St. George, Queen, Kingdom, divorce, this is all too much to take it all at once." I said. "I know, but it's all true, I have spiritual sources I speak with." explained Melody. "Wow, that's amazing." She began to cry, and I felt sad for causing her sadness. I reassured her everything would be OK. We would work things out, as we went through our life's struggles. I was skeptical when I heard I was going to divorce and one of my in-laws would stab me in the back.

Turns out mothers-in-law have a nasty habit of turning on sons-in-law, though. Money came in and left before I could even count it from my pocket, expenses piled up, and I struggled to keep up. Socializing and sharing ideas bonded us as a family to keep hopes up. However, from the beginning of us moving in I felt tension between my family and hers; two families living together will eventually cause a conflict of interest. Yet; when all you have is Love in your heart, Baba, Yahshua and the Holy Trinity will back you up with your requests because Love conquers all.

I should know after what I went through. There was only one way; plenty of prayers and patience is a virtue when divine actions are involved; there is no snapping your fingers. There is Heaven prayer order service – sometimes slower than mail-order yet worth every minute of your life that you have to wait for. Your Love will arrive with open arms and ready to give you a big hug, just like Yahshua did back in 1997 when I stood up on his command and happily agreed when he asked, "Can I get a hug?"

My marriage, emotionally and financially, crashed completely in 2013. I was forced to move out of my in-laws' home due to a final argument with my mother-in-law over false accusations. My advice to this situation; when you plant your seed of Truth, nurture your children with Love and not hate and they will grow with Love forevermore. I arrived at my in-laws late one afternoon and walked into a verbal brawl with my toddler son and his grandmother. Before I could even discipline my son for his actions of disrespecting his elder not following parental guidance, I was backstabbed.

"Take your children and your wife and get out of my house!" yelled Grandma. "Wait, what, what happened? Where am I supposed to take my children and wife, we didn't save enough money to move." I replied. "Oh well, who cares?" yelled Grandma. "Can you tell me what's going on?" I shouted. "Your son is driving me crazy, he doesn't listen to me, he keeps talking back and running all over the place." replied Grandma. "He is just a little boy, they have lots of energy.

Should I smack the shit out of him for you?" I asked. "No, I didn't ask you to smack him. He just doesn't listen to me when I tell him to do what I want him to do." said Grandma. "Where is his mother?" I asked. "She is shopping, and she is not answering her phone." relied Grandma. She continued with her onslaught toward my son and I. Grandma leans down to Xander and gives him the wrong bread to eat. "Xander, your father is a liar, and he is a bad daddy for you!" shouted Grandma. "Hey, what the fuck are you telling him, what's wrong with you?"

Don't tell him that!" I shouted. "Don't tell me 'hey!' Don't say 'fuck' to me!" yelled Grandma. "You calling me a liar in front of my son, who do you think you are?" I asked. "Because you are – you have no money, no house, you've been here for two years!" yelled Grandma. "How much do you think a house is worth; we were at my mother's. We lost the house to the bank because of my sister and her husband." I replied. "Well that's not my problem!" shouted Grandma.

"I know it's not your problem, but don't call me a liar to my son and tell him I am a bad father for him!" I yelled. "Don't raise you voice to me!" yelled Grandma back. "I'll raise my voice to anyone who calls me a liar. Don't flick your finger at me!" I shouted. "Shut up! I'll flick my finger at you anytime I want!" shouted Grandma. "Then I'll flick my finger at you as well, anytime I want!" I yelled back. There it was, the very backstab that Melody the psychic was talking about.

I could not to believe what I was hearing from a supposed churchgoer. She could not take it for more than two years with her own daughter, two energetic children, and me. Help was given even if my pockets were empty. "Xander, your father is a liar and is no good for you, he is garbage!" shouted Grandma. "Did you just tell my son I was a bad father and a liar? I may smell like garbage sometimes, but I'm not liar or bad father to my children." I said. "Yes you are!" yelled Grandma. The only people that ever flicked their finger in my face were my mother and dad, who I love dearly. The others are Baba, Yahshua, Sabra and my children, until they become adults.

In this case, she brought verbal wrath to her front door. Her first mistake was calling me a liar, especially when my 5-year-old's mind was trying to comprehend the argument between daddy and grandma. Words were exchanged, and I had to back off before the situation got out of hand. The police were involved, as well as emergency paramedics. There was a peace officer standing next to me by the front door. Blood pressures were rising, and the paramedics had to intervene to aid my mother-in-law, who was already under household stress.

However, it was too late, the paramedics needed to get her into the ambulance. The brother-in-law heard all the commotion while he was asleep from the schizophrenia pills and awoke in terror from his slumber. "Mom, mom, mom, are you OK?" asked Bruce. "She's OK, we were arguing, and she had an anxiety attack." I replied. "What the fuck did you do to my mom, who the fuck do you think you are, you want me to fuck you up!" yelled Bruce. "First of all, calm down; second of all you act like no one can talk back to your mom.

Who does she think she is telling my son I'm a bad father and liar?" I asked. "She can say whatever she wants, this is her house!" yelled Bruce. "No she can't, not to me or my family!" I yelled. "Shut your fucking mouth, or I'll shut it for you!" shouted Bruce. "Say what, did you just threaten to kick my ass?" I asked. "Yeah, motherfucker come on!" yelled Bruce. There was a thirst for my blood in his raging words. This time His Truth needed to get involved again, tsk-tsk. I was hesitant to have him as supper; he was already spoiled.

I honestly did not know how she let her family walk all over her. Grandma took on the whole household responsibilities many times, leaving her bitter to yell at over energetic children. After heated arguments about how to raise her children and to stop picking on mine, she headed out to the ambulance. Meanwhile, the peace officer was still next to me. "Come on you fucking piece of shit!" demanded Bruce. I could not hold my composure any longer. He was testing to see His Truth be told.

I prepared to pounce on Bruce wannabe Banner. "Arrrgh! Noooooo! Stop!" screamed Bruce. My brother-in-law saw His Truth ready to eat him. To prevent me from putting my brother-in-law in a comatose state, the officer grabbed me before I wrathfully leaped at Bruce. I refrained from touching anyone; however, the officer of the law placed his hand on me. He had to, to stop me from attacking my braveheart brother-in-law who had a long tongue and big mouth, the one who hesitated to save my son at the school park.

When I turned to look the officer who touched me, he had his palms together in prayer. Just then I knew whose side he was on, so I stopped. "I'm sorry; forgive me; he was provoking me into a confrontation." I said to the Peacemaker. "Yes I know; do you have somewhere you can stay for a while until the heat cools off?" instructed the Peacemaker. "Yes I do, I am just getting my things in order with my family." I said. "Get the hell out of here before I kick your ass!" yelled Bruce. "Mutha-fucker!" I yelled. That was the third mistake from my brother-in-law; why do they insist on getting a beat down?

If you are unable to justify your battle, then shut up and sit down before you break. They say my brother-in-law used to lift weights, intimidated others in the streets, and bullied guys in his high school. You can be the strongest and meanest person, machine or devil in this world or out of this world, but provoking me will feed you the consequences of my Father's Wrath. I looked at the officer and turned to look at my brother-in-law standing in living room like supper ready to be served.

I had to remind Bruce again, just in case he did not see the Dragon Slayer the first time. "Noooooo!" screamed Bruce. "Stop!" shouted the Peacemaker. "Forgive me officer, I don't wanna fight him, but he is provoking me to fight again." I explained. "I know; it's OK, are you calm now?" asked the Peacemaker. "Yes, I am calm." I answered. Good, get your affairs in order and head out as soon as you can." instructed the Peacemaker. My brother-in-law witnessed who my Father created; I am sure he will remember that day.

The police officer saved Bruce once more. I took a few deep breaths of logic to exhale my actions. When others who are blind to see Truth, they freak out, and no Word is mentioned of the incident due to disbelief, ignorance or fear. The Truth will set you free if you let Him in. Fear always will hold you back and make you think you are a big shot who enjoys bullying people. Listening to nonsense in their heads providing false truths. You have to be the better person and admit to your mistakes if you have Yahshua in your heart.

No matter what happened in the past, everyone deserves a second chance and perhaps a hug or two. We set aside our differences, recovered, forgave each other, and life went on as usual. I remembered the lessons in life about the required Faith daily; to help me cope with everyday struggles. Why do we forget so quickly from our mistakes and continue to fail, struggle and attack one another? Make peace and fix the problem from within yourself with logic; later on, go get some ice-cream.

Mankind feared Yahshua in the past and avoided accepting His Love and Truth to help them forevermore. Humanity needs to learn from His Truthful past. But we would rather arrogantly deny the Truth and spread false rumors. Society eats the media as truth rather than His bread of Truth. Being loved and speaking His words within your heart brings you closer to him. Never deny Yahshua, even if it means leaving your whole family for him. He who loves other people more than Yahshua is not fit to accept His Love.

Baba requires all of your Love, even more than the Love for your children. For He knows what is right for you in the end and gives you His all. You must do the same for Him without hesitation or question. If you accept Yahshua, He will never disappoint you, He will never deny you, He will never lie to you, He will be with your forevermore. Have you hugged someone in your life lately just because? If you are unable to speak, then embrace their hearts to ease their pain, as your parents. Pay it forward, and He will pay you forever.

The wealth of man should begin with the wealth within their hearts. With the Love for each other, only then can man really become worthy of His Love. As adults, they are still adolescent children bickering over worldly nonsense. They act like young children fighting over possessions and positions. Viewing differences with others creates envy and jealously separates us and isolates our Love for each other. Love should be the breaker of barriers of any difference that we have with each other in this world; to form one family under His grace.

People need to express the four letter word marching on for eternity with Him –Love. See past the color and culture and focus on the Love from his heart for humanity. The history of this planet is on a continuous loop of denial after Yahshua returned to his Father's kingdom – society is a snake eating its own tail, so to speak. Currently; humans allow the evil one to enter their home through freewill and their lust for money. Satan is very intelligent and so self-centered to his own cause.

That dragon knows how to distract mankind away from its true connection to everlasting life. All the chaotic events that led world history was planned by the fallen one and humans. Avoid becoming a part of their path. Instead follow His grace as his eternal blessed flock. Lucifer controls a majority of the individuals who are in power over this planet, who have the most pocket change, phfff. The planet is ruled by cold hearted, demon possessed, evil habited, deranged people puppets who are controlled by psychopaths.

Individuals whom have turned to the dark-side that they would devour their own off-spring and bloodline to maintain their authority. For psychopaths with that type of animosity towards their own kin; what would the population be considered; all you can eat bouquet? The disease within a disease from eating your own species. Judgment will eventually declare Truth righteous forevermore. The clean slate may be His plan if this planet light the fuse of arrogance between each other.

CHAPTER 9

Conquering Your Fears

"Fearless" is metaphorically my middle name and still am for eternity. I remember when my brother, a couple of his friends, and I wanted to ride trails with our mountain bikes. However, this was no ordinary trail, and it sure felt like going down a mountain. When we arrived to the trail entrance, we were unaware of the risks. This scary trail zigzagged down a huge hill hungry for its next victim. The trail was a test of Courage; it looked like a death trap to me.

We stood atop the hill of this hungry monster of a bike trail. I had the worst mountain bike for Baba's test of my bravery. Yahshua was in my heart to help me maneuver through those tragic turns, though. My outdated mountain bike had the weakest brakes ever. The bike was also heavy as an elephant; yet it was awesome because it was mine. You have to make the best of what you have and walk with a limp before you can fly.

We took us forever to see who had the courageous heart out of the group. I was thinking of how to stop or fall off my bike if something was to happen. My brother stood next to me on his expensive mountain bike and two of his friends next to him. This insane trail had such an angle downward it looked 90 degrees straight down. "Are you going down?" I asked. "No!" yelled Sandy "How 'bout you guys?" I asked. "No, you're crazy bro!" shouted Stang. "Bro, are you outta your mind?" asked D-Jay.

"We came all the way here, and now you guys want to head back because you're too scared to go down this trail? Are you serious?" I disappointedly asked. I looked down at the trail and closed my eyes for a moment to pray. Just then, The Champion arrived, stood next to us, looked down the edge, and spoke His Truth. "You guys going down?" said the Champion. We all looked at each other with doubtfully surprised expressions. The stranger looked at me like just before he leaped into the courage challenging trail and said. "You believe in Him, right?"

"Yes!" I shouted. As my best-best friend from renown leaped into the waves of dirt, his response shook me to the core. "Then come on Gandy!" yelled Michael the Archangel. "Michael, wait for meeeeeeeee!" I screamed. I was thinking of who he was speaking of for a second then realized I knew who he meant. The Heroic Archangel who kicked that traitor out of our Father's kingdom was speaking of my Big Brother. "Michael, I'm coming...wait for me!" I yelled as loud as I could. Just as I was ready to leap, my brother stopped me and offered his bike for that faithful occasion.

"Wait, look how he's riding his bike through the trail first!" shouted my brother holding be back before I leaped as well. I focused on his blur and picked up on the hurried lesson of the maneuvers Michael was making and was ready. "Dude, your brother's crazy!" yelled Stang. "Bro, be careful!" shouted D-Jay. I held my breath and jumped into the ocean of dirt. The trail entrance had a slant downward that was almost 90 degrees. The dizzying zigzag trails had turns forcing you horizontally to the ground.

I felt as though I had done this before and had no fear of the turns and deep pits of disaster. I reached half-way through only to be stopped. "Gandy, wait!" yelled Sandy. I heard my brother yelling my name which made slam on my joke brakes in-between the trails. "What?" I shouted back. "Wait for us!" yelled Sandy. "Hurry up and get down, stop being such a chicken shit and jump!" I yelled back. I was trying to lift their courageous spirit to battle this beast of fear. I had added another plate on my fearless armor. I could not waste any more time, I had to continue my journey to reach my battle brother.

To my surprise I heard my brother Sandy courageously yell and take his leap of Faith. Stang and D-Jay followed suit with their battle shouts. I vigorously reached the bottom of the trail and was looking from my heavenly blood brother, however he was gone. "What the, where'd he go? Michael...Michael, where are you? I shouted. *How could he disappear, that's impossible,* I thought. The path at the bottom of the trail was long and straight both ways.

I had seen Michael turn left just I reached his last position. There was wooded forest on either side of the path with trees galore that prevented you from biking through it. The adrenalin rush took no more than sixty seconds to reach the bottom of the path. I looked up and was barely able to see my brother and friends in the tree-cluttered, monstrous hill. I was astonished as to where the blonde-haired blessed archangel had disappeared so quickly. Nonetheless, I am grateful for the inspiration you gave me, I miss you brother. I enjoyed many adventures, even the ones that try to instill fear within me allowing me to conquer with my Father's Word.

Tragedy

I live to conquer fear and tyranny to be victorious in Love's name. The courage was instilled within me from the beginning. Round two, time to sum up my worth. In my case, however, I wanted to go faster, add a jump or two for the second leap of Faith. I had to give up my brother's awesome light weight bike n exchange for my tank on two wheels.

He thought I was crazier than him; he was right, but I prefer braver so, he gave me his helmet. He wanted to go first and I was very proud of him for showing Courage in front of his friends. "Show them wa cha got bro!" I yelled. I patted my brother on his back for encouragement before he leaped into His ocean. Sandy did rather well going down the man-made carved hill trail. I pointed at my friends; My bones were giddy with excitement to fly again. "Who's next, anyone? No one, OK I am going." I said.

Helmet on, weak leg, weak brakes, heavy bike and lots of prayer and Faith for protection; Yah Eesho, here I go again, help me." I jumped into the ocean once more. It was slower at first because I wanted to test my bike's abilities to withstand the G forces that forced you 90 degrees' parallel to the ground while turning. First turn, good enough, more power. Second turn almost lost it; third turn hang on, fourth turn... "Oh shit, No!" I yelled. My brother decided to stop right in the middle of the trail path. I had two choices, smash into him full speed to stop or veer to avoid collision.

I wanted the avoid option; crashing into my brother was not going to do either of us good. It was too late, though, as I was going too fast. The only thing that was able to stop me was a bowl-ditch just a bit wider than my bike. I tried my best to jump over the bowl; however, my tank did not jump nor fly with wings over this pit of doom. I ended up landing my bike's front tire at the edge of the bowl. The halt was so abrupt, my bike was ejected from underneath me and disappeared. After I shook off my dazed impact, I looked around for my bike.

I must have been sitting there for a few seconds. "What the fuck; where'd my bike go, how the fuck...Sandy have you seen my bike?" *WHAM! ~ CRACK!* The seat of my mountain bike snapped at the base landing right on top of my head. The helmet that my brother had given me for safety saved my skull. I bruised my ego and was more enraged due to my bike breaking so soon when Baba and Yahshua wanted me to give my all. I got up, picked up my bike and launched it over my head flinging it down the trail.

When I got to the bottom, I finally super slammed the hunk of steel junk on the ground. "Piece of shit!" I shouted. Now I had to ride a bike with no seat back. My legs were burning with pain from being unable to sit down while pedaling. My brother felt sorrow seeing me in pain and offered to ride my busted bike half way back. Everyone was surprised I was OK and only received a few scratches from my ordeal. The only thing that hurt were my aching legs.

I truly try my best to be the fearless Saint that Baba allows me to be. We called it a day, and I added more feathers to my wings. When Michael the Archangel arrives out of the blue to inspire you with Faith and Courage, follow him. When you hesitate, you may have to wait awhile to get a second chance for sacrifice and bravery to be part of his crew. I am part of Yahshua's Crew, and I am Baba's creation for eternity. Getting in is just half the battle of suffering; keeping His given everlasting title wins you the war.

Build up your Courage, and He will have a title for you if you choose to live up to the challenge at any given moment. Remember to have no fear and no doubt in His power to protect and show you the way to your destiny. Each and every day that you pray, your path with Yahshua will be filled with Love. Without the heart to Love, there is no beloved soul to find and hug. Praying with your heart gets you closer to Yahshua easier than you may think. Pray daily, fast regularly, stay away from the lusts of the world infinitely.

Clear your body and mind of any poison that will interfere with His signal. We are programmed uniquely in such a way that we can actually have a daily conversation with Baba. That may sound impossible, however, He is possible. Somehow Baba lost connection with his children since technology took over their daily lives. Ignorantly the devil set up a mental magnetic force field around Earth to prevent prayers; it is called technological distractions. The masses around the globe have changed Baba's signal to Satan's brain zapper.

The Matrix effect in the reality of the modern human is only but a dream. Most of the people on Earth are still daydreaming about their lusts from society. That dragon knows his time is running out and he is using up all his tricks. Soon; Satan will get tossed in the trash of everlasting inferno. Commit to your Faith and Courage with His helping hand to defeat the evil. I kept Michael's story a secret until my book publication, chapter(s)dedicated to you my battle brother.

Until we meet again someday to fight the good fight alongside Yahshua and our brothers. Michael the Archangel reminds us all the spirit residing within each of us sustains great power. His connection that fuels that power is brought forth with your Faith. The angel, who follows Yahshua the Messiah and serves our All Mighty Father. Michael reminded me of my Courage and Faith to surf with him down that tidal wave with His Word. Anyone making a fool of your Faith or your belief in Yahshua and Baba is lost. If you refuse to try, then you will never know the Truth of His Word.

CHAPTER 10

Baba's Archangels

If you fail when you are trying, never give up carrying on with your cross. When you are unable to move any further, seek help and He will send His Archangels to you righteously. Fear will be absent from your mind, body and spirit when Yahshua is in your heart and Baba on your mind. You can use Courage in any situation if your Faith is larger than your muscles defeating your biggest opponent.

Phil and Shawn –the two who introduced me to puff-puff-pass –and Shawn's brother Sheen and I decided to rollerblade on concrete bike trails stretching for miles. I was unable to keep up with them on skates at the time due to my right leg's muscle atrophy. So I brought my mountain bike to keep up. Though I paced my friends rather easily, the return back proved challenging. I wanted to try the inline skating adventure with my friends. So, Sheen and I swapped blades for bike. Skates on, check, straps tight, check, prayer initiated, triple check.

"You ready?" asked Sheen "Yes, I am ready." I answered. I struggled for a half mile rollerblading with my bum leg that started failing. I had to pause before I kissed the pavement. Sheen waited for me because he had seen me struggle while the others were racing back with their roller blades to test their stamina abilities. "You OK, can you make it?" asked Sheen. "Bro, my left leg is burning and my right is useless" I said. "Do you want a tug back?" Sheen asked. "Tug back, what do you mean?" I asked.

"Hold on to the seat pole and I'll pull you back, just keep balance and don't push with your legs." Sheen instructed. "OK...you sure, I don't want to tire you out." "You won't; just hang on. We gotta get going before they get too far." "OK, let's go." I said. "Hang on bro." replied Sheen. We started out with a slow pace until I became bored and requested more speed. " Are you sure, it is a bumping sidewalk, I don't want you wipe out, bro." said Sheen. I looked ahead and agreed then realized the distance we were putting between Shawn, Phil and us.

I decided to pray again for whatever happens to me if I failed physically again. "I will be OK, bro, no worries; if you get too tired, slow down or I'll just let go." I said. My friend pedaled while I held on to the seat post. It was gradual, and I started to feel every bump on the sidewalk leaning mostly on my left leg.   One leg can support your body for only so long until muscle failure occurs. I tried with my atrophied leg, but it was worthless. Just as I attempted to put more than 30 percent of my weight on my right leg, I hit a bump on the pavement and could not even lift up my legs or jump over it.

When my legs finally gave up, I was falling face first toward the rear tires. I knew I would get scarred if I did not let go. I had to let go and bite the bullet leaning to my left attempting to brace myself with my left arm. *Thud!   Thud!   Thud! Pop!* "Oh fuck, Uffh, Oww, ArrrghFffaaaaaarrrr!" "Oh fuck Gandy, you OK?" asked Sheen "Fuck, I can't move my arm!" I yelled. "Wait, let me see bro, oh fuck!" shouted Sheen. "What's wrong, what's wrong with my arm, what do you see?" I asked.

"Oh fuck bro, your arm is dislocated from your socket!" "Oh fuck, help me Sheen, please. Can you pop my arm back in? Hurry, it fucking hurts!" "Fuck bro, are you sure, how the fuck am I going to that?" "I don't know, do something bro!" "Gandy, Gandy stay awake, bro, stay awake, don't fucking pass out on me!" shouted Sheen. "Shit, what happened?" I asked. "You're passing out, stay awake!" yelled Sheen. "Sheen, just do it, bro, please, I can't take it anymore." I said. I was in and out consciousness while my friend was trying to keep me awake.

I ended up chipping the tip of my collarbone and dislocating my left arm after tumbling to a halt. Sheen was coming up with ideas on how to operate without anesthesia in the middle of nowhere. I prepared for my memorable torture and gave the go-ahead to Sheen. I prayed for mercy and forgiveness because this was going to hurt more than any injury I had stumbled into. "You ready Gandy?" asked Sheen. "Have you done this before? " I asked.

"Yes, my friend from school did the same thing to me, this should pop in the same way." replied Sheen. "Oh fuck...don't fuck up...shit. 'huff-huff-huff...oh fuck. OK I'm ready...oh fuck!" I yelled. "Here goes, push on my leg with your right arm so I don't pull you toward me, just your left arm." said Sheen. "Ok...I'm ready." I replied. "Ok let me see...I'll put my leg over here for support; Ok; I've got your arm, here goes." said Sheen. "Faarrraaaaarrraaak!" I yelled as loud as Baba can hear me as my friend pulled my arm back into my socket.

That was just the socket; I also had a chipped collarbone to deal with. I cannot compare the pain level to a woman giving birth, but I would say pretty close. "You feel better now, its looks like your arm is back into its socket." asked Sheen. "Yes, thanks bro, I couldn't feel or move my arm, freaked me the fuck out." My doctor buddy helped me take off my rollerblades so that I could stand up. My shoulder was throbbing with pain, and I was shocked with pain every time I moved my arm.

"Can you blade back?" asked Sheen. "I'll try...Arrrgh...can't...every time I move my arm; it hurts!" I yelled. "Wait here, I'm going to head back, meet up with Phil and Shawn and come back to pick you up with the car." instructed Sheen. "OK I'm going to sit by the road so you can see me when you're driving up." I replied. "OK, I'll be back as fast as I can." said Sheen. "OK, hurry, I need a joint, bro!" I shouted. My friend raced back to meet up with his brother and friend. I sat in agony near the side of the road waiting for my ride when four guys drive up in a different car.

"Gandy, get in!" yelled the rear passenger. I looked up at him to see if I knew him or if they were my friends who had stopped to pick me up. "Who are you, how do you know my name?" I asked. "It's OK...We're here to help you; get in." said the rear passenger. "Bro listen...Stop asking me to get in the car with you; I don't even fucking know you. I'm waiting for my friends to pick me up...so get lost!" I yelled.

"Gandy, don't worry we're not going to hurt you. We will help you...fuck those guys!" yelled the rear passenger. "Michael...No...Father!" yelled the man next to him. Michael raised his head to the sky then lowered his head in shame and spit on the ground. "Forgive me Father, I meant forget those guys. Forget those guys, Gandy; just get in so we can help you." instructed Michael. "Who the fuck are you to say fuck my friends, fuck you! I shouted. I shouted at Michael as though he was my enemy. I was afraid of my own brothers from my Father. I was seriously lost on this Earth.

I am at your mercy brother for disrespecting you and the crew. Just then Gabriel sitting in the passenger seat turned to me with black eyes and wings that scared me backwards falling on my ass. "Arrrgh! Noooooo! Holy shit...What the fuck are you? Oh God...oh God...please don't kill me!" I screamed. His powerfully glorious wings were filling up the front cabin ready to burst the car open. The driver turned to Gabriel surprised to what he had done. "Noooooo! Please God help me...don't let them kill me!" I prayed. "Hey! What are you doing!" yelled Michael's friend.

Uriel; in the driver's seat; hits Gabriel in his arm to get his attention, while Raphael and Michael take turns yelling at Gabriel. Raphael pokes Gabriel shoulder to snap him out of it. "Gab, why'd you scare him? Change back now!" yelled Raphael. "Gab, change back now; he doesn't recognize us." instructed Michael. Gabriel changes back to his human form, turns his head to me, and smiles with his wide grin. I Love you brother; Love you all forevermore. I thought Baba had made me fearless; yet I was going to shit bricks right at that moment.

I was tough with no chance against a monster with black eyes and wings. I was floored with fear, confusion and relieved I was not eaten. "Two minutes!" shouted Uriel. "It's OK Gandy...he's sorry; he didn't mean to scare you. We will see you later." said Michael. "OK, I'm sorry for cussing at you." I replied. "It's OK, we'll see each other again, don't forget us." said Michael. "One minute, their coming!" yelled Uriel. "Who's coming?"I asked. "They're almost here." said Raphael.

"Gandy, we have to leave; your friends are on their way, but we'll see you again." said Michael. "Thirty seconds, we have to go, now!" demanded Uriel. "Goodbye Gandy." said Michael the Archangel. "Goodbye." I sadly replied. As they drove off, I sat there in shock from arm socket pain, collarbone pain, tailbone pain, and black eyes with glorious wings. I had to make a decision of proclaiming His truth or remain silent. My friends finally arrived as I was in tears of fear, joy and pain. "Gandy, let's go get in!" shouted Phil. "We have to take you to the hospital bro." said Sheen.

"No, no hospitals, no doctors, I'll be OK!" I shouted. "How are you OK with a broken collarbone?" asked Sheen. "It's not broken, it's just chipped!" I shouted. "Chipped? Let me see, does this hurt?" asked Sheen. "Arrrgh, you Muthafucker, what the fuck is wrong with you, shit!" I screamed. "What the fuck Shawn, why are you touching his arm? I told you what happened; you have to prove your point!" shouted Sheen. "I didn't touch his arm, I touched his collarbone." replied Shawn.

"Same shit, stop fucking with him!" yelled Sheen. "You're fucking crazy bro!" shouted Phil. "Didn't you notice I couldn't move my arm when I got in the car, didn't Sheen tell you I got hurt?" I asked. "Well at least now I know." answered Sheen. "Bro, you're a dick, don't fucking touch me again." I said. Shawn decided he wanted to seek Truth from my own agony pressing down on my collar. I let out a roar and growled at my friend for inflicting me more pain to satisfy his curiosity. I never spoke of the incident of Baba's Archangels to my friends; they will have to read my book.

As for Michael, Gabriel, Raphael and Uriel, we will see each other again; I Love you brothers. Forgive me for cursing at you Michael; I was blind at first, but now I saw His Truthful Word within you all. You may think I am crazy, however, do you think you are the only ones on this planet, a planet that does not belong to you? Why have humans become selfish sharing Baba's Love to the rest of the world?

Oh Holy, Holy is His name that none can understand His creations and Love unless accepting His Truth without fear. I was fearless, yet they were Baba's creatures, how fearless can man be toward His Archangels. They tried to help; they knew me from the beginning and I avoided their help because I was blind and lost. His angels are always with us even at birth into this world. Give your trust, Faith and Love to Baba and his son Yahshua. They will send angels to help and guide you through your life of tribulations.

Blessed are the ones who accept Yahshua and YHWH and walk through the valley of the shadows of death unharmed. Help is all around us via Heaven or Earth; you just have to believe in our Father and Yahshua when you ask for help. Some will welcome the help graciously from others in time of need. Others still have the mindset of savages and would rather bite off the hand that feeds them, the dumbasses.

CHAPTER 11

Going Under

When someone arrives to help, thank them and accept their help. However, measure your Faith with theirs; if they have more, jump in. Help one another with your touch and words. Continue with His Quest with Truth, Justice, Courage, Faith and Love. He may send an Archangel to guide you with confidence, as He always did from the beginning to the end. There was a second occasion when my buddy Dr. Sheen helped me when I was in need.

I had taken my two children with me to go to Port Huron beach with Sheen and Shawn's family. We were enjoying the beach and wanted to step away for a quick toke break while the wives were occupied with the children. We puff-puff-passed until it was time to head back to the beach and soak up some sun. I was a heavy cigarette and marijuana smoker trying to stay fit, almost useless in that condition. So, Sheen asked Shawn if he would like to have a race swimming.

Shawn declined, and I accepted his challenge. Our opposition –fast current flowing into shore; our finish line –pass the caution buoys for swimmers. My buddy, who was in better shape than I, he did not smoke cigarettes. We decided to race to a sand mound located just passed edge the border buoy. If you want your heart to stop pumping while you enjoy smoking toxins and attempt a triathlon swim, then make sure you have made out your will. "All right so you know where we're swimming, right?" asked Sheen. "Yep, I see the buoys with the rope." I replied.

"Ready, set, go!" shouted Sheen. We were on our way to test our Faith, frantically swimming to the edge of the borderline to the small island. I was keeping up at first, but my Achilles did not function correctly to point my toes on my left foot and slowed me down every time I kicked to swim forward. I was unable to straighten my foot to push my body through the water. I felt like a vehicle running out of gas and stalling. Eventually I had to stop swimming before my heart popped. Sheen's feet were working as they should for people born without defects.

He reached the sand mound first and waited for me. I was just a few more strokes behind him but the current rushing was relentless. I reached a couple feet near the edge of the mound and my heart was pounding out of my chest ready to seize my organic pistons. "Gurgle – Gurgle – Gurgle – Helarrrullp, huff-huff, Sheen help me, I can't make it, I'm tired." I said swallowing my words. "Come on Gandy. you can do it, the mound's right here. Look I'm standing on it; just a little more; you can do it!" shouted Sheen.

"Buuurlp, ~ Gasp ~ Gasp ~Arrhhhullllp!" I was having my life flash before my eyes, I had to think fast. Relaxing and sinking was my only option before my heart burst out of my chest. Since the mound had an incline of sand leading to it, I decided to relax, exhale and sink to the bottom and try to walk to the mound. I was trying not to pass out while holding my breath fighting the current against me. With every step, I was being pushed back. Just then; a hand reached through the water and pulled me onto the mound just a couple feet away.

"Oh my God…Arrrgh…shit, thanks bro. I thought I was a goner; I couldn't move anywhere. The current kept pushing back just out of reach." I said. "Bro, I thought you had until I seen you go under and didn't come back up, you OK now?" asked Sheen. "Yeah man; much better thanks!" I shouted. "Bro, you need to stop smoking cigarettes." said Sheen. "No shit, smoking, toking and swimming right after is not good." I replied. "You got that right, can you make it back, the current is behind us and with no struggle." said Sheen.

"Yeah, this should be a synch not sink; hahahaha." I replied. "Ready-Set-Go!" Friends are gems, rare to find yet precious to keep. Some of them are counterfeit stones pretending to gleam, but are not worth a box of rocks. No need to fear what they will think of you or how you look. True friends see past what is on the outside and look within your heart. However, friendships are destroyed when they decide to allow the demons to grab them and never let go.

Some friends will move to another location while others no longer have time for each other due to family or work filling up most of their schedules. The ones who were there when you needed them the most. Be grateful for them, forgive the ones who are busy, Love them all. Try to be close friends while still being a loving parent with your children. Your trust in them will instill a long lasting bond. I have noticed children break away from their parent's bond because they are unable to keep up with the changing era.

Some parents would like to instill dictatorship authority over their children with emotionless glares. The wealthy and poor parents are clueless of losing their children to the lusts of the world. However; the parents who follow His Truthful Word; rich or poor; will have the means to enter. Build an everlasting Love with your children to inspire their compassion and prepare the next generation for the royal inheritance within His Kingdom. Your quest to build trust with your children gives them space of individuality to become unique humans.

CHAPTER 12

The Miracle

The Holy Father and Son can show you how much they still Love you. Love them unconditionally to fill their hearts with the Love. The Love they will have for you will soar to heaven and touch the heart of Baba. Sit down with them and have a heart to heart talk like family; you will be surprised how similar your children are when you were younger. Miracles can happen at any given moment on this planet.

My friends and I were once again back at Clutch Cargo, the skinhead brawling nightclub. That night, a stranger's life would be changed forever, though it was from His heart rather than His wrath. It was a fun evening with friends together and a lively atmosphere. Some friends enjoy helping you resolve your problems by giving the answers you seek. Other friends will stand by your side through thick and thin and pull you out of the water. Even if laying on the ground lifeless, there is still hope.

The nightclub was coming to a close, initiating the interior lights to come on to see who was who and the uh-oh moments; it was classic. We gathered by the door like cattle ready to graze of BS and beer. The atmosphere was uneventful until we finally made it outdoors where everyone gathered to exchange numbers and to plan our next destination. The famous Woodward Avenue intersection was notorious after hours. Somehow it was still busy even after two in the morning. The scenario felt like playing the classic arcade game Frogger –sprinting across the road avoiding getting squashed by lead footed maniacs.

However; in this game you may not get back up again if you get hit by a metal beast. Some made it across the road; she did not. I was at the edge of the parked vehicles next to the club ready to leap across the road. My friends were shouting to hurry when I was half way across the road. Just then; I felt someone grab my shoulder. When I turned no one was there but a few people getting ready to run across the road also. One of the individuals was a girl with a couple of her friends near the edge.

When I turned to see what I was supposed to see, a terrible hungry beast came around the corner as she stepped out into traffic. "No, Stop, Watch Out!" I shouted. She had a beautiful smile, golden long hair, full of vigor, full of life; so happy. I was horrified of what had happened right before my eyes. The driver of the beast had made the choice of accelerating toward the crowd in the wrong direction. I was shocked as to how the driver was unable to see the crowd of people exiting the club. What was this, 10 points for every human you knock down?

I was unable to save her in time, I had no powers of running as fast as the Flash as of yet. As Goldilocks turned to notice the hammer ready to nail her to the road, all I could do was watch her eat metal. "Noooooo!" I yelled. The view was in slow motion, as the tank on four wheels hit the pedestrian's legs launching her toward the windshield. She tried to hang on as vehicle came to a stop. Unfortunately, her grip was weak and she was slingshot off the hood and onto the pavement. It was a heart-wrenching sound of a human skull hitting the pavement with full force.

Scrreeeeach! "Uh-Huh!-Uh!" *Thud! Pop!* She was done for; that beast slid her off the hood and body slammed her head to the ground after coming to a complete halt. I raced as fast as my ridiculous legs could get me there for help. She was still, lying motionless on the ground just a few feet away from in front of the v The Holy Father and Son can show you how much they still Love you. Love them unconditionally to fill their hearts with the Love. The Love they will have for you will soar to heaven and touch the heart of Baba.

Sit down with them and have a heart to heart talk like family; you will be surprised how similar your children are when you were younger. She was heading for the victim on the ground to finish her off. I immediately slammed my hands down on the edge of the hood, holding the vehicle in place with the strength of His Power. I was not going to let go of this dragon. It was not going to allow sleeping beauty to be turned into a human pancake. "Stop, put it in park, turn off your car!" I yelled.

The elderly driver was unaware on what she had done; she was in a state of shock herself. I quickly looked over to the unconscious woman on the ground and released my Vulcan grip off the vehicle to approach her. I noticed two women who looked like twins with a ring of flowers on their heads sitting next to the fatal victim. I fell down to my knees next to Goldilocks and prayed to Baba and Yahshua to help me save her. Blood had pooled from behind her head; I felt no pulse. She was dead. I picked up her left hand and held it to my heart; made the sign of the cross on her forehead and placed my right hand on top of her head.

"In the name of the Father, the Son and the Holy Spirit, I beg of you to help her." I prayed. With my head hung low and my eyes closed shut tight, I felt sleeping beauty twitch her finger against my chest as she moaned in pain. She awoke shortly after with groans and tears of pain. "Hi, who are you, what happened?" Goldie asked. "It's OK, lay still, you were just in an accident; you're gonna be OK." I answered.

She tried to get up; however, I prevented her from rising and begged her to remain still until the ambulance arrived. Just then, her mate arrived screaming. "What happened!" said Goldie's Mate. As prince charming reached for her to help her up, I morphed into Wrath, and Baba commanded his Word through my mouth and onto her mate's face. "Arrrahnnnnooooo!" screamed. Goldie's Mate. "Keep your hands off her!" I shouted. "Stop...No!" yelled Goldie's Mate.

After his fearful reaction, I morphed back immediately and instructed him to seek help. "Go call the ambulance, call 911!" I demanded. He started crying and ran for help. After then, I drew a crucifix on her forehead with my thumb and kissed her forehead. "You are going to be OK.I have to go now; your boyfriend went for help and he will be back for you soon." I said. "Gandy, Gandy, come on man, we're leaving, what the fuck are you doing, let's go man!" yelled Phil. "I'm coming; I'll be right there!" I shouted. I turned to her and laid my hand on her shoulder, as her other friends gathered around her.

"I have to go now, just take it easy and wait for the ambulance to get here, don't move OK." I instructed Goldie. "Ok." she replied. As I got up to try to leave, she tightened her grasp with my hand and did not want me to leave. At that moment her mate had returned. "Get away from her, you freak!" screamed Goldie's Mate. "It's ok, I'm ok, everything's gonna be OK, honey." murmured Goldie. "Here, be gentle, hold her hand." I instructed.

I gave her hand to his, as he was overwhelmed with sorrow. He placed his head on the pavement next to her head crying. I got up to leave and meet up with my friends but was interrupted once more. Goldie whispered in her Mate's ear that made him sorrowful; before stopping me. "Wait, wait; what's your name?" asked Goldie. "My name is Gandy, I have to go now, goodbye!" I shouted hurrying to my ride home. "Goodbye." replied Goldie. I ran across the road with another secret to share to the world once more.

However, I decided to remain silent and wait for His approval to share the miracle to the faithful followers of His Word and gentiles alike. I am happy that we have a new member who is on top of the mountain of Faith giving praise to Baba, Yahshua and The Holy Trinity. Your soul also can be transformed forevermore by the power of His Love, blessing your existence to resonate your passion for life. Have no fear on Earth and let the Holy Ghost flow through you to heal and protect the innocent.

If we all channel our spiritual given power to help others, our orbital home will breathe everlasting life once more in His name. The majority of people on earth have been consumed by all the entertainment, media, sports, TV shows, fades and any other distractions to make us forget our most important consumption; prayer. Miracles are signatures of Baba, giving us belief that He still loves us. The shower of Love coming from above feeds our hearts to expand our wings and fly to Him. When your child is born, the miracle begins to grow within them preparing them for their own adventure.

Even if the path they choose gets them lost during their journey, our Love and prayers will steer our children back to His path. We are His servants of life; as the child rises to become servants; Yahshua will be with them also and always. Everyone is capable of a miracle when their Faith has risen to new heights by His Truth and your testimony. There may be many in this world who are not ready to accept the Truth as foretold from the beginning. Many are too overwhelmed by their Earthly, lustful existence.

People will not let go of their planetary possessions to see His Truth manifest right before their eyes to provide them Yahshua's bread. His everlasting mana all on Earth should eat to experience their own miracle of life. Many Saints walk amongst us; many yet to be crowned upon Yahshua's return. Steadfast your body, mind and spirit to accept your crown of Faith, of Truth, of Courage, of Justice, of Love. Be very mindful to keep your pride and ego in check and move forward with your humility and gratefulness. The journey may sometimes be very difficult from the distractions of this world's lust.

If you get sidetracked and have doubt in your heart, prayer will get you back on His path. Do not let anyone bring you down to their level of depression and hate. Just do as Kevin Hart would do –shrug and move on. Kevin's book "Life Lessons" informed people to view perspectives of self-discipline to reach their goals and avoid obstacles of negative individuals. Every person on the this planet goes through those similar struggles. Realizing the bullshit this world must make someone go through; is your first step; the next step is up to you.

CHAPTER 13

Dagger Mouth

Kindness and Love is in human nature. We as humans gradually will evolve to accept our internal and external differences and to live in peace with each other. Unfortunately, my marriage was still sinking, so I gave my children Baba's life vest, and my wife and I had to swim to safety on our own. The argument with my mother-in-law about feeding my son lies about me was too much. I was in fear of Baba and losing everything with Yahshua following a path of liars, murders and thieves.

"I am no liar, murderer or thief!" If I stole anything from them, it was their hearts. When we are young and innocent, we are truthful. We then follow the Truth our parents taught us. Generations will follow His Word. Lying will reward you with a beating by your parents, siblings, friends or whomever thinks you are trying to stab them in the back and get away with murder.

I had no place to go; my mother-in-law, father-in-law, brother in-law, sister-in-law and wife – all except my children –wanted me out of their lives. I did not want to intrude in my brother Sandy's, or my sisters Cindy's or Sandrella's life. I wanted to avoid staying at a bachelorette pad, however I had to ask. I had a couple of other calls to make to my other sister and uncle. "You are more than welcome." said Cindy. "Thank you, Cindy, but two girls and one guy in an apartment may be a bit uneasy for me." I replied.

"I'm thinking of getting my own apartment; if I do I'll let you know." said Cindy. "OK, sounds good...I appreciate your help, Cindy, thank you." I said. Later on that day my sister had called me back after listening to my voicemail I had left her. "It is just for a little while until it cools off here." I said. "OK, let me ask my husband, and I'll let you know if it's OK." Sandrella and her husband recently had moved into their new home and were just settling in. As I waited for my sister's decision, I received a call back from my uncle.

"Gandy, what's going on, I just heard your message." asked Uncle Bee. "Hi Uncle Bee, thanks for calling back. I had an argument with my mother-in-law about Xander's behavior. It got out of hand. and now she wants me out." I said. "It's OK, you can stay at my house; it's empty. Last tenants moved out few months ago, and my father and I live in an apartment." replied Uncle Bee. "Sounds great, I'll let my wife know and call you back." I said. "OK sounds great, talk to you soon." said Uncle Bee.

I preferred to stay at my uncle's home for the time being; it was vacant, colonial and double the size of my in-law's home; plenty of room. "April...I have good news; my uncle's home is empty. He is living in an apartment with my grandfather, pack our things so we can leave A.S.A.P." I said. "No, I can't." replied April. "Wait, what...what do you mean you can't? I just told you we have a place to stay with plenty of room. The kids can play as loud as they want." informing my wife. "I'm afraid we may get kicked out of his home, too; you are barely bringing in enough money.

I'm working and my mother is watching our kids; who's gonna look after them at your uncle's house?" asked April. "Are you serious right now? Your mom is kicking me out of her house. You are my family, and you are kicking me out of your life too?" I asked. Just then my mother-in-law, after recuperating from her anxiety attack, interfered once more with my family affairs. I was standing on the lawn, experiencing my loss and emptiness; seeing the sad faces on my children. They all stood next to and behind my wife providing her support of her decision.

I felt like I was being stabbed multiple times, and my children were trying to plug my wounds with their little fingers. Xander and Lexi could not defend me from being murdered. "Get out of here, we don't need you here; April and the kids will be just fine without you, I will take care of your children." said my Mother-In-Law "Stop telling her what to do; she is my wife and they are my children. I don't want you to raise my children your way!" I yelled. "Oh yes, I will, and you can't do anything about it!" yelled the Mother-In-Law.

"April...April –look at me. Do you still love me?" I asked. "Yes, but I'm afraid I don't want to keep moving from house to house. Anyway I don't like your uncle's house; it's too big for us." replied April. "We won't move...I'll get two jobs, work overtime; get a babysitter; we'll drop them off here in the morning if you want. We'll do something; at least we'll be together. Please come with me." I begged. "No, I'm afraid, I don't wanna leave." replied April. "Does everyone agree with your mother's decision!" I yelled.

Brother-in-law did not speak, he knew what I would do to him again, so he remained silent. "I'm with my mom. I love you, Gandy, but this is her house; it's not my call." answered my Sister-In-Law. "She makes the rules; you will have to leave." said my Father-In-Law. "You see, they're all on my side." said my Mother-In-Law. "I'm sure they are, good for you." I replied. "So please leave before I call the police again and have them take you away." demanded my Mother-In-Law. "Be quiet, I am not talking to you anymore, we are finished here." I said.

April packed my belongings and handed them to me. I hugged my children by the door and assured them that we will see each other again. I refrained from making eye contact with anyone else; I was no longer loved; I had to move on. "Oh daddy...daddy don't leave...I'm sorry...I didn't mean to be bad...I promise I'll be good; I promise!" shouted Xander. "Daddy...don't leave; peeess!" cried Lexi. "Oh Yah Habibi Xander...Oh Yah Habibti Lexi; never...I'll never leave you. It's not your fault, Habibi...I'll always be with you...don't worry I'll be back...don't be sad.

I'm not leaving forever...I'll come back for you...I Love you very much." I said. "I love you, too, Daddy." cried Xander. "Love you too, Daddy." cried Lexi. I kissed and hugged my children long and tight enough to feed my heart for eternity. I picked up my belongings, tucked my wings, and left for my uncle's place. The journey was short but the memories lasted forever. I lived at my uncle's alone for a while. My castle was huge and empty with no children's laughter, no pitter-patter of tiny feet...so empty. I cried many nights to fall asleep; drowning in my sorrows.

Ring ~ Ring ~ Ring

"Hi Bee, how's it going?" I asked. "Did you guys settle in?" asked Uncle Bee. "No...sad to say only I moved in; April decided to stay at her mother's. I don't want to burden you with any drama. I'm trying to deal with it right now." I answered. "No problem, it will be OK. If you want ,your grandfather and I could move back and keep you company." said Uncle Bee. "Sounds good, I would enjoy yours and grandfather's company. Besides, this is your house; you can do whatever you want." I said.

"OK great, our lease is almost up for renewal, we will move back by then. Call me if you need anything." said Uncle Bee. "Will do, thanks Uncle Bee." I replied. After a couple months of solitude, my uncle and grandfather moved back to their original home. I had difficulty understanding our spoken Assyrian language at first, but soon learned as they discussed topics back and forth with each other. I know how to speak Aramaic, Arabic, a pinch of Assyrian, and plenty of English, making my plate full of ethnic.

When we grew up with my dad and mother; they spoke to us in Arabic and some Aramaic; sometimes at home I would overhear conversations with my mother and her friends. Aramaic has a different dialect; similar to the Hebrew language but different in some words of the Assyrian language. I used to know how to speak Greek, however, I replaced it with the English language because there was no one in the United States to continue speaking Greek with. A few months went by; I continued my contact with my separated family to sustain my beating heart.

My aunt and her husband then decided to move in with us at my uncle's home. They had been saving up money to purchase another home while staying at my uncle's. My aunt's husband suggested I save up my money to get my family a new home and it will be smooth sailing from there. He was unaware of how far my wife and I had sailed; we were still lost at sea. This was my uncle's first home; he had a second home in Arizona where most of his belongings were.

The house I was living at was in the process of trying to be sold. My uncle did not want to deal with anymore rental tenants after we all left. He was either going back to Arizona or staying at an apartment again with my grandfather. Uncle Bee stated that he may return to the U.S. military to serve as a translator in Iraq. Sandrella had informed me that her place was available, if I was to move out of my uncle's. I was prepared to accept my sister's and brother-in-law's proposal and move in with their family.

There were conditions to the terms of moving in: my children were not to be left unattended to play with their children, as toddlers fighting over toys would be too much too handle with four going at it. My sister's children were a blast to play with when my children and I visited. Sometimes when children were at my in-laws during school days, I would wait at my sister's till they were out of school; they lived ten minutes away compared to twenty-five minutes. I remember one day when I was playing pretend with a Matchbox car with my nephew; he really loves automobiles, just like me.

At first, I was unable to understand what my nephew was attempting to say until my sister translated his slurred speech. "What's he trying to say, I don't understand?" I asked. "He is saying, 'It is my car.'" replied Sandrella. "Oh, it is your car, OK, then she is my car." I said. "No, my car!" yelled Nik. "No she is my car." I said. We repeated ourselves on whose car was who's for a few minutes like a ping-pong match. "Why are you saying she is my car?" asked Sandrella. "I was waiting for Nik to say, 'my car is a boy not a girl' then I would explain to him she is my beloved car I was soon to drive in every room in the house.

"She, car, beloved, don't get it"? asked Sandrella. "When I sat down with mom one day, she described my beloved Soulmate's name who had the letters car within her name, and she loved pizza or worked there. Nik, do you love pizza?" I asked. "Peeeeezah, yah, yummeeee!" yelled Nik. Great minds think alike; I ordered yummeeee veggie pizza for me and yummeeee pepperoni pizza for Nik to celebrate our bonding.

When the pizza's arrived, Nik and I watched his and my favorite cartoon – "Cars" with Mater, Doc, Sally and Lighting McQueen. In my opinion, Mater, was the daydreaming optimistic tow truck helping anyone in need. Who was Lighting-McQueen, was he lost in the limelight; with the worldly possessions? Some parents will understand the cartoonish parable for their children's minds, some will be unaware and lose their children.

Some cartoons that are being filmed today may show Baba's messages. While other media and other cartoons cleverly show the wrong behavior for our children. Sit down and bond with them. Answer their questions the way He would want you to. True believers of His Word will understand His message to us. The loving bond we have with our children begins a new generation. Spoken to His children; a new generation who have faith. Divine messages and heavenly clues are constantly given to us by our Father in more ways than you think.

You have to cleanse you mind, body and spirit to decode the message. The Quest for Truth is a lifetime of adventures added to you chapter within your manuscript. Eventually every one of us decides to live out their adventure or just sit back and turn on the TV to dream. We are made to inspire one another, to lift our hearts and Love our upcoming generation to new heights with prayer. The most powerful tool to reach our Heavenly Father for help during your life is prayer and Faith.

We need to understand His Word to continue our journey successfully. Baba always tries to reach out to us as we are written in his Book of Life. He wants to make sure that we have a happy ending; when our Love to Him is first and foremost. You may choose your own path because of your free will or you may allow Baba to choose for you and be part of his big picture. The chosen ones will be part for the Epic Awakening of mankind; shall ye seek thy Quest? Will thou Love from within towards humanity? Will thou raise your offspring with His Love, to kneel before Yahshua and receive your crown?

CHAPTER 14

Savage Supper

Time passed, as I was being awakened day by day with visions of my Quest from my Father. I stayed at my uncle's for a while but decided to move closer to my children before winter rolled in. Shortly after settling in at my sister's house; snowflake season arrived with heavy snow and slippery roads. The snow that year was piling up on my sister's driveway. I overheard my brother-in-law speaking to my uncle about a heavy duty snowplow he needed to borrow.

Meanwhile, I was enjoying my just made hot tea with some tea biscuits on the couch. My brother-in-law insisted that I go along with him, just because. "Gandy, come with me, let's go check out your Uncle Bee's snowplow." asked Jay. "Right now bro? Do you need my help loading?" I asked. "No, your uncle and I can manage." replied Jay. "So, why do you need me to come along?" I asked. "Just for fun, get out for a little bit." answered Jay.

"huff; OK fine, at least let me finish my tea." I said. "Just bring it with you, drink it in the car, keep it by the heated vent to keep it warm." instructed Jay. "OK sounds good, let's go." I replied. So we geared up and headed out to inspect the snowplow. The drive there was slippery and cautious as usual Michigan winter weather offers. After arrival and inspection, Tony decided to come back later in another vehicle that had enough hauling space. The weather was terrible, slushy and slippery with a cloak of nightfall.

We left my Uncle Bee's house to head back to Tony's place. The drive back was uneventful until we reached a stoplight. My brother-in-law was talking to his sister on the phone through the vehicle stereo Bluetooth speakers. There were two SUVs and one savage driving a brand new black Charger in the lane to the right of us. We needed to get into their lane when the light turned green. The lane we were in was the entrance to the freeway.

Since the SUV's next to us had all-wheel drive traction, they gained distance from savage's Camaro. My brother-in-law's SUV had 4x4 traction; allowing us to get to next lane over in front of savage much quicker. Obviously, my brother-in-law should have been much more careful and avoided splashing ice or snow on ignorant dumbass' brand new Chevy Camaro on Michigan's snowy weather roads. Ignorance accelerated next to my brother-in-law on the left freeway lane and flips him off.

My brother turns to him and tries to see who it was. I look over and see ignorance flipping us his middle finger then cutting us off getting back into lane into front of us. Yah Eesho, yah Alaha here we go again. "What the fuck was that!" I yelled. Just then stupid slams on his brakes in front of us and nearly causes an accident. "Watch out!" I shouted. "Motherfucker, what the fuck!" yelled Jay. "Forget this crazy ass and let him go ahead of us!" I shouted. "No, I wanna see how tough this muthafucker is!" yelled Jay.

"Forget him, maybe he's in a hurry or just pissed off, leave him alone!" I yelled. Too late; Savage performs a *Stupid Break Check.* "Watch out bro! Is this guy serious!" I was bracing for impact with my hand on the front dashboard while I had my tea in my other. Mind you, these roads were slushy and dangerous to pull stupid maneuvers like that. I would have erased that arrogant fool's whole generation if my children or my brother-in-law's were in the vehicle with us and were injured by the jackal. OK, enough is enough, I thought, this is getting out of control now...until his next bullshit move.

"Noooooo, shit-shit-shit, fuck!" I shouted. "Arrrgh, hold on!" yelled Jay. There was a freeway bridge overpass coming up just around the turn. That idiot timed his brake check once more, trying to force us to crash through the bridge barrier. Our rage was tripled; we did not know what is this guy's problem was. Why did we deserve to be run off a bridge to possibly crash down into the freeway and get injured? After recovering from the snowy bank we were stuck in, we continued over the bridge.

Tony and I noticed savage ignorance waiting for on the bridge near the end stop sign. My brother-in-law accelerates to his location and slams on his brakes and shifts into park. "Gandy, get down with me, let's see what this guy is going to do." instructed Jay. "Bro, why'd you have to slam on your brakes coming over here? Enough with slamming on the brakes already! I yelled. We both get out of my brother-in-law's SUV and see the arrogantly ignorant punk get out of his vehicle with his hand to his back. Oh great; I was about to confront a coward with a gun, here I go again.

Guns will only piss me off; and this guy had already spilled my hot tea on me. I should have stayed home with my hot tea."Watch out, he has a gun...Jay get back in the car!" I yelled. We both ran back into my brother-in-law's car and waited for the next move. "There's no gun...let's get out. I'm gonna beat his ass for doing that!" yelled Jay. "Are you fucking serious, just fucking leave, he's not worth it bro!" I shouted. "No...bullshit; are you coming or not?" shouted Jay. "Fine, this is bullshit!" I yelled.

We exited Jay's SUV and saw the savage beast reach in between his seat and door. My brother-in-law puts his hands up as to surrender. "Stop, think about it before you pull it out, bro!" I yelled. Ignorance pretended once more to have a gun behind the back. That outraged my fumigated brother-in-law. The yelling match began with the savage and my brother-in-law. I stood in front of our vehicle and behind the road-rage monkey's vehicle. Watching the both of them was rather funny; I wished I had some popcorn.

They were worse than amateur boxers who were clueless on how to throw and land a man's punch. "Ball up your fists, and fight like men; come on, it's cold out here!" I yelled. Oh wait something interesting, now they leveled up from a yelling match to a pushing match, finally. My brother-in-law shoved that arrogant fool who was getting too close to his personal space. Ignorance took that offensively and headed back for his vehicle reaching for something behind his driver seat. My brother-in-law jumped back and puts his hands up again. "Get back, bro!" yelled Jay.

"Stop, think twice before you reach for it and bring it out!" I yelled. "Think twice huh, stop huh!" yelled Savage. *Click - Pop;* Savage opened the trunk and headed toward the rear of his Camaro. My vessel was quaking with Baba's wrath; I thought: "Now we are talking, finally a battle, I get to Smash!" I showed Savage my palms up as a gesture of someone who was unarmed. Savage reaches for something in his trunk. I watched him fiddle through his trunk looking for another weapon, I supposed.

"Listen bro, calm down, we don't want any trouble, we're not trying to hurt you." I said. "You guys cut me off, almost ran me off the road!" yelled Savage. "You just tried to run us off the bridge! Why'd you do that? What are you looking for? Your gun, shotgun, what are you looking for?" I shouted. "Gun, no, no gun, I got something better for you, punk." replied Savage. He turned and faced me with his ignorant six-foot tree stature against my five-foot-five peaceful stature.

Ignorance pulls out a huge torque wrench then looks at me while my palms still up facing him. "What's that, a metal bar? You are going hit me with a metal bar? Look bro, I told you we don't want any trouble, OK!" I shouted. "Trouble huh? Well punk, you found trouble!" yelled Savage. I was infuriated by his remarks calling a punk, however, I did not let that interfere. ~ WHACK! ~ With full force, as though he was trying to destroy a piñata, he swung at me as I was blocking my head avoiding impact. Instead, he struck my side ribs; now it's on fucker.

He chose wisely and avoided aiming for my head; that would have spelled Blood for Ignorance, and Baba justifiably would have let me rip the fake ass brave-heart fool in half. **'YH!–Truth!–Feast!'** I proclaimed His Truth bestowed upon me and transformed into Wrath. Savage jumped out of his socks screaming and stumbling over his precious Dodge Camaro to get away. The sorry excuse for a human, filthier than creature excrement, was no longer a braveheart but a jester.

Just before I leaped over his Dodge to rip him in half, my right wing was held by one of His angels who was observing the incident. My battle brother calmed me down with palms together. Soon after, I ended up pounding my fist on the rear trunk in frustration of the dinner that got away; at least I hit something, huff. With my head down, I looked up at Ignorance with growling anger and thought to myself, 'You are so lucky He stopped me. I heard my brother-in-law yelling at yellow-belly after he had struck me.

Tony could not see very well in the dark because we had some distance between us. If he saw me, insanity would begin. "You hit my brother; ha punk, huh, come on, fight me, come on punk!" yelled Jay. "Bro leave him, it's OK, don't hurt him!" I shouted. "Come on fucker you want some too!" yelled Jay. "What the fuck? What are we playing? Football? Do you guys even know how to fight!" I shouted. My brother-in-law tried to tackle the civilian quarterback. Savage ignorance takes another swing with his makeshift metal sword at my brother-in-law and nicks him at the top of his head.

That just pisses off my brother-in-law, he blitzed him and takes him down just shy of the ten-yard line, hahaha. They end up tumbling on the ground until my brother-in-law had him in a headlock. I wanted to clap –good move, good move, nice takedown. However, Ignorance still had his torque wrench in his hand whaling at my brother-in-law's head, back and anywhere he was able to strike him. Now that pissed me off; he fought dirty. Now I had to score a goal with your head, I thought. I saw Ignorance land a few blows while my brother-in-law yelled in pain from the impacts.

I rush in for the FIFA penalty kick moment. Ignorance was about to become unconscious after contact. "No, don't kick him in the head!" shouted Jay. That was the second save for savage, seems like He may have had something else in store for Mr. Soccer Ball Head. My Father forbids us to kill, one of his commandments; rather, I put them in a comatose state, no less than one year, la-la land. "He keeps hitting you with the wrench; stop hitting him with your wrench, punk!" I shouted.

At this stage, they were both on the ground. I knelt down next to the beaten jester as my brother-in-law had him in a head lock. *Whoosh! Thud! Thud!* Ignorance swung at my head, as I blocked his attempts with my forearm. "Get away from me, you freak!" shouted Savage. I reared my Thor Hammer fist ready to make pancake brain on the road. "Who you calling a freak?" I shouted. "No, I will get fired for fighting, don't hit him!" yelled Jay. "What do you call this– playing? We *are* fighting!" I shouted.

"I'm just holding him for the police to get here, call them, I got him!" yelled Jay. "You sure you got him?" I asked. My brother-in-law grabbed a hold of the wrench to stop Savage from swinging just in time. I started to dial 911 on my cell phone to instruct the authorities to come pick up some trash on the road that was left behind. "Let me go!" shouted Savage. "No!" yelled Jay. "If we let you go, are you going to keep fighting us?" I shouted. "No I won't fight!" yelled Savage. "Are you lying to us?" I yelled.

I examined Ignorance trying to see if something was shining through, and I saw a fear in his eyes. "Let him go bro, he's telling the truth." I told Jay. "No, he is going to hit us again!" shouted Jay. I turned to Ignorance, leaned to his face with my balled up fist and flicked my index finger. "Are you going to do something, if we let you go?" I asked. "No, I swear!" shouted Savage. "Let him go Jay, he promised." I said to Jay. "Right?" I asked Savage. "Yes!" yelled Savage.

As the savage man was distracted and loosened his grip on the wrench, Jay was able to grab it from him and throw it down the road. He let go of the terrified fish and jumped out of the way to avoid any more confrontation. "Come on, let's go; the cops will come get him." said Jay. I was laughing inside; the comments my brother-in-law had made were hilarious. Ignorance was not going to stay there until the cops arrived, too funny. "Huh, if you say so bro." I replied. "This your hat, not any more, go get it!" shouted Jay. My brother-in-law tossed savage's winter cap over the bridge; classic.

We returned to our vehicle as the arrogant fool went to gather his weapon and race back to look for his winter hat. Obviously he loved that hat so much he rushed over to Tony's driver door attempting to open it. "Where's my hat?" shouted Savage. "If you touch my car, I'm going to get out and beat your ass!" yelled Jay. "Tell him it's over the bridge, you threw it overboard; put your window down, man, he can't hear you." I said. Just then, I notice Ignorance run behind our vehicle heading for my door. I thought, "Look at this kid, he is going to get hurt again; maybe chewed upon this time."

My brother-in-law made sure the door was locked. Savage attempted to open my locked door and rears his weapon back to smash my window; perhaps to become brave once more. I tried to open my door to speak to this brave brat who was testing my nerve. "Where is my hat?" screamed Savage. "Unlock my door! Let me out!" I yelled. "No! Just lower your window!" shouted Jay. "Are you kidding me bro, unlock it!" I yelled.

I manually unlocked my door and opened it as Ignorance leaped back and hid his metal sword behind his back. "If you swing that at me, I'm gonna hurt you!" I yelled. "Where is my hat, what did you guys do with it!" shouted Savage. "Maaaan, are you serious; fuck it's cold out here!" I shouted. I shut the car door and opened my window. Perhaps he needed it more than my brother-in-law had thought before throwing it over the bridge. So, I politely pointed in the direction where my brother-in-law threw savage's hat.

"Look over that ledge, he threw it down the freeway!" I shouted. When Ignorance headed for the ledge of the bridge, I instructed my brother-in-law to drive back home. "Go bro, I'm done with this shit." I instructed Jay. We drove past Ignorance and made a right turn on the service road next to the freeway heading back home. Ignorance really loved his hat so much that he sped past us only to slam on his brakes in front of us once again. "Watch out!" I yelled.

I should have changed his title after that move, yet he was still a coward and perhaps needed the authorities to pursue him. Ignorance sped away in his Dodge Camaro fishtailing on Michigan snowy roads. Dumbass. Oddly enough, he handled that stunt maneuver rather well; he should have been a stunt driver instead of brave jackass. Shortly after an officer called my phone and provided their location where to meet them to identify the suspect. Surprisingly, the Dodge Camaro racing pro was captured within a few minutes.

We had to go through the process of pressing charges against Savage for assault and endangerment. They wanted to give us a hard copy report and verify an injury. Paramedics examined me and saw my bruised side ribs; the bruise was the size of my thigh; causing irritated nights of restless sleep. The courts delayed proceedings by constantly rescheduling; that was bullshit. My brother-in-law's sciatic nerve also caused him pain besides suffering bumps, bruises and a welt on his head from tussling on the ground.

I was branded with a 7-inch bruise on my rib that was very painful at bedtime and when my children wanted to jump on daddy. My memorable bruise was Baba's reminder of his mercy that night on the bridge. I never will forget that day; I am forever grateful to Baba and Yahshua. After months of waiting to see Ignorance and provide him with a new title at the court proceedings, we finally seated ourselves on the bench outside the courtroom after speaking briefly with the prosecutor. After two frustrating hours pass with the courtroom doors shut, no one was to enter.

Oh yeah, I am taking names and will see whomever is attempting to enter at His gates. Have a good day or life for that matter, ladies and gentlemen and Mrs. Your Honor; who supposedly was managing the dock on this vessel we are traveling in. Were there more ignorant participants in the courtroom with deceptive proceedings? Savage brave hearts were all around in this world that I walked upon. Choosing to bully others only angers Him, and they encounter his wrath through me.

However, only my flesh was bruised; my heart needed mending until my Love arrived to rescue me from my sadness. I had to keep searching for her until we hug once more, forevermore. This time, I will not let go of my soul, my breath, my beloved, my Sabra, Baba's glorious child. I was on a mission of Love throughout most of my existence on Baba's planet with adventure after adventure. How many would pass up a Quest from our heavenly Father? I pray no one would succumb to fear and build their courage to serve Him.

Our season of spring arrived to lift our moods from our chilly winter. Living with my sister and her family, I was still working as an IT consultant. GK Services, LLC was still operational; however, a bit slow in obtaining sufficient income for my family. My wife and her family were anticipating success in such a short period of time. Starting a company is never a failure but a gradual learning experience like any endeavor you encounter in your life.

You must have the "I will keep trying, I will succeed" attitude. Unfortunately, my depression kept my addiction to marijuana constant. Moreover, Michigan had legalized the distribution of marijuana as medicine to patients legally. My attempt to quit was sidetracked by the plan to help those in need that require organic pain relief rather than popping pills. Smoking fogs the mind, sometimes disconnecting our signal from Baba. The cannabis will inhibit the person from completing tasks or cause social irritation with vulgar behavior.

Satan may hear them more often than Baba or Yahshua when smoking that dragon. You can still accept Yahshua into your life prior to inhaling that demon smoke. You can always count on Him helping you. The devil has tricked many of His followers in the past; why would today be any different? Mankind must realize that Yahshua may arrive at any given moment. Our Father will give the power to his Son to imprison The Evil One for 1000 years for shedding the blood of His innocent children.

After a short probationary period that dragon will be gone for good. The Traitorous Dragon will be tossed in the Abyss of Nothingness for eternity, freeing mankind of the dumbass's interference forevermore. The light bearer tried to learn from his Father how to accept Love rather than feast on stale rotten souls; dumbass continuously fails. The lovingly born human starts out being good; who raises them defines humanity. Why do people fall to manipulated truths by the masses and follow them to edge of the cliff to jump off?

Avoid doing that; instead laugh at the devil's face with your strong Faith. The Evil One will try to trick everyone until the chess match is over; the glory of Baba always will prevail for eternity. The dumbass who betrayed The Father does not know how to play truthful chess. Avoid speaking lies yourself and knocking your own chess piece over. Your life is His game of Truth, not your game that you may think you are playing. Your actions will ripple through the course of history and you will change the chess moves he had already planned for you or others.

To stay on His chess board; Love your family and neighbors as Baba loves you and instead sacrifice your disgusting habits. Avoid losing your children to hate, or Baba may well lose you as well. Humbly reach out and help each other and He will see the true nature of your Love. People can be cruel and bitter to each other when they are unable to live up to the requirements they were expecting of one another. Forgive them and remember what you have done to cause those actions against you so that you may correct your trespasses.

Give them the means of support to lift their spirits once more to their lives in love and joy, even if you are no longer together. Those who can forgive their worst enemies can have the biggest treasure of Love and live for eternity. Let your arrogant past go, and Yahshua will hold your hand and lead you to YH's eternal kingdom. Humans will have a choice that will test their will and Love for our Father and Big Brother. If Yahshua arrives and requests that you to leave the ones who do not Love him, would you?

Would you leave the ones you have love for, your career, your lifestyle, and follow Him? Would you take the risk of humility to follow His Quest through the flames unharmed? Will your heart withstand the immense pressure of the physical and emotional strain you may face? Will you be brave to fight the forces of evil with no fear? Are you the chosen ones who will join His good fight with Yahshua's Saints? For any human who follow His Truth will hear the trumpets blow.

They will feel the Love of their Father who has written their name in his Book of Life. Many have also lost their ways by means of degrading music, prejudice acts, hatred, temptations, lust, lies, theft, slaying, etc., etc. Lucifer makes that type of lifestyle pleasing to the human eye with their pockets full and heads delusional with the fake power. If you want real power, pray to the creator of the original power –His unlimited power.

CHAPTER 15

Baba's Conscious Atom

In the end, we will all be together when forgiveness and Love co-exists within our hearts toward each other. Unite with each other as a family and come together as one to celebrate in His heaven on Earth. We all matter in His eyes; the creation of us with the matter from His universe. Did you know that Baba's particles really do exist in the space between us? Baba has the final Word of those particles of atoms, space, time and gravity; He controls all.

Science never will be able to measure or solve His Word. Yet; scientist seek self gain Recently, a scientific program had me pondering how man was trying to decode Baba's language with science.. The test –have a stationary particle gun shoot atomic particles against a backboard that could be measured visually with an instrument. The particles drew a picture of vertical lines with dots on a backboard.

The particle gun was aimed just a few inches away from the first board with the thin vertical slits through it.   The objective of the experiment was to visualize and record how many particles would go through each vertical slit and land on the rear board. The scientists would initiate the test and receive the same results over and over again. They let the gun run its programmed course of firing particles for the time allowed. The scientist left the lab and returned. They were fascinated with what they witnessed on their display board. The pattern they were expecting was no longer normal.

The scientist noticed most of the particles were going through the first vertical slit on the board and not the second. Some of the particles did not go through any of the vertical slits and landed on the first board near the gun. Continuous experiments were attempted getting the same results while the scientists observed the stationed gun. Every time the scientist would leave the room or turn off the video recording, the consciousness of the particles took over creating His original masterpiece.

Baba likes to tickle the brain stems of smart humans to let them know who is boss. The scientists try to figure out the universe with quantum physics to the infinite probable outcome; squared. Metaphor …"That is illogical, Captain, what are they trying to accomplish?" asked Spock. "I'm not sure of what to tell you, Spock; they're human." replied Kirk. To understand Baba's language and appreciate all that you have and all that He can give you, sacrifice your dirty deeds and praise Him daily. Ask for forgiveness of your sins to be seated and eat supper with Him.

You will miss out on life if you avoid at least trying; you may actually Love more. You have or had the same feeling when you hugged your family or children. Would you like to feel how the child feels when Yahshua hugs you with Love? Yes, you do; do not be afraid of what His awesome power can provide for you in exchange for your awesome Love. Many have tried yet so few have succeeded to even get close to our teacher Yahshua the Messiah due to fear or ignorance or denial.

To understand his existence; is to have no fear and believe in Him. Why does man think death is the final answer to this life? Yahshua's thoughts and powers are immeasurable whereas man's consciousness has yet to understand a speck. People should have the; "Yes, I will stay on the path" instead of "No, I cannot give that up"; mentality. Even the ones who are lost can be found and shown the way of Love. In many cases, even being faithfully lost will lead you to Yahshua. He can provide you with strength and courage you need to continue.

For example; I met a man who went through a life changing experience after witnessing Truth. Troubled life ended him up in prison where he was attacked by twenty men. During his stay before the attack; he turned to Yahshua and repented of his wicked ways. My friend's choice guided him to victory with His Word. His life had turned from bad to good overnight after having his own encounter with Yahshua the Messiah. Everyone who is at the brink of losing all hope in the darkness will end up being found with Yahshua's Love for you.

He will shine upon your darkest hour and have you raise your head to praise your true Father in heaven. He will guide you to salvation to eat the bread of his body and drink the wine of his blood. Remember Yahshua's sacrifice for you; so that you may show him how much you Love Him. He may ask you to sacrifice your old self to become a new being with His Word. If you are suffering, have no bitterness toward your fellow man or woman, for the sacrifice you must endure is for His mercy and grace to rain upon you.

He may introduce you to someone who could be the one who is there to help you or show you the secrets of the Universe. Have gratitude for Baba for giving you the opportunity to have the life that you desire for your sacrifice and determination to better yourself to praise Him. Show Baba you can give him your very best even in your worst days of frustration. Never give up your Faith and devotion, keeping yourself clean in this semi-filthy world we currently live in that tends to taint the heart.

Have no fear, for His words are Truth, Justice, Courage, Faith and Love protecting you throughout the universe forevermore. We are like children gaining knowledge through life to prepare ourselves for the spiritually eternal graduation. Suffer like a wounded warrior, study his spiritual songs of Love, prepare you spirit for Baba's and Yahshua's ceremony, and finally hug them both. They have unlimited power throughout the Universe, guiding you every step of the way. The path they can provide you overwhelmed with His miracles to say the least.

Connecting to people who have His Strength of Faith bonding together as brothers and sisters from renown. The people who are compassionate toward others have an easier access to His Kingdom, as they humble themselves with humility. Be like saints of His Word marching side by side with Yahshua leading His Truth. The rejoicing of the human spirit connects us all with Our Father with songs of Faith. We must all lift our head up high and praise our King of Kings for our everlasting life.

CHAPTER 16

Battling Brutes

In my Father's book, our names are all written with the story of our lives on this Planet. The year medical marijuana was legalized for qualified patients. My friends and I decided to start our own delivery service for those patients who were in need of pain relief. I tried to avoid delivering later than 9p.m. However, one last call was received and we obliged our MMMP patients because our motto was "We Care We Deliver."

The strange part was the amount requested; the patient requested the full amount the law allowed to be transported. Two and a half ounces were packed and stored for delivery after we finally agreed on the price of $500. The patient sent me a text message of his address, and I replied with an estimated time of arrival. The drive was about an hour and I wanted to head back home to enjoy a smoke or two while the night was still young.

I wondered why someone would want to pick up their meds at a party store. I had texted the patient to let them know that I was waiting for them. The place looked busy, and they mentioned they had a home nearby and would like to pick up the meds at their father's place of business. It was legal, so where the transaction took place did not matter to me, so long as they had their proper identification before purchase. I was waiting in the parking lot for at least fifteen minutes before texting him again to let me know if they were a no show or late show.

His reply texts had me act like a pinball driving from home to business to excuse after excuse. Finally, the last text indicated he was on his way and he apologized. I let him know I would not wait any longer than ten minutes. To my surprise, he needed two other men to aid him in this transaction. Oh boy, here we go again; yep, you guessed it, supper time. I greet him and his two other friends, as I scan them quickly. More brave hearts to battle, and I was already irritated.

"Hi, you took forever, I was about to leave, you had me driving everywhere." I said. The patient was standing near my open driver side window twisting his empty glass juice bottle looking ever so nervous. "Can I see your MMMP card and your ID?" I asked. "It's missing." replied Devon. "Wait, what? Are you fucking kidding me? I drove all the way out here, waited two hours for you, and now your card is missing!" I shouted. Devon looks at his posse with a face of: Is this fool for real yelling at me in my hood?

"You had plenty of time to find your card, even if it was lost; you could've at least let me know ahead of time. Who are they?" I asked. "These are my friends; they just came along just in case." replied Devon. "Just in case of what?" I asked for each of his friend's names, and they either gave me their real or fake names, no matter; I was ready for them. I had been raised in the streets of Detroit, and everywhere I traveled was a human braveheart confronting me. People with that type of mentality need to turn off their act of bravery, or someone will remind them of true bravery earned justifiably.

Like I said before, if you play games with me, I get frustrated and take names. If you Insult me, I will give you His Truth to short circuit your brain. If you touch me with your bravery, I will devour you. The patient was very, very nervous. "You OK, you look nervous; are you guys cops? This is legal you know; if you would like, we can go to your house to get your ID?" I asked. "Can't find my ID either." said Devon. "Wow, no MMMP Card and no ID; you are full of surprises tonight." I said.

The three amigos looked very nervous, as our conversation was exposing more and more of their planned intentions. "Relax bro, I am not going to hurt you; it's no big deal. If you wanted weed to buy and sell, you should have said that from the get-go. I will help you; but if you sell to children, then we will have a problem. If you play games with me, then we're done. Are we good? I asked. "No bro, no games, we can get rid of it and in a couple days flat and call you for more." replied Devon.

What was I supposed to do, break the law or help someone that is living in conditions hard enough to survive? I was there; I knew what that felt like. "OK, I will help you." I said. "Show me the weed." requested Devon. "You want to see the weed? Why, you don't trust me? Do you have $500 on you right now? I'll show you the weed if you show me the cash." I said. "Yeah-yeah, I got the money, just show me the weed so that I know you have it." replied Devon. His remarks were amusing so I had to laugh and give him a peak.

I used to play this game in the hood; sometimes they just screamed. "See; here it is; all two ounces of it." I said. I opened my oversized briefcase showing them the marijuana for this memorial occasion of ours, and their eyes lit up. "Let me see it again, take it out, hold it in your hand." said Devon. "OK." I replied. I gladly replied by taking out the bag of marijuana to show them once more and feed their curiosity. Did they not know that sometimes curiosity may shorten the pussy's nine lives?

"You want to toke to try it out first before you buy so much? You may not like the taste. You don't wanna waste your time buying something you don't like." I said. "OK, sure right here in front of the store?" asked Devon. I was tired and wanted to head back home. Taking over the situation with orders rather than questions made the ordeal much more manageable. "No, how about away from the front of the store; get in my Jeep, we can go for a spin." I instructed. "You want me to get into your Jeep with you?" asked Devon.

"Us too?" replied Devon's friends. "Yes; in my Jeep, you guys too." I said. "Nah, we're good, we can pull up back there though." said Devon. "Back where?" I asked. "Just toward the back of the lot." said Devon. "Fine by me; you guys getting in? I can drive you back there." I replied. "That's ok; we'll walk there." said Devon. "OK, see you guys there." I replied. The patient and his friend huddled up for their next move. How typical can you get with that type of body language?

They were luncheon meat in plain sight. I placed my Jeep in park and waited for dinner to arrive to my den. "Where are we all going to fit?" asked Devon. I point at my prey and instructed him to sit next to me since I was about to serve him up some supper. I also instructed his two friends to sit in the backseat. I looked back at the rear passengers and notice my child's car seat was in the way for my guests to be seated at the table. "Oops sorry about that; let me get that for you." I said.

I politely moved my daughter's seat toward the middle of the rear seats for the desperado's two bodyguards. They were going to get a story of their lives and some peace pipe bonding. "Get in." I instructed them. He looked like he was in fear of something or perhaps someone, maybe having second thoughts; who knows? I would have avoided doing anything if they kept their hands to themselves. Within a split second after their fearless leader sat in the front passenger seat, He decided to grab my briefcase. "YH!"

"Noooooo, don't!" shouted Devon. Both of his pack scream in terror and run behind my Jeep into their darkness, but this wolf was bolder. He decided to grab hold of my briefcase to see who would win our tug of war. "Wait, don't, what are you doing, where are you going, are you serious bro?" I asked. Holding on to my briefcase, he attempted to reach for something behind his back, tsk-tsk. So I had to show him more of His Truth. "Arrraahhhh, noooooo! screamed Devon. I was puzzled on what to do with my dinner –eat it or let it go.

Devon witnessed His truth that would last him eternity. I gave him one last chance before he disappeared into the night. "Do you really need this weed, bro?" I asked. "Yes I do." replied Devon. "Are you sure?" I asked. "Yes I'm sure." said Devon. I saw fear in his eyes and felt pity for him, so I released my grip and let him have my briefcase. "Wait bro, I'm not going to hurt you, I promise, don't leave!" I shouted. However, his friends were screaming for him to run. He had no choice, he was their leader.

I was trying to show him the right path to His salvation if he would just have stayed. With all the commotion I unaware of an additional dilemma that occurred after the theft. I had my personal paperwork in one of the briefcase pockets. I shifted my Jeep in D for devour. Ignorance was trying to hide in one of the car wash bays located behind the party store lot. I approached ever so slowly, passing each bay, like a lion sniffing out its prey; the cornered hyena was quivering against the wall clutching my briefcase.

Did he not know I was driving and he was running –where was he going? Fortunately for Devon, he was quite nimble. My large cumbersome 4-wheel lion was too big to turn quicker than my hyper-hyena. I sped after Ignorance hoping he would drop my briefcase, as he realized3000 pounds was trying to devour him. "You 'bouta get popped!". I shouted at the runaway hyena as he decided to jump over fence at a nearby homeowner's backyard.

I was avoiding causing damage to my vehicle or property of others, just wanted to snag my snack from my drive-by window. Oh well, maybe dinner will show up to my den of residence after all; yummy. I never had any worries with anyone trying to bushwhack me; there was no need to run, as I will be waiting for you. There was plenty of room at the supper table. However, they were afraid to sit down. They preferred fast food to go. Lesson learned? If you are unsure on how to serve supper outdoors, then stay indoors. By all means, avoid attempting what I had gone through to test your bravery unless you had already passed your test of Faith.

Baba or the Evil One gladly will provide you that test of Faith. Will you be ready? How much longer till He notices you? In my case, I was ready from the beginning of His thought of me. through my life and forevermore. There should never be any doubt in yours or anyone else's heart about His Word. When or if you carry your crucifix for Yahshua, avoid dropping it. If you do, lift up and carry on until that day comes where you are called upon.

If you can endure the pain, then you are already blessed. If you are unable to take the pain and suffering, He will definitely hear you cry out for help and mercy. He may show up to ease your pain or send one of His angels to mend your wounds. Have no fear and accept His help without question or doubt. Doubt brings fear and fear causes you to lose your Faith and allows the evil one to drain your energy to finish you off. Raise your head up for His strength to guide you through your turmoil. Cast out the evil one and his demons in the name of Yahshua.

He will fill you with Love, and your Faith in Him will always allow you to prevail. Never let anyone intimidate your Truth because of your stature; they have no idea how big your heart is. They have no idea the power of Our Heavenly Father, who can crush your enemies with one thought. Battles are won by words; wars are won by prayers. If your opponent is unaware on how to play chess of life, then the game is over before it has begun. We as humans must realize we are our own doomsday weapon ready to make our own race extinct.

Hatred fills the hearts of many because Lucifer is playing his game with the weak, the wicked, and the warmongers. Keep your Faith with Yahshua and Baba and allow them to shield you from evil. The other humans who bully the world with terror will join the Evil One for Eternity in his Pit of Dumbasses. There are many, many people who think they are brave, tuff turf, wanna-be-soldiers of Earth. Even if they came right out of the military or from the spawn of hell, bullying or devouring anyone they meet, they eventually meet His Wrath; me.

Then, they can shit bricks after I show them His Truth. He who diffuses a confrontational situation before it ever begins, is a true Saint of His Truth. Treating each other as brothers and sisters is the solution; rather than estranged enemies enraged with hatred in their hearts. Hate is your real enemy, defeat the feeling of hate within your hearts and you will sit at His table to eat for eternity. All who are exalted with forgiveness could enter His Kingdom. All who show mercy could enter His Kingdom; all could, how many do?

We were not breed to fight each other; we were born to help each other in time of need. The Devil, his demons, and humanity's traitors coerce people to fight each other into obliteration. Lucifer has zero love for humanity. Zero. That old dragon fools the whole world with his wrenched lies and promises. Mankind still falls into his traitorous trap and swallows his poisonous sap, hardening their hearts as the deception oozes down society's throat until they choke and gasp for a remedy. Humans will seek restitution given to them by any means to ease their suffering.

Lucifer will make the false antidote easy to swallow; yet difficult to escape. To defy the lie, mankind needs to endure the birth pains of this world as Yahshua pained for their sins. With every step, a human endures pain and requires a Truthful relief. Most of us have been lost from Truth for many years due to the lust and greed of this Earth, and the constant demand for the struggle for power and wealth. Humanity's path is not being solely directed by its own accord, though.

The mind of humans at a certain point can be distracted from the real Truth when evil is involved. Media can provide you that distracted path; however it is up to the individual to choose the right path. The connection to Baba always will be embedded in humanity's DNA. Therefore, the path chosen always will constitute the outcome at the proceedings of humanity's actions. Those who have been placed on Earth to serve Baba and Yahshua will be called upon to Judge. To enforce His justice and aid humanity against the terrines forces of evil.

Show the humble side of your soul so that He may be pleased with you. Show them your Love, so Yahshua could sit next to you when it is supper time. Yahshua mentioned that some of the people will be unable to get into heaven because they are either ignorant or fearful to accept the Truth. He will take one and leave the other. He gave you that option called free will, allowing you to choose your destiny or fate. Even your loved ones will be unable to save you from purgatory if you committed a sin.

CHAPTER 17

Baba's Chess Match

Each person has his or her own responsibility to keep themselves clean when our teacher Yahshua the Messiah returns. I agree with every single Word Yahshua the Messiah had said in the past, especially when I met and hugged him in 1997. He always had been my Truth; so for Him to choose one and leave the other, you should be thankful that is he keeping you and throwing the other off Baba's planet.

Baba has higher authority over you and gave you a Quest to complete. If someone tries to offer you an easier way out, would you take it? Or would you continue your mission of struggle and suffering to search for His Love and live in peace for who had commanded you to move from the beginning? I choose to at least try; those who want the Truth spoken to them or given to them need to pray and prepare before they can start their blessed Quest.

For the ones who prefer to take care of their affairs first and take on His Quest later, bury your dead. If you were arrogant to begin with, go graze elsewhere, and "Avoid touching me when you leave."Let me tell you this –if you deter someone's path who has been chosen for his/her destiny to spread His Love, then you should have walked in their sandals through sand, suffered, and became humble. You could have gained more knowledge, empathy, humility and become a Saint you should have been today.

You may be ridiculed, belittle or intimidated, however; they have become the jackass no one wants to ride in the end. That's because something other than speech comes out of their doubtful mouth: a dagger. You agreed to follow Truth, so follow with Faith, no fear from anyone on this Earth; be courageous and devoted for you are almost there to win your Grand Prize of Glory. Life is a set of clues leading you to your destiny that seem to never end yet necessary to earn your ticket on His starship with your beloved by your side who He led you to.

If your time on this Earth is important enough for you, then search for Yahshua. He will lead you to Him to claim the Love you have. He also may toss you into your infinite abyss of nothingness if you slack off sinning. You literally have to bleed from within for Him to win anything you ask for, even when you get pierced in your heart or suffer from childhood to adulthood. A lot of people will try to throw you off your path of searching for His salvation, your Quest of destiny, or your true Love.

When they deny Him or your Quest to succeed and avoid cheering you on, keep going no matter what happens. They will be left behind and lack the meaning to comprehend the language of Love spoken to them. Making them lose interest and getting lost in their own desires, move on. There is nothing to see there but slumber walking around. Searching for a Soulmate takes either a long time or a short time; be patient, Baba will intervene when you are ready to find each other. Why should I let man determine my destiny for me since Baba had already chosen for me?

Avoid following man's advice when it comes to Yahshua's Word of advice; you will get lost or eaten. The awesome part of being an IT professional is you enjoy being hinted coded messages or directed by my Brother; you should accept him – He is an adventure you would want to accept. A lot of people have missed their ship or were missing their tickets to board when He docked to Love them. I have been onboard for quite some time now. Yahshua is your captain to His starship; do not lose your tickets and avoid being late; I will be waiting for you.

We are sailing through the cosmos in His starship, to His destination of paradise and awesome galaxies. However, the cosmic journey will have to be delayed unless the chess match that is ensuing for the battle of the souls comes to an end. In my opinion; everyone may think that Lucifer was in charge of the Earth, when he was merely an equivalent of a lab assistant for Baba. While Baba tends to other matters, Lucifer stays behind in the lab to complete a simple task. Baba had instructed Lucifer to avoid attempting any creations until he gets back into the lab.

Lucifer agrees and continues with his boring tasks. Lucifer was possibly thinking he may be able to do a better job or perhaps tackle His immense duties on his own. When we speak of Baba, we can relate to the creation of the universe. Lucifer glances over to notice a manual for creation. Lucifer wanted to make his Father proud and decided to go at it with his own creation. Lucifer begins to mix the Speech, Smell, Sight, Touch, Hearing and Thought ingredients. Unfortunately, the main ingredient was hesitantly avoided.

Substituted with another ingredient that was hazardous and made a disaster for millenniums to come due to the horror that was created from ignorance. The main ingredient that was required was Love. Lucifer was unaware of the correct amount to use compared to thy Great Father. Ignorance grew within Lucifer and selfishness sat the loser down to play an earthly chess match with Baba. That ol' dragon is about to lose to Baba with the biggest chess match upset in the history of mankind and universe.

Love always wins when it comes to His creations; He is always the correct ingredient in any recipe. At this point, Lucifer is in check in the game of cosmic chess. Every move made without Love loses for eternity. Love starts from the top and trickles its way down the mountain of your fruit and shines for eternity. When the Love starts from the top of the cloth and trickles down to their flock, it better be Love for our Teacher rather than Love for the Lust.

The leader of all churches is in Rome; they trickle down blasphemy to Yahshua by cloaking their hearts pleading allegiance to Lucifer. If you are able to consume the drunkenness of the Vatican, then you have betrayed your first Love and have taken theirs and placed it on top of your dome for the world to see in shame. When you belittle my Brother, He sends wrath from his Father to crucify the traitorous vipers. Who have poisoned His blood from within to spit at whoever approaches for the body and blood and receives lies and betrayals.

Placing a small crucifix on top of the Vatican dome and claiming to be the head church means that to even title yourself as men of Baba and or Yahshua was a disgrace. In addition to the disrespectful act, the Vatican gives homage to Lucifer in its cellar, becoming the traitor of our Beloved Bread. Scholars went as far as to rearrange the English language to confuse the masses to praise the false son. The lie grew in addition to the incorrect spelling of Yahshua's name from the proper English language. Simply put, prayers are like food to Baba and the Devil.

When families are crushed by ignorance, selfishness and betrayal, it causes hatred toward one another. The whole foundation that you had built from seed to tree withers away and dies, unless you sacrifice your ignorance, selfishness, arrogance, lies and betrayal. Ignorance plays a big role in chipping away at your foundation. When two people unit as one, they must take the good and the bad from that person. You must ask them politely to sacrifice their bad or unwanted habits.

Submit to unconditional Love to strengthen your foundation, and only then will you have the opportunity to soar to His Universal Love for eternity. The unselfishness affection of the human spirit toward another is seen by our Father as favorable behavior. Caring for each other opens the connection to Yahshua to hear our plea for help. Through The Holy Spirit, Baba will reach out to us to cease our pain and anguish we suffer from; do not give up – give yourself time.

CHAPTER 18

I Was Lost, I Found My "Caro"

Time is little of what we have to ignore the keys to His Kingdom being lost when they are in plain sight. People will even be blinded by their loved ones with the daggers that exit their mouth and pierce their loved one's heart. In my case, I was about to fall with the sin of adultery. I was still married yet separated for years because of betrayal, loss of Love, ignorance, and arrogance.

Being denied intimacy or Love from your own mate will cause any man to wander into the arms of a sinful woman, a viper to finally bite you into nonexistence or wreck your home. My denial for affection lasted more than seven months when I finally decided that Lust was better than Love; at least I can get it whenever I wanted it. So I made that decision and set out to acquire some funds to complete my desires to sin; I was going to fall. I had called my business partner to acquire any funds that were owed for services rendered from our clients.

He had informed me that three clients had invoices due and we were able to collect payment. I had collected from the first two clients; the last client delayed payment for our services. There was service call at a pizzeria to replace some defective cameras. I knew the previous owner who I had befriended and met the new owner of the pizzeria that had also befriended me and made me his brother instantaneously. My partner and I had installed security cameras at the pizzeria in the past with the previous and new owner that still had a balance due.

I also was given information from my business partner to speak to a manager at the pizzeria of a break-in incident that had occurred a week prior. When I arrived, the employee behind the counter indicated that the manager was not there at that time, so he gave me the managers number. I had called the manager of the pizzeria to setup an appointment. She was requesting to access the DVR for a prior recording of a break in that had occurred. I had other clients to tend to before I was to meet up with her at the pizzeria just before noon.

When I arrived at the pizzeria and was greeted by my befriended brother. We shook hands and I informed him that I was here to speak with the manager to access their CCTV system due to the intrusion that had set off their alarm. My befriended brother had instructed me to come in and head to the back of the pizzeria to access the DVR system. I entered the side door, unaware of what was about to happen to me that day and perhaps for eternity. I was only interested in acquiring the funds I needed to sin for lust and fall due to lack of affection from my separated wife.

I concentrated on getting my job done and leaving as quickly as possible. There is a place and time for everything and everyone. The time was just right, the place was just as He planned it, and I had to seize the moment or she would have left my life for good. I continued down the aisle in the pizzeria, until she came from around the corner and stopped my heart. I was in awe when I saw Yahshua momentarily standing behind her holding both arms outward as to gesture "my gift to you."

I pointed with my finger for a second at Sabra then followed Yahshua who hovered away, made a right turn, and vanished into the wall. I had no idea how many people were in the pizzeria. Sabra was making the same following gesture to Yahshua behind me. "Huh, that's strange because someone was behind you." I said. She turned around for a second to see who was behind her and turned back again toward my direction. "I thought someone was behind you too." replied Sabra. "You mean your brother? He is behind me, by the counter?" I asked. "No I mean right behind you was someone else; I don't who it was, not my brother though." replied Sabra.

Touching Her Soul

Yahshua gestured with his arms, as though the father of the bride was releasing his daughter to the groom during a wedding. We dismissed the miracle and greeted each other; we were both logical and rational. I reached out my hand and connected with hers.

Once we touched, it was as though I knew this woman from the past somehow. After greeting ourselves, we began to talk about the break-in incident at the pizzeria. Sabra asked to install an application to view live and recorded feeds from the DVR. I was unable to keep my eyes off her and had some force driving me to touch her again. I began asking Sabra questions about what was stolen or broken during the forced intrusion to the pizzeria. Sabra indicated that nothing was damaged or stolen, which was quite odd.

"I think someone that works here may have something to do with it; they were showing up on and off for a whole week." informed Sabra. "Nothing was broken or stolen?" I asked. "No, just the back door was opened, the alarm went off, and ten to fifteen minutes later the police showed up." replied Sabra. I leaned over, inhaled her essence, went blank for a few moments, gained composer and spoke Aramaic with her. "Do you know who here had their friends walking around back here?" I asked.

"I don't know who's friend he was, but I know he was tall with blond hair and blue eyes." replied Sabra. The DVR was located above the drop ceiling tile, which required a folding ladder to reach. I had to obtain some settings from the DVR. We needed to install a remote application on Sabra's laptop. I asked Sabra for a ladder to access the DVR above the drop ceiling. I wanted to make sure the cables were seated on the modem and DVR for remote access. She headed to the back of the pizzeria to acquire the ladder for me.

I was impressed by her strength and strong will. I was a bit intimidated by her get-back stare, like she was ready to pounce on me if I attempted to help her. I was in awe over how she was handling the establishment like a professional in charge of any situation that may arise. I was hesitant at first; however, I insisted on providing my aid for her as a gentleman would. After inspecting the DVR, the wiring checked out OK, except the DVR had no monitor to view any live feed or recordings.

I was unable to do anything without the monitor attached to the DVR, so I needed to use Sabra's laptop to access the DVR through the internal network. I installed the necessary application to access the DVR through the pizzeria's network. After tweaking the required settings on the DVR to view the live and recorded video feeds, I was able to access the DVR. Sabra came by to view my progress and touched my arm, which threw me into another Loving trance for a brief moment.

"Would you like some coffee?" asked Sabra. "Yes please, I would Love some, thank you very much." I replied. "What would you like? I Love Tim Horton's coffee; it's my favorite." said Sabra. "Really, why?" I asked. "I Love the way Tim Horton's coffee tastes; other brands of coffee are too bitter for my taste." replied Sabra."Coffee tastes like coffee to me; however, let me try your Tim Horton's coffee; I'm sure it will taste good." I said. "How do you like your coffee?" asked Sabra.

I should have responded: "I like my coffee sitting next to you enjoying your glorious aroma overpowering my coffee" but instead said: "Two cream, two sugar, thank you." Sabra had left the pizzeria to get some coffee for her, others and I. While Sabra was away, I continued retrieving the data for viewing. One of the persons that I remembered she had mentioned to me who was arriving periodically was a taller gentleman with long blond hair. While I looked at the CCTV data recordings, Sabra returned with some coffee.

I honestly can tell you it was the best coffee that I had ever tasted. When I say "I would drink or eat, anything Sabra would make, even if it tasted disgusting," I would enjoy every sip or bite and swallow her love. I would sacrifice my existence for her Love. Love for a person or people allows you to walk through oceans, as Baba splits his water apart for you. I would lay down my life for this woman I call my Soulmate. Sabra is the woman who Baba had created waiting for me to reunite with her soul. Just a few moments away from Sabra felt like an eternity of empty loneliness within my soul.

She would fill my cup of life with every embrace. I would melt with her everlasting warm embrace in the chilly nights. I kept dreaming how we would be together happily ever after in Love and ruling our own galaxy. We would travel on His bridge sharing His story of true Love from heaven to everyone who have Faith within their hearts. When two Soulmates are united by our Holy Father, an immense force is felt throughout the Universe. The force so strong that it will defeat the evil with one unified heartbeat of Love.

The emotional ties between two souls bring together parallel universes into coexistence with peace, Love and joy. The energy shared between two Soulmates can jump start the sun after it has finally extinguished. Pray to reunite with your Soulmate; He will reunite you both forevermore.

Once More I Beg of Thee

My heart was beating faster and faster trying to figure out what to say to Sabra when she returned from her cigarette break. How can this be happening again, how did I end up here?

There was only one explanation that I could think of. Yahshua was leading me to my Soulmate and steering me away from sinful damnation. I was so grateful to Yahshua being part of my life; He never failed me. I had a sigh of relief when Sabra had returned with coffee and stood next to me to access her laptop. Yes, her glorious aroma overpowered my coffee. As I was next to her, some uncontrollable force to touch her again came over me. I turned my head to look at Sabra and she had a few strands of hair covering her eye.

Like a child who was curious, or a man who is passionately in Love, I reached over with my right hand slowly; gently moving her hair away from her eye and wrapped her worth-more-than-gold hair around her ear. After doing so, Sabra looked at me surprised for touching her. "Why'd you do that?" asked Sabra. "Oh my God; I'm so sorry, Sabra, I didn't mean to touch you. I was just moving your hair away from your eyes so you can see better." I replied. "It's OK, thank you." said Sabra. "You're welcome." I replied. Sabra excused herself to have a cigarette.

I wanted strangle my hand for touching her. However, I decided beating my head against the metal shelving was a better idea. After a few knocks to my noggin, I composed myself and returned to investigating of the perpetrators who had set off the alarm. I kept searching the video recording on the week and day that the incident occurred. Sabra returned and walked past me and headed to the front counter of the pizzeria.

I attempted to refrain myself from glancing while she had walked past me. Some force was pushing my head toward her direction, as she had walked past me. I was staring at her aura emitting around her body and the strength of her thigh muscles. I have a fascination with the leg muscles since mine had functioned improperly for years. I thought maybe she could help me, perhaps whip me back into shape. She had strong thigh muscles that could kick anyone into next week. I shook my head from my daydream and continued with the video search. After a few moments, I was able to access the recordings and was shocked on what had happened. "That is impossible!" I shouted.

"What's impossible?" asked Sabra. I showed her the strange missing data for the week that the individuals had arrived at the pizzeria. "What do you mean?" asked Sabra. "This is our DVR system, I have been installing and programming them for over a year now. The DVR does not erase only specific days. You can only erase the whole recording on the hard drive or the hard drive would fail and not record any video at all."

I informed Sabra. What was strange about it was it had stopped just at the week of the occurrence and continued when I had arrived that day. Plus, the video was continuous without a pause, showing static, then recording again. "Hmmm, that is strange." I said. I was in fear that she was going to be angry at me thinking I deleted vital information. I had showed Sabra the impossible missing video recording that she had requested. "Where is it?" asked Sabra. "Look, the moment the door opened the video recorded static on the cameras viewing the door outside and in here, until they left." "How is that possible? Is it broken?" asked Sabra.

"I'm baffled myself; our DVR can either erase all data or the hard drive stops working and doesn't record any at all; you cannot choose what to erase. DVR's do not do that due to police investigations needing the full footage; you can't erase just portions of it." I replied. "Are you sure no one messed with the DVR to erase the video?" asked Sabra. "Well, unless you allowed someone to use your ladder; get above your drop ceiling, access the DVR without a monitor attached and guessed their way around the DVR settings to delete anything at all." I replied. Just then,

Baba's light bulb tuned on in my head. I remembered the supernatural event that happened to me in 1997 when Yahshua visited me. When I encountered Yahshua in Detroit during my childhood, He mentioned that He would return to see me, sometime before or after my forty-fourth birthday to heal me from my suffering. I was in her presence when Yahshua showed up; I was 41 years of age. While staring at Sabra, I thought to myself, "Oh Yah Alaha is she the one, Yah Eesho is she the one? You stood behind her, she is why you led me here?"

"Love finally filled my empty heart. Did Yahshua mean this day He would see me again? If you seek His Love, then you are seeking Yahshua, the messiah, the son man, our teacher, our big brother. He brings two hearts together to beat as one forever and ever with His Word of Love. What was I supposed to do, get on my knees and ask her to marry me the moment I gazed at her beauty? That would have landed me in the mental hospital if I would have explained to her who led me there. I had forgotten about my past intentions of sinning, my past life, my past sadness and misery of being alone.

All the worries had fallen off me when I had accepted His Grand Prize for keeping my Faith. He knew I was going to fall into the pit of adultery and never return. I was devoted from the beginning, and He saved me again from the worst disaster ever that I was going to commit. Yes, my wife and I had been separated for years, yet we were still legally – and in my case, morally – married. If I wanted to begin my life with Sabra, I had to follow through with my separated wife's request for a divorce.

I never cheated on any woman or betrayed any person who would hold Baba's commandments close to their hearts. I had told white lies in the past; however, I stopped my dagger from coming out of my mouth toward others without forgiveness, you may face doom; do not be prideful. I informed Sabra that I was unable to retrieve the video she requested due to it being supernaturally missing. "You mean I can't see who had entered the pizzeria the past week?" asked Sabra. "That's right, I'm sorry, the recording is missing."

I showed Sabra how the video recording was continuous with no skips in time frame. The recording showed static while still recording the supernatural occurrence, then back to normal video recording. If someone stopped recording manually, they would stop the recording briefly then continue recording. You would see time frame skip while viewing the recording. "I'm confused myself how this happened." I informed Sabra while keeping my composure from all the excitement tingling throughout my body from just being next to her.

Overwhelmed and excited; just to be this close to my beloved. She gives off such immense Loving energy, she is mightier than the largest Tesla coil. To avoid ruining this moment or frightening her away; I did not blurt out: "Sabra, you may think I am crazy, however I am your Soulmate," that would have ended my future with her. I was still trying to figure out exactly how to the recorded data was deleted while the other recordings from the previous days and today were still available. Due to required further investigation of verifying if the internet hard drive was malfunctioning.

I informed Sabra that I would have to take the DVR hard drive to see if I can install it in on another machine to verify that it was not the DVR at fault. In the meantime, I had instructed Sabra on a few shortcuts for a few applications on her laptop to make her work tasks easier and faster. "Would you like to get a cup of coffee someday; I can show you more features of the software on your laptop?" I asked. "Sure, that would be great." replied Sabra. I prayed silently to myself thanking my Father and Yahshua.

I figured I would start off slow and grow my rapport with this woman whom I was blessed to be with. I setup remote access on my phone to verify it worked correctly and to watch over my beloved if those individuals should decide to return for a second attempt during the day. I also setup remote access to the pizzeria on Sabra's phone and her laptop to view live feed. I assured Sabra I would keep an eye on the store while we figure out what happened to the recorded data. I wanted to help her and keep her safe for eternity.

I placed the DVR back atop the drop ceiling after removing the hard drive for further inspection. I met up with Sabra, who was taking a cigarette break outdoors behind the pizzeria. I noticed Sabra sitting in her vehicle while her girlfriend was standing next to her talking. I greeted her girlfriend I wanted to stay forever next to my beloved. I had quit smoking for quite a few years but wanted to stand by my Love, even if it meant dying slowly for her. So, I asked for a cigarette just to stay. It tasted disgusting, and I was getting dizzy from just one.

However, I was willing to die for her; what was one cigarette compared to years of suffering that I had endured without her? We talked for a little bit, then Sabra finished her cigarette and went back inside to take care of business. I still had my disgusting cigarette lit and conversed with her friend outside while trying not to vomit from the taste. Her friend had finished her cigarette before me and walked back into the pizzeria. I noticed Sabra was not coming back out, so I began to inhale the smoke stick quicker to get back to her.

Wow, big mistake after years of non-smoking; I should have just tossed the cigarette. I thought I was going to topple over right then and there. I gained clarity after a minute and entered the pizzeria. I had seen Sabra standing next to one of her employees and wanted to update progress of her DVR system. I walked into their conversation of who had what nickname when they were younger. "Hi, I'm Gandy." I said. "Hi, I know you from somewhere." asked the stranger. "You do, from where, I don't remember you." I asked.

"At your brother's home during one of his family gatherings; I'm Sabra's second cousin and your brother's brother-in-law is my uncle." said Sabra's second cousin. "Small world, cuz, nice to meet you." I replied. This was going to be easier than I had thought. She is so smart, beautiful, strong, loving, caring, full of life and energy. Courage and Yahshua led me to my beloved for my devotion to Him. Who would ask for anyone else when she would save my heart from the most severe earthly disaster. "Gandy, what is your nickname?" asked Sabra.

"My nickname, what do you mean?" I asked. "My friends and family took a few letters from my name and nicknamed me." replied Sabra. My thoughts were fumbling over each other trying to compose myself staring into her glorious galaxy green eyes. "Oh, like Gan or G, my friends called me those nicknames." I said. "No, how about a different nickname for you, can you think of one for me?" asked Sabra. After reciting a few nicknames for her, she disapproved of each one.

"Hmm, I am don't think of one at the moment, however I will let you know when I have one for you." I said. "Try to think one that will fit you." said Sabra. "Oh I know – can you say Jéjee?" I asked. She repeated my given name from My Father in Heaven who passed on to my mother and grandmother had given me when I was old enough to understand language. "Hmmm, Jéjee...Jéjee...not sure what do you think?" asked Sabra. "Nah, no good, think of something different." replied the cousin.

I look at him with disbelief while trying to bond with Sabra, like he was on a mission to sabotage our destiny to be as one flesh for Him. "Do you like my nickname, Sabra?" I asked. "Pick a different nickname!" shouted the cousin. "I think Jéjee is a very befitting nick name for me!" I shouted. I was staring at Sabra dreaming of the Love and Joy sounds from her of breath, calling me by my nickname when she needed me for anything, anytime, anywhere. "How about Gotti?" asked the cousin. "Gotti, what's a Gotti?" I asked. "What do you mean Gotti?" asked Sabra.

"You know, John Gotti, cause of his hair." said the cousin. After he explains who John Gotti was and what he stood for; I wanted to send him on his way for picking a name associated with the Italian mafia, a fucking criminal? "Nah, I don't think so; I don't want a nickname of a crook; pick something else." I said. "You say it, Sabra." said the cousin. "Gotti, Gotti, I'm not sure" replied Sabra. Since he changed her mind after I had given my nickname to my Love, I was frustrated. Yet, it was no matter; I was here and was grateful all the same to be near her that was all that mattered.

"What do you think, do you like it?" asked Sabra. I was imaging happiness every time she calls for me, even if she calls me any nickname she would choose for me; even if she agreed with a nickname of a thief, I'm not crook; however, I will steal her heart. "Gotti, Gotti...if you like it, I will." I informed my beloved. "You sure?" asked Sabra. "Yes, I am very, very sure, Sabra." I replied. I excused myself and headed back to Sabra's laptop and began to finish up the tasks that were still left.

After a few moments, Sabra came by and stood next to me while I informed her that I would need to take the DVR hard drive for further diagnostics. I explained to her I would return the DVR hard drive the following day. I was extremely proud of her intellectual abilities to learn given instructions rather quickly. "Well done Sabra, you're a fast learner, I'm proud of you." I told her. "Thanks, I do my best." replied Sabra. I reached out my hand to shake her hand and noticed my hand was extremely filthy from handling the drop ceiling and ladder.

I avoid spreading any germs or grime; from airborne or physical contact as much as possible. Cleanliness is close to Godliness; close to our Father's Kingdom in any situation; even an effort to remain clean is appreciated. Clean and cook for your loved ones to show your gratitude of their Love. Being clean also goes a long way in health and tranquility. Imagine Baba's kingdom; do you think dust exists there? Everlasting life starts with a clean heart and mind; the body follows suit.

With daily prayer to Yahshua, Baba will refuel your soul daily to combat the forces of evil. If all the church congregations prayed to the correct Messiah, we would have paradise on Earth much sooner.

Saving My Soul

Dust has no place in the kingdom of Baba; neither does anything else disgusting. My thoughts of infidelity and sin were dismissed from my mind and heart when I met my Soulmate Sabra.

I had a new mission in life, a new beginning, a mission that would lead my beloved and I to the stars in heaven. Memories of my mother immediately echoed in my mind of my true Love. I was not going to leave this woman's side even if the Earth cracked in half. I was at peace near my Love; in awe with her beauty. Astonished with her mental superiority toward her abilities as a professional. Her personality was making me giddy like a teenager having his first crush. I wanted to carry her and fly away and live our lives together happily ever after.

After Sabra reaches out her hand for a handshake, I noticed my filthy hands ready to dirty my beloved. "I'm sorry, my hands are dirty, let me go wash them." I said. "You don't have to, it's OK." replied Sabra. "Are you sure, they're dirty; I can go wash them it'll only take a couple of minutes." I insisted. "Yes I'm sure." said Sabra. I was unwilling to contaminate my flower with anything filthy; I wanted to keep her clean as close to godliness. "How about a hug instead?" I asked. "Hug?" asked Sabra. "Yes, just a friendly shoulder hug; here like this." I replied.

I gave Sabra my side shoulder to her side shoulder, a sibling hug for all the help she provided me. I felt a spark; then chills jolted me with more energy, Love and Faith. What she informed of next literally rocked my world. "Will you excuse me for a minute, I'll be right back?" asked Sabra. "Sure, I'll be right here." I replied. Moments later Sabra returned to give me some news that would rock my world.. "Gandy, may I talk to you personally?" asked Sabra. "Sure, you may ask you whatever you want." I replied. "Do you believe in Soulmates?" asked Sabra.

"Soulmates, of course." I agreed. "If I told you we are Soulmates; would you believe me?" asked Sabra. "We are? Are you serious, wow, you'd be an awesome soulmate." I said. "Are you serious, you would accept me as your wife?" asked Sabra. When Sabra said *wife*, I lost it. I wanted to cry and cry to empty my tears and drink from her lips to refill my dehydrated body. Staring at her eyes, I saw His Universe; her blessed existence was flowing through me for sustenance. "Oh yes; yes, I would want you as my wife, who wouldn't want you as their wife, they'd be crazy not to."

"I'm gonna rock your world, if we ever get together and get married." "Yes please; rock my world. When is this going to happen?" I asked. "Soon, but you have to go through some rough times before we do. Don't give up." instructed Sabra. "I would never give up on you." I said. "Don't. I won't give up either. Do you promise?" asked Sabra. "You have my Word; do you promise?" I asked. "I promise; there is one thing though." answered Sabra. "What's that?" I asked.

"You cannot contact me, or come see me, or argue with my brothers during that time." instructed Sabra. "Are you serious, I can't see you or talk to you?" I asked. "Yes, you have to wait. Can you do that?" asked Sabra. "Yes, I can, I don't want to lose you." I said filling my eyes with tears. "You won't; I don't want to you lose you either." replied Sabra teary eyed. After hearing Sabra inform me of my close future and take an oath of Faith; we were sealed as one flesh. We awaited our reunion with the help from our Father, Son and the Holy Spirit.

She wanted to excuse herself for a moment; however, I gently grabbed her arm, as she began to walk away. Slowly; my hand rubbed her arm until reaching her hand and fingers tips, as though I was holding on to my dear life falling away from my beloved. I startled His glorious angel in doing so. "Wait, no, please don't go!" I shouted gently holding her arm. "Hey, no, it's OK, I'll be right back, I promise." said Sabra. "OK, I'm sorry for holding you like that, I didn't mean to scare you." I reassured her.

"It's OK, wait here I'll be right back; I just have to find out something." instructed Sabra. "OK I'll wait here." After a few moments, Sabra returned to stand next to me and continued foreseeing my future. She let me know that she had the abilities of a superhuman; at lease that was my interpretation of my hero of the household. "You're going to scratch your chest with your fingernail or something sharp into a shape heart, a letter I and a letter U and I would get your scratch on my chest." informed Sabra.

"Scratch my chest in a heart, are you serious, how?" I asked. I did not allow her to touch me at first, I was so dumb, however; I did not know what would happen if I did. She attempted to touch my chest to show me how I was going to engrave a heart shape and letters on my chest. "Wait, stop, what are you doing?" I surprisingly asked. "I was trying to show you how you were going to do that." replied Sabra. "You can show me on your chest." I said. "Like this heart, this letter I and the letter U." instructed Sabra.

"Oh I see, when I do that you would get the imprint on your chest from me?" I asked. "Yes." replied Sabra. "Wow that's wonderful; weird, but wonderful." I said. "Can I do something else?" requested Sabra. "What?" I asked. "Can I touch your face?" asked Sabra. "My face, why?" I asked. "Because I want to remember the shape of your face." replied Sabra. "That's weird." I said. "It's OK; sorry I brought it up." said Sabra. "No, no, I want you to, you can rub your hands on my face." I said. "OK, you ready?" asked Sabra. "Ready; wait, are your hands clean?" I asked.

"Clean, wait, I'll go wash them right now." replied Sabra. "OK." I said. "Ok I'm back; ready?" asked Sabra. "I'm ready." I replied. "OK, I'm going to run my palms down your face." instructed Sabra. "OK." I replied. Sabra gently rubs her soft hands on my face and I feel as though Heaven is touching my face; the gentle rub of everlasting Love. Sabra rubbed her hands along my face and awoke my hungry spirit with her everlasting Love. "How'd that feel?" asked Sabra. "That felt great, could you do that again, please." I requested. "Again, OK." said Sabra. When Sabra began to rub her palms down my check, I gently held her hands and kissed both of her palms. "Why'd you do that?" asked Sabra. "I'm sorry for scaring you, felt like the right thing to do. Your hands feel good on my face, do you want to try again? I asked. "Next time, I promise I'll rub your face every day." said Sabra. "That sounds great, I'll look forward to your caresses." I said. "There's something else too; hold on I'll be right back." instructed Sabra. "There is, what?" I asked. "You're an important person, and you're going to do something very important.

You're going to find out who you are." said Sabra. "Who I am?" I asked. "A saint." replied Sabra. "Say what? A saint, I'm not saint." I replied. "Yes you are; I don't know which one, but you are." informed Sabra. "Wow, this is a lot to take all at once." I said. "I know, tell me about it." said Sabra. She absolutely shocked me out of my socks with her statement. Saint, soulmate, beloved wife, her yummy palms, what else? I needed to take the DVR hard drive to a different DVR at our office and verify if the pizzeria DVR was at fault.

"Sabra, I'm almost done here, I need the hard drive to take with me and I'll contact you tomorrow about the video status." I informed her. "OK, thank you." she replied. "You're welcome." I left the pizzeria with the DVR hard drive that had the missing data of the intrusion and the visitors. I informed my business partner of the impossible missing data and we both confirmed that the DVR had no issues. We also confirmed that the pizzeria hard drive was functioning properly and the missing data was a result of a supernatural phenomenon.

However, I already knew who had erased the specific data. He showed up to save me in 1997 and again in 2014. In my case, Yahshua stood before us and behind us. I remembered when I asked my mother that Eesho would have to approve my soulmate. In this case; He allowed me to witness His daughter standing before me with all of His might residing within her. My Sabra, my Soulmate, my Beloved, my Caro, my Princess awaiting my arrival to slay the dragon of this world and set her free.

Embrace me my Love so that I may feel our Father's Love; forevermore. I explained to my business partner that Sabra was my soulmate. The following day, I arrived with the hard drive to complete the project from the day before. I saw her again, and she was just as eternally beautiful as the day I meet her. Who can work for hours in an environment near heat, grease and food and still look blessed; Sabra can. We greeted each other, and I refrained from shaking her hand because I wanted to stay focused.

I was trying to avoid losing concentration when I stood next to her; noticing her aura emitting from her existence. I knew she was the one I was going to be with for eternity. I wanted to take it slow and speak of Love gradually, not blurt out my feelings for her and frightening her away. I would visit her socially every day, to look into her eyes and see my Baba Alaha's Holy Kingdom. Her Glorious Galaxy Green Eyes of Divine Truth embraced my soul with every glance. I would have purchased pizza every day from her to continuously see my beloved and fill my soul.

I never knew true Love could feel this way just after seeing my Sabra for the first time from renown. I did not know I should have waited to engage in close physical contact with my genuine, one of a kind Soulmate. Just like in Yahshua's case, there a forbidden touch in effect until a hug is requested then let the ceremony begin. Sabra is an angelic woman sent to Earth by Baba.

She is the Beat of My Heart

When Baba made woman for man, He also created true Love for the man. Her true Love will light His way for me; to find her in the dark maze of this world. I can see her soul and inhale her Love from across the Universe and arrive to her rescue. If you are seeking true Love by way of Truth and Faith, be patient and He will guide you to her supper. It felt wonderful seeing my beloved once more; her beauty will resonate throughout the Universe. Her glorious emerald green eyes are more precious than the most valued gem on this planet and beyond.

I wanted to run my fingers through her hair all day long and forget my worries. I would massage her every aching muscle every day to relieve her of any daily stress. I would be her personal bodyguard for eternity, defending her honor with any wrongful touch. A Divine Soulmate is blessed in every way, born on this Earth to spread His True Love to inspire Faith in all. Love is an immense vibration of joy flowing through the body tickling every fiber of your soul when you embrace each other.

Love is a calm feeling when the two unite to show their eternal Love for each other who were meant to be from the beginning. Sabra, your blood floweth through my heart and pumps my life source within me forevermore. Upon arriving at Sabra's pizzeria, I installed the hard drive into the DVR and used Sabra's laptop to access the DVR's settings for programming through the internal network. I had informed Sabra that the missing recording was irretrievable due to the strange selective static interference.

After about an hour of work, I had completed my task and educated Sabra on how to use the DVR program on her laptop for viewing video recordings remotely. She was pleased with me and that was more refreshing than drinking ice cold water in a hot desert. I wanted nothing from her other than allowing her to jump into my heart so that I may live. "Thank you so much, Gandy, how much do I owe you?" asked Sabra. "Oh no, it's OK, no worries, just pay for the hard drive and that's it." I replied.

I refused to accept money from her for my labor, for she was my sustenance giving me strength to labor for her. I finally surrendered to her demands and agreed to charge her labor. Since it was my decision of how much to collect; I chose to invoice her one-hour worth of labor instead of six hours. "No, that's not fair, you should get paid for your time you spent working here; I'm going to contact your boss to find out you guys charge for labor." said Sabra. "Oh-no, oh-no, please Sabra, it's OK, I'm serious, it's my time, I can charge what I want; I just want to help you." I insisted.

She made a phone call to my business partner to confirm the amount and returned to agree to the price of the equipment being replaced. "Tell me what I owe you for your time, Gandy." asked Sabra. I felt butterflies in my stomach; I wanted nothing monetarily from her, just her preciously priceless Love. She insisted oh paying me monetarily; me; pay me monetarily? Lean forward and drink from my lips with yours my Beloved, I will be paid in full infinitely.

"Fine, since you insist on paying me; then I will only charge you $50 for the five hours, since it's my decision on how much I should charge for my time." I said. After her disagreement in regards to all fairness of my compensation, I finally agreed and she wrote me a check for my services. I felt sad with guilt because I wanted no payment from her, only her Love in my arms. I would give her what she needed and much more. I would ease her pain every day and night and reassure Sabra that our Love would conquer any obstacle that would get in our way.

We would beautify our surroundings with His Word, Love and our Faith. I would show her the secrets of the universe and Yahshua would guide us to Him. I would educate her with the knowledge that I had gained from His hug in 1997, the day Yahshua arrived to me. I would teach her the ways of my Big Brother of True Love, would show her my Faith. I would stand by her side if the Earth shook and the skies fell. I would spread my wings and lift her to safety with My Father's name on my forehead.

I would embrace the Universe within my beloved as she was from the very breath of my Father Baba. We would count the stars as we pass by each planet in our starship; exploring the galaxies within her eyes. The essence that Sabra provided is my sustenance to thy soul. She would bring new meaning to every Word that I exhaled to her from the bottom of my heart to my last breath. True Love will overcome any hatred, bitterness, daggers or any other wrongful actions this world may throw at us.

My Pure Love – Pure Joy – Pure Soul

True Love will be our shield against any entity that will attempt to stop our Love for each other, for we will prevail with His Word and inherit the Earth and Galaxy. Everyone around the world shall read the story of our unity that conquered every doubtful thought on this planet. My services were complete and it was time to leave; I was praying I would see her again. I kept my professional composure; so, I thoroughly washed my hands to present them clean to my Queen.

"Well, we're all set Sabra, if there's anything else you need, please don't hesitate to call me for help." I said. "Is that it, is it all good, is the DVR system is working fine?" asked Sabra. "Yes, everything is working fine, and you'll be able to access the system remotely." I replied. "That's great." she complemented. "Everything is all good; it was a pleasure meeting you Sabra, thank you so much for all your help." I said. That's it?" asked Sabra. "What's it, yes, I washed my hands; see they are clean, what do you mean?" I asked. "Just a hand shake, that's it?" she grinned.

"What do you mean, my hands are clean, look see, I promise." I replied. "You know what, forget it, just forget it!" shouted Sabra. "No wait, what, no it's not it, don't leave!" I yelled. "Tell me Sabra, tell me what you want from me, I'll do it!" I shouted. "How about a hug, can I get a hug?" asked Sabra. I was praying, *Oh Alaha, Yah Eesho help me, should I touch her again, what will happen this time? I'm dead, I'm seriously going to die if I hug this woman right now.* Oh my heart was pounding more vigorous than a hummingbird's when Sabra requested a hug, just like Yahshua did that historic day.

"Come here, can I get a hug?" asked Sabra. "Are you serious, right now, look, my hands are clean." I said like a dum-dum. My beloved's face had saddened; I was about to lose my soul and drown in the deep sea of emptiness. I looked up, and closed my eyes... "Yah, Alaha help me; OK, I'll hug you. Both hands or should I hold my briefcase in my hand, should I set it down?" I asked. It's up to you." replied Sabra. "OK, I'll hand to it; you ready?" I asked. "Yes, I'm ready." said my True Love.

I inhaled her Love and exhaled my worries, made the sign of the crucifix on my chest and head then jumped into her sea of Love. Sabra lifted up her arms to wrap them around my neck while I embraced her waist holding her close and tight. Our heads touched, and we snuggled into position to hold each other for eternity. Oh my Love, you are so peaceful, so calm, as though we had disappeared into another time. I was unable to hear our surroundings anymore, just her heart beating upon my chest.

Oh the feeling, oh the emotion, the glorious touch of an angel who stops the fabric of time and eternally Loves you with all her might. Her creation as a woman has no equal in the Universe, for her eyes sees the Love of my Father, and there rests her glorious soul who feeds me forevermore. Her embrace took us to our own Galaxy where we ruled for our Father. The uniting of two souls bread from Our Father's hand sets forth a check-mate throughout the Universe. His winning move of everlasting Love conquers forever and ever. "Oh Sabra, I missed you so much." I whispered.

"Mmmmmm" hummed Sabra. During our embrace I felt her get startled. "Don't let go!" shouted Sabra. "I won't; don't worry, I got you." I assured my Yum-Yum. She tightened her hug while I embraced her close and tight. We touched our heads together and become as one once more; forevermore. I was embracing my Father's Love and felt his grace. Oh how her heart felt glorious beating at my chest. We were in His Universe, motionless as our hearts stopped time. Oh my Love, you are so peaceful, so calm, as though we had teleported to another time with our embrace.

I was unable to hear our surroundings anymore, just felt her heart beating next to mine. As our one soul was becoming two; we returned from our engagement to prepare for our Holy Ceremony. ~ **BANG**! ~ Aaaarrrahhh! yelled the pizzeria staff. We were startled apart from our eternal connection. I am unsure what it was, perhaps someone in the pizzeria that had banged something on the metal counters located in the back. "What was that loud noise?" I asked.

"Don't know, sounded like someone was screaming." replied Sabra. "Could've of been the lady in the back chopping up some vegetables, perhaps?" I asked. "Don't know; how did it feel...our hug?" asked Sabra. "It was good, great to be exact." slurring my words as I gazed into her galaxy eyes. There were no words I was able to share with my beloved Sabra; no language on Earth has no expression of feeling of soulful Love. No sound justifies His Word of her creation for my eternal sustenance. His drink are her lips to my soul, His food beats within her heart for my joyous fullness.

I answered her question looking into her eyes. Her glorious green eyes opened His window for me to the Universe. I wanted to kiss her forevermore. "How did it feel for you?" I asked. "Like we fit." said Sabra. "That's great, I agree." I relied. "That's it, just *great*?" asked Sabra. "We fit like a glove...like a glove." I replied. My gaga-goo-goo mental calibration was unable to form words. My tongue had been shocked with the energy of her soul.

Her eyes, her green pasture eyes were kissing my heart, and I wanted to become her Sheppard to our flock. As we pulled our heads away from each other, our lips were close...oh so close. Our noses could have rubbed like Eskimos. When Sabra caressed my hair; her touch curled my toes with the euphoria of Heavenly Love. Looking upon thee, I witnessed the gates of heaven open up to let me in. Oh my Love, we blended our spirit to form His loving color of Truth, Faith, Courage, Love and justified His Word. I leaned forward to drink from her lips; she leaned back, we were not ready to wed...yet.

"What do we do now?" I asked. "Should we let go?" asked Sabra. "I'm not sure." I replied. "I guess we can let go now." she instructed. I did not want to let go of her, I did not want half my heart to let go. Her embrace was like fresh spring water in the scorching desert. Her aura was drawing me near to His Truth. Sabra's voice was like my echo I would listen to her songs for eternity. "OK, did you hear that loud noise?" I asked. "What was it?" asked Sabra.

"I don't know, I had my eyes closed when we were hugging." I replied. "I'm not sure either." said Sabra. "Did you kick the metal counter next to you with your foot?" I asked. "No I didn't." she replied. "Maybe the lady behind you cutting up the vegetables made that loud noise?" I asked. "Did you make that loud noise just now, with your knife or anything else? asked Sabra. "No, not me, I am cutting tomatoes." replied the staff member. "Wasn't her." said Sabra. Unsure what the loud noise was; we sadly had to say good-bye.

"If you need anything else, please call me anytime." I informed beloved soul. "OK, I will, thank you again, Gandy." she replied. "You are most welcome Sabra; it was my pleasure serving you." I said. "It was a pleasure meeting you as well Gandy " I turned and walked toward the front door and prayed: 'Yah Alaha will I ever see her again?' We had known each other for only twelve hours sharing stories, advice and our loving bond with each other. I felt her past when our bodies and mind were as one.

Feeling disappointed in myself after leaving; I do not know why I was unable to tell her about how my mother described her. Maybe that was too soon; maybe I would have scared her away? I knew she was the woman Eesho approved of; the one my mother excited me with. The next day, I was metaphorically hitting my head on the wall because of the information I withheld to unite two genuine divine Soulmates. So, out of desperation I ended up texting Sabra. OK, for all of you who are seeking, take my first and last advice, "Do not text your beloved with a cell phone to express your Love."

I was ignorant; I sent a text messages to my Love stating we are Soulmates, met Yahshua in 1997, and needed to speak to her before it was too late. Imagine someone you just met reading that text; they would think this person is crazy. Yes, my cake went flat; I received rejection from my beloved. I felt like I had lost my life for good; I felt a part of me just died. I began to phone my angelic Love multiple times, no answer. I wanted to climb the highest mountain and jump off without a parachute.

Lost in Love and shocked that I was lacking Courage to phone my Love and tell her the Truth instead of texting her. I was unable to function properly from lack of food, lack of sleep, lack of energy, lack of Sabra. Other than my mother, I had never felt a bond for a woman so strong in unconditional Love. I was determined to win her heart as my dad had reminded me would happen. However, I had no idea how I would do that. I survived on prayers and Faith for my true Love.

I prayed for Divine intervention to help me succeed with my Quest for Love with my beloved Sabra. I never was going to give her up, for Yahshua was with me whenever I needed His help. She is the clarity to my sanity, the remedy to my insanity. She is my natural Love drug that soothes my aches and pains of my lonely broken heart. Her presence brightens the saddest days and lifts my spirit.

Crazy in Love

Sabra; you give my heart peace and Love on Earth or anywhere in the Universe.

My only chance was to seek help from a higher power beyond my control on this matter of Love of the soul. I was a soul lost at sea looking for Sabra's beacon to guide me home. The seas were rough and my beloved had turned off her light because of my arrogance. I had to hear her voice once more, I had to explain myself or I would lose her for good, I would drift into loss of her Love into darkness. I was at my office, thinking how I can reach my beloved without her avoiding my calls. I despise deception; I am neither jester nor fool.

However, I was a fool in Love and was in fear of losing my bread for someone else to consume. I had used our office phone to dial Sabra, praying she answer to her hear angelic voice. Dear Baba, it is her, help me Baba, help me say something to her, give me the Courage. "Hi, who is this?" asked Sabra. "Hi Sabra, it's me Gandy; do you have time on your hands, I need to speak to you." I replied. "Where are you calling me from, I haven't seen this number before; whose number are you calling from?" asked Sabra.

"I'm at my office using my friend's phone; you weren't answering my calls. I had to reach you to tell you something." I explained. "What'd you want to tell me?" asked Sabra. "This may sound a bit crazy, but my mom told me about you and meeting you; she said you are my Soulmate." I informed her. "OK, that's it, I am hanging up now, I have no time for this shit, I'm no one's Soulmate, you're crazy, it was just a hug." fumed Sabra. "Oh God, oh no; wait-wait, please wait, don't hang up, stay on the phone with me."

I moved the phone away from my ear and held it to my broken heart as I prayed; Yah Alaha please help me, what am I going to do. "I didn't want to scare you away; I didn't mean to hurt your feelings. It's a long story; I just wanted to talk to you over some coffee." I sadly said. "First you text me to be safe as I leave the pizzeria while watching me over the cameras; then you text me about me being your Soulmate. Sounds to me like you're stalking me; I am hanging up now and calling your boss." demanded Sabra.

"Oh no, oh please wait, Sabra, stay on the phone with me, please. I was only trying to help you because your business was broken into, and I just wanted to look after you. How can you say it was just a hug, didn't you feel anything between us? Then why did you not want to shake my hand and wanted a hug instead? I was trying to be professional, but you requested a hug, and I said yes." I explained to Sabra. "I was just trying to be friendly." she replied. I was crushed. My ship had slammed into a giant iceberg, tearing a large hole in my heart and I was sinking rapidly.

"I'm done, I'm going to hang up now and call your boss!" yelled Sabra. With my head hung low I was drained; I had to agree to my Love's demands as I replied sadly. "OK Sabra." She hung up the phone with me, and I sat down at my desk avoiding tears just in case anyone had come into the office. A few moments later, my business partner had called me trying to find out what happened and I had explained everything to him. My partner stated that I was accessing their DVR system and watching the pizzeria.

"Yes, I was just trying to keep an eye on her, just in case anything else happens, I was just trying to help her." I said. "Well, I am heading over there now because they want me to change their passwords on their DVR system." replied my business partner. "That's fine; as a matter of fact, I will delete my DVR app right now, I'm done." I replied. Before my partner finished talking, I had one more application to delete. I was about to remove the app used to watch over my beloved whom Yahshua had led me to.

I accessed Sabra's DVR system one last time praying she was there so that I may see my Love before I would forget her beauty. Upon accessing the system, my heart was once more beating for survival when she appeared on the screen. I had to think fast and had taken a few still shots of my beloved to save on my cell phone. I then deleted the DVR application on my phone for good. I was heartbroken. I ruined it; I was such an idiot. While saving her image into my mind for eternity, I received a call from my brother Sandy.

I had mentioned to my brother about my Soulmate that I had found. I informed him of the name our mother had provided for me. "Hi bro, how's it going?" I asked. "How's it going; how's it going huh, what did you do, do you know what you just did?" asked Sandy. "Did what did I do?" I asked. "You know who I just got off the phone with?" asked my brother. "No, I have no idea who you got off the phone with; tell me." I replied. "I told you to wait; I told you to slow down. I asked you don't text her; they have a family emergency.

I couldn't reach them to get you answers you needed!" shouted my brother. I was unaware that Sabra's relative was ill in the hospital. I stumbled over untied shoe lasses; rushing into her arms. I was such a fool in Love unable to wait for help from others. "Now her brother, who owns the pizzeria, wants to file harassment charges, stalking charges, and anything else they could think of. Even your so-called best friend Netman called you crazy for thinking that girl was your Soulmate." explained my brother.

"No-no-no, why, I was only trying to help, I was just trying to look after her. Let him try to press charges, I will press charges for false accusations. Why are they doing this to me!" I yelled. "Because you jump in without looking first, because you can't wait and wanted to find out yourself without anyone's help. Now it looks like you lost it or her. Good job, bro!" shouted Sandy. "Shit, what am I supposed to do now? I didn't mean to disrespect her or her family." I said.

"If you want her, then go get her, but you need cold hard facts that she is your soulmate to prove your point." instructed my brother. "How am I supposed to prove my point with cold hard facts when mom is gone?" I asked. After a few minutes, our conversation was over, and we hung up. I slammed my cell phone on my desk in tears, and then I got another phone call. "Hi, this is Gandy; how can I help you?" I asked. "Yes, is this Gandy; OK good; this is Sabra's brother." replied her brother. "Oh hi, how are you, listen I just wanted to apologize for..." I said.

"Listen bro, I need you to stop calling my sister. If you need anything, you can get a hold of me instead." said Sabra's brother. "I just wanted to explain myself to her over a cup of coffee that was all, honestly." I formed him. "Did you hear me? Do not call Sabra. Do you understand?" asked Sabra's brother. I had no choice, she loved him more than she loved me. She thought I was crazy; she thought I was stalking her. I thought I had lost her for good, I felt like I was doomed for the rest of my life. "Yes, I understand." I replied.

We both hung up the phone, and I was done, burnt to a crisp and ready to be thrown into the trash because no one believed His Truth. Why did I do that what am I going to do now. Was she unable feel my Love for her, was she unable to see our future together, why did she fear me so quickly after our hug connected us? I was a bit chubby, yet she still hugged me; I was a mess, yet she still touched me. I was lost, yet Yahshua guided me and stood behind her; He showed me the way to Love again. I was willing to exchange my life or sacrifice anything to get her back.

That is what He meant in regards to sacrifice, I will exchange everything unhealthy in my life in exchange for her Love forever. Eureka! I also will kill the demon that gripped my life for so many years and never let me go. My longtime deceitful temptation for over twenty years was Mary J. The demon that seduces your mind, the one that entered your life for so long, must be sacrificed. I still had bad influences clinging onto my life and had to let everyone and everything go. I had to change my life completely from the inside out.

I had to prove my point with cold hard facts for her. I needed to erase my past to begin a new future with my beloved Sabra. Ever since I was seventeen years old, the demon clung on and tempted me for more than twenty years. Avoid drugs, alcohol, bad influences, bad habits and just outright wicked behavior enter your life and take control. If not, you are going to crash and may never recover or lose them. However, if you crash and are unable to get back up, you know what to do you right? You know, remember, remember?

The Big Guy, remember? Have you always wanted to ask someone for advice? Have you ever begged someone to help you up after you have failed so many times? Have you ever prayed to guide your next step before falling into the bottomless pit? Crashing brings out the worst and the best in us humans. We have to learn from what we have done in the past to avoid repeating the mistakes of our future. Humans have such a short memory span, even if a person spoke with you just moments ago. They would forget what they had watched on the news within a week.

How strong do you think their Faith can carry them from the time of understanding His Love? How many times do you remind your children to remember what you had instructed them to do? Each person has to look within themselves for the energy and belief that is required to survive in this world with His Word. Make the choice, make the decision, follow through and get a hole in one. Avoid jumping into the bottomless pit that you may never be unable to climb out of.

If you are cautious, listen to the advice of others that have experienced your situation, you may have a chance to avoid the struggle, disaster or mistake you are about to make in your life. If you become stubborn and make your own decisions thinking nothing will happen to you. Then be prepared for your hardship; your hardship in life. I found her; I touched her, when I should have resisted doing so. But, I had to; Yahshua stood behind her, and she is glorious. When Yahshua came to me in the year 1997, I had to reach out and touch Truth, Love and Faith.

I had to reach out and hug her as I hugged my Big Brother. She would rock my world, be there in the morning for my hugs and kisses, the one who I will sing to, serenading her sweet soul to sing along. My prayers were answered when Sabra and I met, bonding with our first hug. Breakfast is ready my Love, rise and shine. Allow my Father to speak to me through your eyes, caressing your soft lips upon mine, nourishing my soul with your breakfast, lunch and dinner heart.

You are dessert forevermore, my baklava. Baba created thy Love, for thy shall never thirst nor hunger any more, forevermore. Yahshua shown your heart to mine; let us beat to the sound of His Love drum as one. The tone of your voice, my Love, shall sing along with Baba's angels whom shall follow your harmony in a choir of His Truth and Love. Yahshua's everlasting Love will guide us to His kingdom hand in hand showing the way to all we follow knowing Faith and His Word.

CHAPTER 19

The Fast

I prayed to Yahshua and Baba for her touch, our embrace, our lips to be everlasting. I could never live without her after He led me to her. My mind hand her thoughts, her aches and pains I felt, her gentle touch reminded me of heaven. She would complete me with every breath I take day or night. Sabra's essence is like Father's everlasting tree of life who would be my loving sustenance even after the end of time and forevermore.

True Soulmates have the most glorious feeling; with every thought of their existence, they sense each other. I will feed her my life source eternally: "Yah Alaha, Yah Eesho, I will give up everything you ask for, I will cleanse my soul for you. I am grateful for your Truth in my arms, her Love in my soul. Sabra; to be mine for eternity, I beg of you." I prayed to my beloved Father and my beloved Brother. He gave me a visit to remember, a mission to accept without fail, a Quest to change the world; should I accept.

Yahshua said to me, "I am here for you; everything will be OK." when he met me in the flesh in 1997. I knew I would win; my Brother never lies for Baba is Truth from the beginning and never-ending. I set out on my quest to transform myself from within to be a shepherd; like a beacon of Faith for my beloved, for my teacher, for my Heavenly Father, for my family and friends, the dragon slayer of the world.

Yahshua was about the offer me a position that no other human should ever pass – a position with T.H.E.M – a part of the Holy Trinity's organization. His Solider of Truth-Justice-Courage; a man of Faith and Love like no other in the Universe for eternity. I rolled three marijuana joints for what was about to happen to me, to ease the pain for my initiation into the Holy Trinity, the transformation for the Quest. Please; do not associate marijuanna with Yahshua; nor what I personally went through, nor is this part to inspire you to smoke marijuanna thinking your going to meet Archangels. Do not!

I smoked to ease the pain, however, this last smoke was the last to fast my body, mind annd soul. The demons did not want me go through the fasting process and quit smoking. The night felt unimaginably horrifyingly terrible for the demons knew what was about to happen to the world. The fallen were battling with Baba's Archangels to stop my initiation. I gave my Faith and Love to my Father and Brother to guide and protect me during the transformation process. I left behind everyone that was still smoking marijuana, I left everything in the past, I demanded that anyone that would get close to me to avoid touching me.

I fasted for one week, eating bread and water and giving up any unhealthy foods entering my body. I loved more, cared more, strengened more; living for His cause who my Love Yahshua set me out to complete. I was a new man, a different breed, a better, stronger, faster Jéjee. I was forty-one years young and looked and felt like an Archangel. I had disciplined myself with Yahshua's guidance.

Forever grateful for His Love, I wanted to please Him, I desired His Love forevermore, His Word for eternity. His crew reminded me of my destiny, constantly following me every step of my way. Speaking from HisWord to my heart. My surroundings were filled with clues and guides toward my next step closer to my Soulmate and my destiny. I lost unwanted pounds, vulgar thoughts, unhealthy living and gained more knowledge to focused and fine tuned my Baba-gifted abilities. I will also remember the Words of Truth fromYahshua had said to me in His own words in 1997: "You will be fast, strong and much more."

I was yet to find out what "and much more" meant when My Big Brother spoke to me. Nonetheless, I am extremely grateful for your hug Eesho, for you advise us, for you Love us, for you grace us with your mercy. I am joyous for Yahshua being there for me, to be accepted into His life. I refused to crack or go insane as most people would think. I am His Dragon Slayer; there is no cracking or hacking me for I subdue the matrix.

I am the Saint who pierces the hearts of evil, initiated into Baba's elite crew of Truth, Justice, Courage, Faith and Love. I am His to command at any given moment. Everyone who accepts His Quest or path within their hearts and life, must sacrifice to succeed. You must suffer to show how much you Love Him. You must endure the pain as Yahshua indured pain inflected upon him. You must be brave before you accept your Quest, having no fear during your journey. Choose your path to Truth and Courage, and you may also be the metaphorical Neo who helps humanity unplug from the lie.

You can follow His Word and shine your heart in the darkness of society or within your own family. Be the Peacekeeper and the Warrior of your household, unconditionally loving and forgiving all members. I am infinietly grateful for being accepted to His Quest. I am no Evangelist, I am Jéjee, The Dragon Slayer, born by His Word. I live my life in Truth, Justice, Courage, Faith and Love. How will you live your life? When will you show him your Courage and Faith?

CHAPTER 20

Ignorant Daggers

When will you express your Love how He wants you to express your Love to everyone else? Now is the time before it is too late; jump into His Truthful ocean and swim to Yahshua's shore for some on time. Walk with His son on the sands of time to speakwith your heart.Accepting the Quest from Baba is a very high honor before your graduation by your teacher, Yahshua the Messiah, guiding you through life along the way.

He will grade you on the compassion you have for others that despise you, treated you harshly or took advantage of you. You must study to forgive the ones who betrayed you. You must excel to the top of your class and become the valedictorian of Love. When you drink from His cup, you will have the Word within your heart ready for the big test to you may pass and graduate. After my initiation to Baba's elite crew, I had instructed my family and friends to refrain from touching me, even the children and elders.

I was to wait until my beloved and I are finally reunited. Then, blessings will be spread to all who truly have His Faith within their hearts. Some, however, are reluctant to keep their hands to themselves after specific instructions. I forbid my own flesh and blood family from touching me. I was heartbroken over why I had to do that, especially after so many years of affection giving and receiving. I wanted to surprise her, perhaps maybe then she will say yes to joining me for a cupof coffee. I set out to acquire a chariot for my beloved rather than just any vehile.

There are vehicles and there are chariots, I prefer chariots for rescuing my damsel in distress. What better chariot than an exotic chariot near a local dealership for my first attempt – a 2014 Lamborghini Galardo. "Good afternoon, name's Gandy; forgive me, I can't shake your hand at the moment. I see you only have one model in your showroom, where are the others?" I asked. "Good afternoon, the owners of the dealership are bringing in newer models to fill the showroom later today." replied Lou.

"Oh I see, how about this one?" I asked. "Are you interested in purchasing one today?" asked Lou. "Perhaps; I would like to test drive her first, I want to get to know my car much better." I smiled from within thinking of my beloved Sabra. "Yum", my beloved's nickname from my heart, my mother's breath, and His Word. Why Yum; you may ask? Have you ever eaten your favorite food? How did you feel when your tongue spoke to your brain? Do you hunger for your beloved to drink for her or his lips? Yum.

"That model has been paid for already and is expected to be picked up." informed Lou. "OK, that's fine, how about the Maserati that are in the next door showroom?" I asked. "Tell me, what are you planning to do; maybe I can help you pick the right one?" questioned Lou. "Where shall I begin? Let me tell you a story of meeting and hugging Yahshua." I finished telling my story of my encounter with our Teacher in 1997 and my Quest to win the heart of my beloved Sabra.

The Lamborghini sales manger was teary-eyed and eager to help me in any way possible.

"You don't need a Lamborghini to pick up your soulmate. You need something more luxurious than speed in your Quest for Love." said Lou. "I'm not sure what you mean; these aren't good enough for my beloved?" I asked. "If you want don't want to feelevery bump on the road in these chariots, you need something much smoother, more to her liking." Instructed Lou. "What do you have in mind?" I asked.

"Go see the sales manager at the Aston Martin dealership; he will have what you need in your Quest for Love." replied Lou. I wanted to hug him for all his help, however refrained and extended my hand in friendship brotherhood for believing in Yahshua and His cause. "Thank you so much for your help, have a great day." We shook hands, and I set off to the Aston Martin dealership to speak to the sales manager there. Upon arrival, I noticed the sales manager sitting at his desk typing away on his keyboard.

He approached me to shake my hand, and I hesitated, placed my palms together as to pray and explained. "Whatever you do, don't touch me in any way; I will explain myself later. In the meantime, show me what you have available." I instructed the Aston Martin sales manager. "We have these models available." said the sales manager. He pointed at the Aston Martin Rapide S. "This is the Aston Martin Rapide S; costs $238,000; here is the convertible model cost a little bit more." explained the sales manager.

"Hmm, they're nice, I prefer the hardtop model though; what's the name of that model?" pointing at a 4 door model. "Oh that's the Vanquish, cost $280,000." replied the sales manager. The sales manager explained the different models and features in the Aston Martin showroom. They were all nice machines; yet were they good enough for my Queen to sit in? "They all look great, I'll look around, and if I need something I'll call for you." I told the sales manager. "Take you time; I need to finish up some paperwork in my office." he replied.

There were a couple of convertible Aston Martin chariots that did not suit the special occasion. The one that I needed was called the

Aston Martin Rapide S. The cost of that hunk of metal is worthless compared to His Word and Her Love. There was also another chariot that was hiding toward the back of the showroom. It was called The Vanquish; that was for another occasion, and I decided to ask my Father for that one, too, for our Quest. I had asked the Aston Martin salesman for the keys to the Repide S to see the interior dash light up. The salesman, however, turned into a liar and out came his dagger from his orifice.

"I'm not surewhere the keys are; someone must have taken them. I'll see if I can find it for you." He replied quickly reaching for his desk drawer pretending to search for the keyfob. The dumbass salesman thought I had never been to a dealership before. After inspecting the Auston Martin Rapide S interior for comfort, I leaned over to the passenger seat and imagined, " You look gorgeous my Love; how are you guys doing back there, are you enjoying your ice cream?"

Feeling the moment I wanted to experience in reality; I stepped out of the Rapide S and headed over to the sales manager. "Did you get a chance to find the keys to the Rapide; I just want to see the interior light up." I waited patiently. "No I'm still looking." replied the sales manager. I was sitting in the winged chariotte while also oberserving and waiting for the sales joker. After almost thirty minutes of waiting, I wanted to request a test drive. Perhaps he wanted me to sound a bit more serious about his rustable piece of junk.

"Hey, sorry to bother you, I would like to test drive the Rapide S; do you think that would be possible?" I asked. "Sure, that would be fine, I need to make a copy of your driver's license beforehand." replied the sales manager. I handed him my business card along with my drivers license. He made copies of them and returned my ID and proceeded to look up a few things on his screen, perhaps looking up my credentials. If the sales manager only knew how important my credentials were he would be ecstatic to aid me on my Quest, no, I was his interruption.

"Are you a churchgoer?" I asked. "Well, yeah, kind of, I went to catechism, I guess you can say I'm a churchgoer. Why do you ask? asked the sales manager. "Good enough. Do you believe in our Lord and Savior?" I asked. "Where are you going with this?" questioned the sales manager. I raised my eyebrow in suspicion and began with my story of meeting Yahshua in 1997. Within a few minutes, another gentleman, who was the district manager of the dealership, arrived. "Would you excuse us for one minute?" he asked.

"Sure, by all means, take your time." Excusing myself, I headed back to the Rapide S and adjust the seating and mirrors for the test drive. While seated in the chariot, the sales manager and district manager were heading my way. The district manager walked passed me with a grin on his face. I had a feeling that they were conspiring a foul plan against me. The sales manager's whispher and the district manager's grin said it all.

I set forth to connect to my Sabra, who Yahshua and Baba had led me to and two humans were not going to deter my Quest when all they cared about was their precious vroom-vroom commission on wheels. The importance of Love for your brohters and sisters is extrememly more important than any wealth nor any material possesions. All things made on Earth are made by machinces that were constructed by other machines or man. They become distractions to the true nature of humanities existance; the Truth in living as oneness with our Father to provide for us all; instead of man-made.

CHAPTER 21

The Stab

When you have more Love to give, He will give you more Love to spread to the ones who are less fortunate than you are; just be true. "Hey listen, I have to leave for a meeting, and I need to lock up because no one will be available in here." said the sales manager. "Maybe I can return after your meeting is over, and we will continue where we left off?" I asked. "I'll be busy all day in the meeting."replied the sales manager.

"OK that's fine, maybe I can come back in the morning when you are not too busy?" I asked. "Sure, sure that would fine, just call before you arrive so that I may know you are coming. I'll have the keys and get the car prepped for you." replied the sales manaer. "Oh I see, that would be great, do you have a business card?" I felt estranged, deceit was at hand; he looked at me with annoyance, as though I was wasting his precious time looking for a key fob to Earthly possessions.

Moths, rust and time eat your earthly stuff; it is just a vehicle, move forward. "Sure, let me get that for you." The sales manager rushed to find his bussiness card. I had to wait another days, she was worth the wait. I have waited many years, one day is just around the corner, it is no big deal. "OK, here is one." said the sales manager. "OK, good, thank you." After inspecting his business card; I turned to walk toward the front door of the showroom. "No!" I yelled, shocked on what he had done.

After I had specifically instructed this fool at our first encounter, he had broken the ultimate rule of disobeying my instructions and touched me. There was an immense drain of energy from my body when the sales manager tapped my right shoulder. "Come back tomorrow, I may have something for you." instructed the sales manager. I froze for a moment and turned to face this tall person who broke our oath. I looked at his face that was lit up like a fake christmas tree with eyes wide open, as though he had envisioned something wonderful. I did not know what he experienced when he touched me.

I did not even let my own children touch me while going through a fasting stage of my life. However, I took his Word for it and would return tomorrow. "OK, I'll see you tomorrow." I informed the sales manager. I arrived home with my beloved on my mind. Everything was going to be OK. His Word lifts my spirit on every occasion, even when commands are broken by humans. I had no clue as to why that man touched me after instructing him from the get go to avoid touching me. I stayed devoted to my fasting, my new Quest, my clean soul, my beloved Sabra.

The following day arrived as slow as the new year ringing out the old. I headed to the office in the morning to handle a few quotes and invoices that needed to be completed. It was a sunny day with a few clouds; that was fine for my Loves to go out for ice cream and enjoy the day together. I left my office and headed to the Aston Martin dealership early in the morning to make sure no meetings took place that early. I had a feeling that daggers were flying everywhere from the sales manager in the showroom.

I arrived like Yahshua, a thief in the night, eager to find out the Truth. "Good morning. I apologize; I was unable to call you first before arrival. I was in the neighborhood and decided to stop by to see what you have for me." I said. "Well, I am extremely busy. You should have called first." replied the sales manager. "No worries; I assume it will be quicker this time to test drive this chariot. I can wait; were you able to find the key to the Rapide S from yesterday?" I asked. "No, could you give me a moment while I finish up this report for a client?" he asked.

"Sure, that is fine, take your time." I headed over to get acquainted once more with my Love's chariot. I sat in the driver's seat, took out the owners manual from the glove box, studied the steering wheel paddle shifter, buttons, locations of all gadgets and more then decided to look under the hood of the Rapide S; however, I needed to have the keyfob for that. What a beauty she was, a fine-tuned machine with a V12 engine that I was denied to hear roar or light up the instrument panel.

Within moments, the same district sales manager from yesterday arrived at the Aston Martin showroom. Oh great, let me guess, another surprise meeting.I have been in the corporate industry for many years; I know how they play their game with their shiny dagger meetings. As I walked around the showroom, the sales manager approached and said he had to leave for another meeting. "I have to leave for a few hours and need to close up the showroom." informed the sales manager.

"Excuse me; you have to head to another meeting. I just arrived; why didn't you get the car ready for me since yesterday, like you said you would?" I asked. "We don't let customer's test drive our vehicles due to adding miles." replied the sales manager. OK, this guy is about to step into his own hole that he had just dug for himself to lay in until he is devoured. He would have saved me a trip back to the dealership if he would have told me that excuse in the first place.

"You mean to tell me, if I was any other customer that came in here, and decided I would like to purchase this Rapide S, that I the customer have never driven one before, looked at the one I was interested in and requested to test drive before purchasing, you would tell me 'No, we don't do that because of added miles.' What are kind salesman are you?" I asked. At which point the tall dumbass twig Aston Martin sales manager approached me. Standing in between the Rapide S driver side door and me.

He leaned down as though he was scolding a young child. "First of all, let me tell you something; do you know how much this car cost?" he asked. "Excuse me, did you just ask me if I knew how much was this car, as though I couldn't afford it? Based on what? I don't care how much this car costs, you don't tell your potential customers that!" I shouted. I looked up at luncheon meat fordisrespecting me; I had no clue why. I was dressed to impress and to melt in my Sabra's hand.

I was going to pick up my Soulmate for eternity, and this tall punkass was about to get chopped down to size. "No I did not say you couldn't afford it!" shouted the sales manager. "Yes you did!" I yelled back. "Are you calling me a liar!?" asked the sales manager. "Yes, as a matter of fact I am, you asked me, and I quote: 'First of all do you know how much this car is worth?" Do you remember saying that to me a few seconds ago or did you forget?" I asked.

All the while Mr. District Sales Manager in charge of the privately owned dealerships was standing near the back of the showroom ready to leave. "I am no liar!" yelled the sales manager. "Sure you are, first you told me you were couldn't find the key to the Rapide S yesterday, and today you refused to hand me the key, even after I gave you my word that I would never start the Rapide S in your showroom. On top of all that, I told you not to touch me right when I came into your showroom yesterday, and you still touched me. Who do you think you are? Are you unable to understand simple instructions!" I yelled.

"That's it, I am through with you, I have the right to refuse you service if I choose so." fumed the sales manager. "Excuse me, 'Refuse me service?' You didn't sell me anything, what service, how do you call that *service*?" I asked. I had to block the cobra from spitting venom at my face. If this guy would have laid his filthy hands on me to lead me out the door, Baba's wrath would have turned him into a pretzel. However, I am a very peaceful man unless my life is threatened or you test Him, then He will let Truth and Wrath take over. "You need to leave, right now!" yelled the sales manager.

The dagger-wielding Aston Martin sales jester barked this stupid orders. I looked at this treasonous traitor with disgust and wanted to throw him overboard. "You're kicking me out of your showroom because I called you a liar!" I shouted. "That's right, and I refuse to listen to you calling me a liar, so I need you to leave." replied the sales manager. "OK, that is fine, but you're still a liar. Have a good day,liar." This man made the ultimate mistake of his life by tapping me on my shoulder behind my back.

People like to be brave, but be cautious if you touch and you're not righteous with Him; then you are going to suffer His consequences and wrath through me. I had instructed my own family and friends, even my children, not to touch during my transformation fasting. Do you think Yahshua would allow this back stabbing peasant to touch me when I had my back turned? I told my Father on him. No, Yahshua could make examples out of jesters like this fool who reached without permission and who thought he was in control, if he wanted to.

I decided to head to another dealership within that automotive strip mall. When I arrived at the Corvette dealership, I remembered who had sent me to Judas and headed his way. I arrived at the Lamborghini dealership to speak to the teary-eyed sales manager. "Hi, how can I help you?" asked the sales assitant. "Hi, I need to speak to your sales manager, is he in?" I asked. "Just one moment, I will get him for you." replied the sales assitant.

I stood there thinking about the sales manager at Aston Martin and how sorry I will feel when wordgets to my Father. A few moments later, in walks the Lamborghini sales manager. "Gandy; hi, how'd it go?" asked Lou. "Why did you send me to your friend thinking he was going to help me? He just kicked me out of the showroom. I asked him to take a vehicle for a test drive but he just wasted my time." I explained to Lou. "I see." he replied. "I was also aggravated with the way he touched me when I had warned him to avoid touching me when we met.

When I returned the following day, he treated me with disrespect." I added. "Well, these are exotic vehicles, and we have none for test driving." said Lou. We stood next door of the Lamborghini showroom which housed Maserati chariots. "Wait, let me get this straight – if I was a customer that entered your showroom and wanted to purchase one of your Maserati's, you wouldn't allow me to test drive before purchase?" I asked. "Correct." replied Lou. "Turn around and look outside." I instructed him. "What am I looking at?" asked Lou.

"Do you see all those Maserati's parked outside in the sun, rain, and whatever elements beating down on them?" I asked. "OK?" he replied. "None of those Maseratis are for test driving? There are more than ten of them out there. They are withering away out there, you have none to test drive?" I questioned Lou. "That is our policy, there are no test driving our cars." replied Lou. "Fine, I need to speak to the head of this dealership and to the Aston Martin dealership." I requested. "Excuse me?" asked Lou.

"You heard me, I want to know who your boss is, the owner of these dealerships." I insisted. "Oh, OK, you need to see the district sales manager located at the Jaguar dealership." said Lou. "Thank you Lou, have a good day." No handshake, no glance, no nothing for these Judases. I was in shock that this guy at the Lamborghinidealership flipped 360 degrees on me too. Even after I shared my lifechanging story and had him teary-eyed,he was afraid of his superiors rather than His Truth.

We will change the world in whole for the better or one example at a time. These dealerships were just the beginning and only crumbs compared to the whole supper that He is about to serve to the world. The lost flock cherish junk more than their salvation; when He arrives, what will they do, trade in their junk to get in? Everyone I come across gets a chance; once they make their choice, they are stopped from boarding my starship, scrutinized by Him, and allowed to board or turned away to find their own way home.

Yes, they are junk, they rust, they dissolve; however, your hearts are forevermore thanmeaningless items that you unable to take with you when He asks you to come home. A vast majority think that you have to die on this Earth to see our king Yahshua again. They are very wrong. I tell you this, if He came to help me in 1997 and then finally led me to my beloved Sabra where Faith and Love to Yahshua were consistent, then He will come to you and aid you in whatever you seek. I sought adventure, Truth, Love and knowledge.

My true love Sabra; your are the one who I call my Beloved, the one who I would stand by me through all of my nights and days. The one who keeps my ship sailing through rough tides. You are the one I was meant to be with, written in His book. I headed toward the district sales manager's office and noticed the Aston Martin sales manager standingoutside looking for worms in the grass. "You are next, Judas." I yelled at him driving by slowly, pointing at him, while I asked my Father to provide him the Truth he needs.

After I arrived at the Jaguar dealership where the district sales manager was located, I walked in and was greeted by a Jaguar sales associate. "Good afternoon, how may I help you?" asked the Jaguar sales associate. "Yes, I need to speak with your district sales manager." I replied. "Yes sir, one moment, please be seated." said the Jaguar sales associate. "No, thanks, I will stand." I replied. Within a few minutes, in walks the same ignorant individual that was probably coherssing the Aston Martin sales manager or vice versa.

Oh great, I just walked into a trap with treason at hand. "Oh it is you – what is the deal with your sales manager at your Aston Martin dealership?" "What is wrong with him? He has every right to do what he wants; he is in charge there." said the district manager. "Oh really, and his title gives him the right to touch my shoulderwhen I warned him to not to lay his hands on me the moment I walked into the the Aston Martin dealership?" I asked. "Well, that is between you and him, I had no idea what he did.

I am extremely busy; what is it you need from me?" replied the district manager. "I want to speak to the owner of all of the dealerships– no managers, no supervisors – just the owner, you know what that means?" I asked. "Yes sure, let me get you that information you are asking for." After leaving his office to gather the information, he returned with a business card with the owner's name. "Where is this person, I need to speak with him. Is he here?" I asked.

"No, he is located a few miles away at another office, the owner is on vacation; however, her son is available to speak with." informed the district manager. I set off to meet up with the owner of the businesses. After fifteen minutes of driving to the owner of the dealership's office, I show up with some advice on how to handle selling Love instead of junk.I show up at a Ford dealership with the new vehicle showroom under renovation and two contractors seated within. They both looked baffled as to why I was there.

"Good afternoon, I am here to see the owner of the Lamborghini, Maserati, Aston Martin and Jaguar and whatever other dealership they own; I need to speak to the owner, is he here?" I asked the staff. "The owner, uh, not sure what you mean?" replied the staff. "OK, maybe you don't know what's going on with my situation. Aare any of the owners here?" I asked. "Yes, the owner's son is in the upstairs office, if you would like to speak to him?" replied the staff. "Yes, have them come down here, so I can speak to them if they don't want me upstairs." I said.

After a few moments the staff memeber returend with some news from the owner. "The owner informed me to have you go see Holly at the Aston Martin dealership; she will take care of you there." he instructed. "Go back to the Aston Martin dealership and talk to Holly, this is what the owner's son informed you, correct?" I asked. "Yes, that is correct." replied the staff member. "Ok, thank you very much; have a good day." So, I set off again back to the Aston Martin dealership to speak to a supposed Holly; maybe she replaced the ignorant owner's son.

You have to have determination and persistence to get where you want to go, otherwise, if you become the ball within the pinball machine and get smacked around. If you do get smacked around; get as many points as possible before the game is over; shatter the glass if you have to. Another fifteen minutes of driving to get there, and as I arrived, no vehicles were in the parking lot of the Aston Martin dealership. No matter, I was heading to speak to Holly, who may have an actual beating heart.

Maybe she can help me rescue my beloved from her locked dungeon of frustration, weary eyes, and lonesome heart. I exited my vehicle upon parking and headed for the Aston Martin showroom doors to speak to Molly and get the show on the road. To my surprise, the showroom doors were locked. "Oh great, here we go." I whispered. I had just been duped again;it was time to tell on them, to tell my father Baba to get involved in this matter. Since no one was available at the Aston Martin dealership, I had no choice but to leave and head back home for results of my actions and prayers.

I was almost at my vehicle when I noticed someone parked in the back of the Aston Martin dealership. An elderly gentleman walked out of the dealership from the rear sidedoor like a coward, and along with him came out the district sales manager from the very same sidedoor. I had saved all of their images in my mind for Yahshua to see who had interfered with our Quest. The first example could be the Juda sales manager, for placing his filthy hands on me when he was verbally warned not to.

The others will follow suit when He thinks the time is right. I continued to walk to my vehicle to leave and also noticed the Aston Martin Judas sales manager unlocking the showroom doors. Seems like they were all in on it together, more food to feast on – chain them all together like the devils they are, perhaps. I placed my headphones on to listen to some relaxing music, and finally the icing on the cake showed up. One police patrol vehicle zipped by, slammed on its brakes, and headed back my way to enter the dealership. I wondered if this was for little 'ol harmless me?

After all I Love law enforcement; they represent the arms of Justice; I was heading to that career at my earlier years in college before I had to suffer through my first rushed yet nesscasary marriage. I had nothing against them, all I had was Truth. The first officer pulled into the dealership parking lot and a few minutes later, another showed up. "Oh my, you need two huh?" I asked. I looked at the owner of the dealership's son. Yes, he was cowardly, hiding behind locked doors.

He did not want to face me in person like a man would when I arrived to his office to speak to him. Instead, they sentme driving back and forth like I was their joke. I will have the last laugh when I take possesion of their businesses and treat customers with respect, even if they walk in with their pajamas. When they called for backup, it was a failed attempt to trap me. The coward was arrograntly unaware of who my backup was. Baba is in control of the humanity's chess board; playing the game of my Quest.

He just needs a make a few moves on the chessboard to eliminate the obstacles, mydestiny will proceed as planned. I have waited these many years; I follow him infinitely. In the case of jackals, you do not have to wait too long for supper to fall right in front of you to feast on without getting your hands filthy. However, I was going to avoid eating trash; instead I am throwing it out for society to sweep them away as usual. "Good afternoon officer, how can I help you?" I asked. "Good afternoon, what seems to be the issue here?" asked the peaceofficer. "Issue, what issue, with me?" I asked.

The second officer parked next to my vehicle to get a better look, supposedly to find invisible weapons or anything suspicious. I notice the first officer's eyes glance quickly over my shoulder to his partner; I had put my Wrath Mode on standby. No one is to touch me except a select precious few. You could be the Pope, and I still will not let you touch me. That wolf is way too filthy to begin with. After you get hugged by the son of Baba, you can smell the human heart. The filthier they are; the more you try to avoid contact and get contaminated.

Fasting is a must when you accept the challenging Quest. You must be devoted to the Faith of the Father, you must make ultimate sacrifices. You must never turn back, for it will be treasonous to the Wordwhohas been with you from the beginning. Would you stab your father for raising you, for telling you secrets, for showing you classified information? Will you betray Him for loving you unconditionally and feeding you His Truthfor your survival? Think twice and look up; enough said.

"May I see your Identification?" asked the peaceofficer. "Sure thing; there was no issue here officer, just a belligerently deceptive Judas sales manager who is selling junk instead of Love and decided to kick me out of this showroom for calling him a liar." I informed him. "Nothing else happened?" he asked. "Yes, they had me driving all over the place; I was trying to speak with the owner of the dealerships only to come back here and speak to a nonexistent Holly and run into you two officers." I replied.

Before the first officer turned to head toward the showroom to speak to the three jackals standing inside, I needed to add a checkmate move. "Oh, yes, one more thing, when I first entered the Aston Martin dealership, I warned the sales manager not to place his hands on me at all. I touched Yahshua, and I'm going through a fasting process. I didn't even let my my own family touch me, not even my children. Who does that Judas think he is for touching me?" I asked. "Oh really, he touched you when you asked him not to touch you?" asked the peaceofficer.

"Correct, he thought he was a big shot; but instead he turned out to be a dumbass." I explained to him. Both officers stepped inside the Aston Martin showroom to get the other side of the story from the two cowards and their leader, king coward. After a few moments, both officers returned and headed to the second officer's patrol vehicle to discuss further matters of this awkward situation. I could not hear what their discussion was all about but approached me with a surprised look on their faces. "Here is your identification back and your business card." said the peaceofficer.

"Thank you, I appreciate your help officers; I apologize for wasting your time with all this mix up." I assured them. "They informed us that you are no longer allowed on any of their dealership properties." instructed the peaceofficer. "Oh really, is that what they said, I'm no longer allowed on their property, over what, a test drive for one of their junk? It's OK, their time will come soon, He makes sure of it." I proclaimed. He looked at me puzzled while the second officer was heading back into the Aston Martin dealership.

"We have to go back in and let them know your agreed to their terms. Is there anything you would like for us to tell them in return? "No nothing." I replied. "You sure? OK." said the peaceofficer. "Oh wait, as a matter of fact there is something you can tell them. Tell them – I will be back, however, I will not set foot on their property, no trespassing. I will return to own this dealership along with all their other dealerships. They just made a big mistake." I told the peaceofficer.

"Nice move, I'll let them know what you told me; well done." he replied. "Thanks, have a good day officers." I left the Aston Martin dealership with a victory over worthless peasants selling expensive junk. I headed back to my office to contemplate how their actions would set off chain reactions, making them examples of His power from the Word of Truth, Justice, Courage, Faith and Love alongside His almighty son, Yahshua. Do not be afraid to follow your heart to His Truth; your Faith will guide you through the fires of the abyss untouchable.

Know that He stands with you as your Father forevermore; He hears you reaching for Him within your heart. Yahshua will embrace you as His brother, standing with you in your time of triumph or suffering. Everyone must realize that Their power of Love for you is limitless. For you are always in Thier thoughts, you are always a part of His family, your name was written. Baba's book of life expresses His Love for His children, forevermore. Remember to be humble and Love yourself along with your brothers and sisters of this world, for He Loves them as well.

Do not belittle anyone just because they are less fortunate than you are. The repurcustions afterwards when you stand in the acuqsations and affairs building will say otherwise. We all must realize that we are all connected through our heavanly Father as one. Killing each other because of the color of our skins or sounds of our ethnic language is obsurded and condeming. We have been seperated with religion a long time ago and must see our Father as the only oneness you will need on His own planet.

CHAPTER 22

Baba is the East, and Sabra is His Heart Who Feeds My Soul

This world tries to break our Faith, tries to destroy our family; try as they may, His Word always will checkmate them all. I was determined to see my beloved once more after things had settled down from the unjustified accusation of harassment charges or classifying me as a stalker coming from my Soulmate's siblings breath. I had called the pizzeria she was managing and ordered some food to pick up for dinner later that afternoon.

I was nervous; what if she is there, what will I say, what shall I do, should I get on my knees and beg for her forgiveness, should I apologize for causing her and her family any harm I have caused them? "Yah Alaha help me; Yah Eesho help me. I beg of you, I Love her too much to just let her go." As I prayed, I had no idea what I was about to go through.

Yet, with His Word within my soul, not even a mountain will stand in my way, as Baba splits it in half and I walk through it. I pulled up to the pizzeria, took a few deep breaths, and exhaled any jitterbugs that may have still been in my gut. Sabra gets me all tongue-tied speaking gaga goo-goo to her; true Love does that to a person. I kept thinking of my mother's advice of meeting my true Love for eternity and my dad's advice of how she will not be able to recognize me in the early stages of our first meeting.

However, my dad stated that I would win in the end. I was praying she would hear my heart cry out for her. "Here I go, Eesho." I whispered. Walking into the pizzeria, I see my longtime befriended brother, Sabra's brother. "Hey, how is it going, bro?" I asked walking past the counter however there was no immediate reply from him. With a disgusted tone in his voice and frustrated expression on his face he responds with disappointment. "Hey, how can I help you?"

"Hey Hart; I just ordered some pizza to go, I apologize for taking a bit longer than usual I had to take care of things at the office before I left for the evening." I said. "Oh yeah, here you go." He drops the pizza on the counter and heads back to his computer screen pressing some buttons. Kind of an odd behavior from my buddy who had hugged me, kissed my head, and called me his little brother. My buddy who had now forgotten me and left me outside in the hail storm. I was still happy to see him because he was going to be a part of my family and I his.

As I grabbed the food that I had ordered, I leaned over the counter to see if I could at least get another glimpse of Baba's perfection before I left to prepare for another Quest. "Thank you for the pizza, bro, I'll see you again, we will talk some more." She was unavailable, and I had an empty feeling in my heart from missing Sabra so much. I reached out my hand for a firm blood brother handshake, and I received a feathered grip in return.I was being treated like trash, useless to anyone.

After shaking his hand, I looked at my palm, as though I had been cut, and the flow of blood was unable to stop draining from my heart. I rubbed my palm that my blood brother had shaken against my chest to stop my heart from bleeding dry. I remembered when Yahshua's friends had betrayed and denied him, still knowing their brother when they came for him, my friends and family were doing the same thing when I proclaimed His Truth and my endless Love for my Sabra.

"Why is this happening to me, Baba; these people are my friends, my family, they accepted me, they welcomed me into their personal lives – why are they doing this to me?" I prayed to Yahshua. "Was I no longer good enough for them because I was divorced with children, poor, older, walked funny, looked funny? I did not do anything wrong, she stood in front of Eesho, as did I." We connected like His DNA Lego pieces. I wanted to prove to everyone she was worth His every Word, every breathe, every heartbeat. We are His thought made in His Kingdom; we are from one soul made into man and woman.

We were meant to be together because Baba and Yahshua led me to my beloved Sabra. Why do scuffers no longer believe in Love, why do they replace compassion with selection of credit worthiness, age, rumors, fear, selfishness, self-worth. Why do they still look for the qualities of a man or woman's worthiness in earthly possesions or monetary gain in their own eyes of judgment? Would Love have more worth than any wealth you try measure to it? Do you seek any other detail when unconditional Love is all that matters?

She had seen the old me, wait till she sees the new me!We will be together my day, my night, dream, my Soul. Yor are my beginning and my end, my one and only, my CAR that runs on the fuel of my Love, f or you are my True Love, for every kiss you give me I will give you infinite in return. Just wait and see, we will be happily ever after, forevermore. Every cell within my being had instructed me to change, to better myself for the next Quest that was about to begin shortly after I had finished this book of many.

My journey already had begun when I accepted the Truth from Yahshua to change the hearts of many on this planet we call Earth. When I was asked to take on His Quest, I was blessed to accept my destiny to change the world with the help of Baba, Yahshua and the Holy Trinity. I agreed and signed my life over, hugged Baba's son, and He accepted. I had changed my life to where even my whole family would be unable to recognize me. My seeds would be joyous to hug their new daddy once again; always.

More Faithwas gained for my blessed Quest than ever before;Courage and Love is out of this world with His blessings. I eased my sorrow with training, healthy eating, eliminating disgusting habits. Vulgar words and thoughts were gradually being erased from my memory banks until they not spoken. I cleansed myself from within to shine for my beloved, for Baba and for my eternal friend, teacher and my brother Yahshua. The yearning of Sabra's embrace once more, forevermore.

Thoughts of my beloved Sabra every day and dreams every night reach to heaven to guide her to my arms. I prayed with all of my heart and soul to Yahshua to unite us as we were written in His book on one flesh. I also prayed to Baba to disallow any other man approaching my Sabra for their taking, their bride. Unaware I had rushed into this dramatic situation unprepared but realized that my dad's claim meant I had to suffer for her Love just a bit longer until we were together again.

My journey was painful, passionate, terrible, tragic, adventurous, courageous, loving and humble, a journey revolving around His Love. My creation was from the beginning of Baba's loving thought, as all of you are. We all play this game of chess we call life everyday we awaken. Just allow Baba and Yahshua to take over and allow destiny to get in your driver's and passenger's seat as you enjoy your destination to Love. Every person who believes in Him will win, even in the worst of odds, nor shall ye taste death. The words that our Father speaks are of Truth forevermore.

The Father of heaven is about Truth, His entire family is about Truth, no lie stems from His Word. Once you accept the Truth, He will be apart of you with every breath you take and give. The Word was proclaimed from the beginning that Truth and Love always prevail. Love follows Truth as a child follows aparent to salvation. Love for His creation began ions ago and never will cease to exist. Love conquers all hate at home, work or world. Love keeps you alive and destroys your enimies with His command.

Commit to Baba's request and Yahshua will guide you to victory and bring you home to True Love. I had awaited many years for the right moment to find Sabraand win with HisWord. I had suffered many years since my first steps in pain. I had endured many obstacles that most would give up because of pain and anguish. Fear has no place in my heart nor should fear be within yours. When I hugged Yahshua; I knew who I was and still am. When I accepted his Quest, I began the journey to Truth.

When Baba introduced me his Love; I hugged Yahshua and my beloved Sabra; and understood the Universe and the Love He has for His creations. In the beginning came sound, and Baba's voice created life. Just pray to our Father in Heavenand have patience. Accept Yahshuainto your heart and have no fear to seek Him; talk to Him; Love Him and finally spread your arms wide and ask Him...

"Can I get a hug?"

May Yahshua guide you to his Father's kingdom.

May Baba bless you, your family and friends for eternity.

CLOSING NOTES

Upon completion of my book, I had prayed to Yahshua and Baba to reunite me with my Sabra. Praying endlessly that she would remember me day and night; I awaited patiently for my prayers to be fulfilled, for His Word is Truth. My path in my life is to follow Yahshua wherever he may lead me. I am honored and grateful to complete my Father's quest in slaying the dragon and embracing my beloved Sabra. The stories of my life are true as Yahshua, Baba, his angels and the people I Truthfully encountered are witnesses to my testimony.

When I hugged Yahshua, I was shown Truth and eternal Love. My quest had begun the moment I was born. My longing to be one with my beloved soul was found and I await thy lips Sabra. They knew my destiny bestowed upon me by my Father in heaven. I was being lead to my destiny by Faith, Love, Truth, Courage and Justice. I am on His path to save my soul and others, forevermore.

My desire is to eat Sabra's True Love and to be strengthened by His Word. I pray that we soon will embrace endlessly, my Love. You are the air that I breathe and who I give my last breath to. I beg thee thine drink from thou lips and eat from thou heart. For thou art thine bread of eternal sustenance, thine kiss, thine hug, thine Love; forevermore.

I Love you Baba, forevermore

I Love you Eesho, forevermore

I Love you Family, forevermore

I Love you Sabra, forevermore

I Love you Brothers and Sisters, forevermore

Hallelujah
Praise Father in Heaven

www.ingramcontent.com/pod-product-compliance
Lightning Source LLC
Chambersburg PA
CBHW070015100426
42740CB00013B/2503